D1520566

Unfaithful

UNFAITHFUL

Love, Adultery, and Marriage Reform
in Nineteenth-Century America

Carol Faulkner

PENN

UNIVERSITY OF PENNSYLVANIA PRESS

PHILADELPHIA

A volume in the Haney Foundation Series,
established in 1961 with the generous support of Dr. John Louis Haney.

Published by
University of Pennsylvania Press
Philadelphia, Pennsylvania 19104-4112
www.upenn.edu/pennpress

Printed in the United States of America
on acid-free paper
1 3 5 7 9 10 8 6 4 2

A catalogue record is available from the Library of Congress.
ISBN 978-0-8122-5155-5

For Mae

CONTENTS

Introduction: The Adultery Metaphor 1

1. Adultery as a Sin and a Crime 14

2. Adultery as Freedom from Sin 24

3. "Two Kinds of Adultery" 36

4. "Legalized Adultery" 49

5. True vs. False Marriage 60

6. "His Adultery Is Proved So Clear" 78

7. Adultery Among the Free Lovers 93

8. Feminists and the Marriage Question 103

9. Adultery as Social Protest 116

10. Adultery as Civil Disobedience 134

Epilogue 158

Notes 173
Index 205
Acknowledgments 213

The Adultery Metaphor

In her 1855 fictionalized autobiography *Mary Lyndon*, Mary Gove Nichols described her liberation from an unhappy marriage and her discovery of true love with her second husband and fellow reformer Thomas Nichols. By the time she published the novel, Mary Gove Nichols was a well-known lecturer on health and physiology and a leading practitioner of the homeopathic water-cure method. She was also an outspoken critic of legal marriage, asserting that it deprived women of their physical and moral autonomy. Her abusive first marriage had inspired this radical view. As Nichols wrote of her relationship with Hiram Gove, "A conviction had long been growing within me that marriage without love was adultery."[1]

What did Nichols mean by this curious statement? She and her first husband had been legally married. Neither of them had an extramarital affair. Instead, Nichols used this metaphor of adultery to call attention to the personal violation of obligatory, loveless sex within marriage.

Nichols's usage was not idiosyncratic. A number of mid-nineteenth-century reformers, including women's rights activists, abolitionists, spiritualists, communitarians, bohemians, and free lovers, shared her critique of unhappy, hierarchical, and brutal marriages. They used the adultery metaphor together with the far more ubiquitous criticisms of marriage as a form of slavery or prostitution.[2] But the term "legalized adultery" uniquely characterized, and condemned, unwanted or unwilling marital sex in a lifelong, monogamous bond as a betrayal of the self, or individual agency in matters of love. Unlike—or, sometimes, in addition to—the marriage metaphors of slavery and prostitution, the adultery metaphor enabled activists to address controversial topics of women's equality, desire, and right to consent within the institution of marriage. For Mary Gove Nichols and other reformers, love—not the law—created marriage and legitimated sexual intercourse.

The strange metaphor of "legalized adultery" conveyed a particular critique of marriage, and a particular agenda for its reform. Between 1830 and 1880, an array of activists viewed the legal, social, and cultural institution of marriage as an obstacle to a more equitable society. As historian Helen Lefkowitz Horowitz describes it, a growing number of midcentury reformers began to place "sex at the center of life."[3] Early feminists identified the question of marital rights as equally important to political rights. Other reformers deemed the marriage question more fundamental to the transformation of women's status. The most radical activists, known as free lovers, demanded an end to the constraints of legal marriage. They argued that individuals had a right to choose when and whom they loved, advocating a form of serial monogamy. More moderate marriage reformers, including women's rights activists and spiritualists, believed that love, choice, and happiness were essential to marriage. When marriages failed, they advocated liberal access to divorce. These activists differed in their attitudes toward legal marriage, insofar as the moderates still had faith in the institution, but they shared the fundamental insight that marriage should be a voluntary, loving relationship, and used variations on the idea of adultery to convey wrongs and harms *within* the legal bond of a marriage.

Activists defined marriage as love, and adultery as the opposite. To promote their controversial message of marriage reform, they traveled across continents and oceans; they lectured and reported; they also dabbled in new technologies such as Pitman's shorthand, the pseudoscience of phrenology, and religious mysticism. Their debates over how best to challenge legal, monogamous marriage scandalized their contemporaries: newspapers and colleagues homogenized marriage reformers and disparaged them as free lovers, cranks, and dreamers.

With few exceptions, historians have been similarly dismissive, relegating them to a sideshow of nineteenth-century reform.[4] But this book concludes that marriage reformers were more successful than we think. Some of their ideas faded from the view because they were marginalized as eccentric, but others were mainstreamed because they were unremarkable or unobjectionable. And the adultery metaphor, however strange or incongruous, helped advance reformers' shared perspective—and ours—that only love makes marriage.

*   *   *

Marriage reformers' criticisms of the legal institution in the nineteenth century, described in these chapters, were one episode in a larger transformation of marital and gender relations. It began at the end of the eighteenth century, when Enlightenment thinkers proclaimed the individual right to pursue happiness, continued into the early twentieth century, with the rise of companionate marriage, and may have culminated in the slogan associated with the Supreme Court's 2015 decision on marriage equality in *Obergefell v. Hodges:* "Love Wins."[5]

During this period, individual choice, mutual love, and companionship gradually and unevenly became the key requirements for marriage. They replaced earlier concepts of marriage as a consolidation of labor, reproduction, and family wealth. In companionate marriages, couples wanted a "love match," or to find and marry their true love.[6]

This historic transformation began during the American Revolution and the confusion of war, when Americans rejected community and family control over marriage in favor of individual choice and romantic love. A growing number of Americans began to engage in sexual relations outside of marriage, and men and women entered and exited romantic unions at their pleasure.[7]

Following the Revolution, most states responded by recognizing a right to divorce. Though divorce had been available in some colonies, access expanded in the decades after the war. The rationale for revolt against Great Britain, the right to withdraw from an undesirable compact, buttressed this legal revolution. Divorce did not become commonplace, but its availability further distinguished the United States from England, where it was impossible for anyone but the aristocracy to secure a divorce. As divorce became established in American state law, politicians also placed restrictions on access, demanding fault or guilt in one party. The two most restrictive states were New York, where adultery was the only ground, and South Carolina, which offered residents no means for divorce.[8]

The sexual turmoil of the Revolutionary period might have undermined marriage in some respects, but in the Early Republic, marriage also gained renewed importance as the fount of political and moral virtue. This change had significant implications for women. As American women and men continued to choose spouses based on mutual regard, leading thinkers articulated a new public function for marriage and reproduction: women's responsibility as guardians of civic virtue and personal morality. Such political ideals rationalized the expansion of women's education, but also placed greater pressures on their behavior.[9] As models of sexual virtue, women gained moral influence over their husbands and children. Though women did not have political rights, they extended this moral authority beyond the home, to their neighborhoods, churches, and voluntary associations. The upwardly mobile middle classes adopted sexual purity and restraint as a sign of their respectability. Evangelical Protestants also prized sexual morality, defining all extramarital sex as licentious and sinful. These groups identified women who did not conform to the ideal of premarital purity, whether through choice or coercion, with prostitutes.[10]

While middle-class wives garnered moral authority from this standard of sexual virtue, it excluded many impoverished, working, and enslaved women, who did not have the same resources or protections. For enslaved women, in particular, the equation between morality and marriage made sexual purity unattainable. Viewing their own marriages as essential to the production and reproduction of property, slaveholders barred such legal bonds between enslaved men and women. Enslaved African Americans defied this restriction by defining their loving relationships as marriages, but these relationships were vulnerable. Slaveholders pursued their financial interests without regard for the standing of slave marriages, even those they had created through force. Masters bought and sold husbands, wives, and children, separating enslaved families with impunity. Such antimarriage practices allowed slaveholders to label African American women as inherently promiscuous for engaging in sex outside of wedlock. Slaveholders also viewed enslaved women as sexually available. As former slave Harriet Jacobs wrote, southern laws that decreed that the child follow the status of the mother meant that masters' "licentiousness" did not "interfere with avarice."[11]

These circumstances led abolitionists to denounce slavery as undermining the marriage vows of both blacks and whites. American slavery, one group of activists asserted, was a system of "legalized adultery, piracy, and murder," highlighting the illicit behavior protected by its legal and customary status.[12] Here, abolitionists used adultery in its conventional definition, demanding that the religious and civil laws of marriage be enforced, but they also critiqued the crimes within an accepted, established institution, a strategy that would be adopted by marriage reformers. Abolitionists further demanded that marital rights be an essential goal of emancipation.

Paradoxically, many Americans elevated the political, social, and moral value of marriage at a time when the institution's dominance appeared threatened on several fronts, and by several things, including enslavement, romantic ideals, divorce laws, and lived experiences. Influenced by Enlightenment thought, Americans expected more from marriage. In its ideal state, marriage created a happy, permanent home, with a loving, hardworking husband, and moral, nurturing wife. In reality, loveless, incompatible, and even violent marriages coexisted with contented ones. In response, from the 1820s through the 1840s, some states expanded the earlier-established grounds for divorce to include cruelty or drunkenness, and added omnibus clauses that gave judges wide discretion. These state differences created a marketplace for divorce, and in 1852, Indiana became the chosen destination for most divorce-seekers because, to the horror of marriage defenders, it required no prior residency.[13]

In this context, Americans understood adultery to be a tangible act with specific meaning: the sexual betrayal of a spouse, a violation of the Seventh Commandment, a crime in most jurisdictions, and the basis for divorce or "criminal conversation," a civil action. Nineteenth-century marriage was as much an institution of law as of God. The Seventh Commandment instructed religious Americans that adultery was a sin. While many devout Protestants agreed that the act provided a biblical basis for separation or divorce, they viewed monogamous marriage as so sacred and binding that remarriage by the guilty party, the adulterer, became another breach of the commandment. They viewed a life of chastity as the only moral response to adultery and divorce. New York recognized this religious ban against remarriage in its laws. Other states, such as Connecticut, did not. Religious Americans worried that such statutory diversity detracted from the holy character of marriage.[14]

Adultery was a sexual act that had public consequences. In most states, as in most European countries and their colonies, adultery was a crime. Nathaniel Hawthorne's 1850 novel *The Scarlet Letter* was one reminder of this colonial history in Puritan Massachusetts. His depiction of the plight of Hester Prynne condemned such laws and the moral hypocrisy of civic and religious leaders. With nineteenth-century marriage reformers, Hawthorne's novel valued "mutual happiness" and "sacred love" over "human institutions, and whatever priests or legislators had established."[15]

Mother England had since let its criminal adultery laws lapse, but these statutes were a persistent reality in the United States, and those who violated the law risked arrest. In 1856, communitarian and free lover James A. Clay published *A Voice from the Prison* to protest his six-month imprisonment in Augusta, Maine, on charges of adultery. Though he proclaimed his innocence, Clay denounced "the marriage law" as the "deepest and biggest root of the tree of evil." "The laws not only endeavor to hold together what God has not joined," he continued, "but put asunder what he *has* joined." Other accused adulterers also faced prison sentences and/or fines. Only New York State, which remained exceptional in stipulating adultery as the only possible grounds for divorce, was unusual in failing to criminalize adultery. In their laxity on criminal adultery and their restrictiveness on divorce, New Yorkers followed the lead of the British.[16]

Aggrieved New York husbands and other American men also had the option of pursuing a civil suit through the tort of criminal conversation, known colloquially as "crim. con.," or the act of having sex with another man's wife. Notably, women did not have the same recourse, an indication that lawmakers were more concerned with the impact of wives' sexual transgressions than those of their husbands.[17] "Crim. con." cases had long been a staple of the sensational press in England and the United States. These articles depicted the scandalous, titillating behavior of British aristocrats and American political, religious, and business leaders. They also contradicted the paeans to domestic bliss that otherwise dominated American culture.[18]

*   *   *

The marriage reformers described in this book entered the conversation at this moment, when marriage had been both elevated and endangered, when the frontiers of marriage and adultery had become part of a political agenda, and when adultery carried specific legal and religious meanings. These reformers' ideas about marriage and adultery first emerged in the 1830s in the midst of an evangelical campaign against sin. Founded by ministers and their female parishioners, the moral reform movement sought to abolish prostitution and sexual licentiousness more broadly, and behaviors, such as adultery, which fueled the growth of prostitution (Chapter 1). These reformers saw adultery as the problem, and marriage as the safeguard of moral and social order.

But some evangelicals associated with these moral reform organizations soon proposed an alternative understanding of adultery and marriage. John Humphrey Noyes, among others, began to view marriage as a selfish institution that deflected attention from God. Perhaps marriage was the problem, he suggested, and adultery the solution. Within the larger context of communitarian experimentation in the 1840s and 1850s, Noyes built a community with a small group of devoted followers that abolished monogamous marriage, and eventually moved it to the Oneida Community, where they implemented complex marriage, or sanctioned adultery.[19] Their practices were not adultery, Noyes argued, but an expression of God's love among true believers (Chapters 2 and 3). Noyes prized mutual consent as essential to complex marriage, but he ultimately relied on his own spiritual authority, as well as state laws regarding sex and marriage, to regulate the sexual activities of his female followers.

In contrast, other communitarians, especially followers of French socialist Charles Fourier, developed a secular justification for the abolition of marriage, one that challenged patriarchal and male privilege (Chapter 4). Expanding on Fourier's ideas of passional attraction or affinity, Stephen Pearl Andrews touted the concept of "individual sovereignty" in his utopian experiment called Modern Times.[20] In his view, women as well as men had a fundamental right to self-determination in matters of love. For Andrews and his followers, the individual was the ultimate authority, and marriage, with the collusion of church and state, confined and restricted the individual.

Both Andrews and Noyes embraced the label of "free love"—and Andrews and his followers were among the first to use the phrase "legalized adultery" to question the validity of sexual relations in a loveless marriage. Adultery was one way for these activists to talk about sex, and since reformers variously used the word to mean both a figurative state and a literal act, its meaning will be contextualized throughout this book. Their nineteenth-century audiences easily recognized adultery as a serious issue. For marriage reformers, however, the concept of "legalized adultery" placed sin, crime, and betrayal *within* the institution of marriage, as well as outside of it. The metaphor of adultery became their shorthand for loveless marriages. Through the adultery metaphor, marriage reformers reimagined marriage as a loving relationship between free, consenting individuals.

And through this metaphor, reformers placed the marriage question at the nexus of the antislavery, moral reform, communitarian, spiritualist, free love, and feminist movements, linking causes that historians usually treat as separate and distinct.[21]

Within these movements, more moderate marriage reformers dealt uneasily with free lovers' philosophies. Some of these reformers, including spiritualist and feminist Mary Fenn Davis, agreed with radical free lovers that marriage should be based on love and consent, but she also agreed with evangelicals and most other Americans that marriage was still an unbreakable spiritual and material union between man and woman (Chapter 5). Spiritualists, women's rights activists, abolitionists, and phrenologists idealized "true" marriages and believed that love created pure, uplifting, and enduring bonds between individuals. Unlike free lovers, these more moderate reformers did not call for the abolition of marriage, instead urging individuals to find and marry their true love. Significantly, while their advice rejected free love, it also shows how far these ideas had infiltrated other social movements and the broader marriage debate: even reformers who believed in monogamous, legal marriage tacitly endorsed facets of the adultery metaphor when they conceded that love was the basis of harmonious and genuine unions.

But feminists, free lovers, and other reformers did not view marriage exclusively as a political question. They attempted to put their ideals of marriage into practice, viewing their intimate relationships as laboratories for the larger reformation of the legal and social institution.[22] A small number of activists had open marriages; most did not. Activists thought love—rather than a legal vow—was the only way to ensure sexual fidelity, and to prevent both literal and metaphoric adultery. With this tremendous faith in love, activists also experienced disillusionment. In addition, their very participation in social movements, which brought them into contact with attractive strangers and radical theories, created stress in their marriages. Like other Americans, reformers experienced acts of adultery in their own marriages, and the resulting divorces and scandals confirmed their opponents' fears. As the troubled, scandalous marriage of Mary and Sherman Booth illustrates (Chapter 6), marriage reform had shaped both the ideals and imaginations of those who followed them—but it was difficult to navigate heterosexual relationships by the standard of true love, or to entirely supplant the more conventional, legal understanding and boundaries of marriage.

In the midst of overlapping and competing conversations about marriage, free lovers initiated a marriage crisis on the eve of the Civil War. The Unitary Home, an urban experiment in communal living that housed journalists, writers, spiritualists, and bohemians, all of them influenced by Fourierism and free love, was at its center. In the pages of American newspapers and on the podiums of reform conventions, these activists denounced marriage as legalized adultery and prostitution, loveless relationships that degraded husbands and wives, and forced women to exchange sex for financial support (Chapter 7).

The women's rights movement, which had recently coalesced in a series of national conventions, became their principal target. Free lovers, including Julia Branch, a resident of the Unitary Home, viewed the women's movement as misguided in its increasing focus on political over marital rights. Branch argued that marriage deprived women of their moral autonomy because marriage, rather than individual character, determined women's sexual respectability. Disavowing and protesting any connection to free love, women's rights activists nonetheless borrowed some of the free lovers' worldview, advancing similar arguments for mutual desire, individual happiness, and liberal divorce (Chapter 8).

Both the slavery and adultery metaphors provocatively connected free love to women's rights. In the mid-nineteenth century, the two movements shared ideas and personnel. Feminists criticized the laws of marriage; free lovers promoted their views on women's rights platforms. While free lovers argued for the end of marriage, women's rights activists sought legal and political equality to reform the institution. Ignoring these differences in emphasis, the national press coupled the two movements, predicting that sexual license and societal collapse would follow in the wake of women's rights. After the Civil War, "free love" increasingly became a slur and weapon. Concerned with potential damage to their movement and reputations, most suffragists vigorously denied the association, and scholars have followed their lead, overstating the divide. Yet women's rights activists and free lovers alike argued that marriage should be a reciprocal, dissolvable contract.[23]

Attacks from ministers, editors, and authors who defended the laws of marriage increased over the course of the nineteenth century. After the Civil War, marriage's defenders began lobbying for new restrictions on divorce.[24] They also embraced the 1873 Comstock law, which outlawed the mailing of obscene materials, placing reformers at risk of arrest for even writing about conjugal love. While marriage reformers argued that their proposals improved marital and social harmony, their opponents argued that free love, spiritualism, women's rights, and communitarianism undermined the social and moral order, contributing to divorce, prostitution, illegitimacy, and polygamy.

Marriage reformers, for their part, also condemned polygamy, and denied any association with the marriage practices of the Church of Jesus

Christ of Latter-day Saints. Joseph Smith, the founder of the Latter-day Saints, had introduced plural marriage in 1841, and it continued to grow after his murder in 1844.[25] The Oneida Community's complex marriage especially drew unfavorable comparisons. Noyes rejected attempts to link the two movements, and viewed the Oneida Community as participating in a larger conversation about marriage with free lovers, communitarians, and other reformers. Victoria Woodhull mentioned the Latter-day Saints only to note that both monogamy and polygamy upheld male privilege: "I need not tell you that Mormonism is practiced in *other* places beside Utah." For these reasons, the marital experimentation of the Latter-day Saints is beyond the scope of this book.[26]

In the 1870s, amid this harsher and more vociferous criticism, marriage reformers continued to invoke the adultery metaphor to criticize legal marriage; they also adopted more confrontational tactics. Inspired by the success of the Civil War in ending slavery, they launched their own battle against the legal and social conventions of marriage. They turned the act of adultery into a form of civil disobedience (Chapters 9 and 10). Radical critics of marriage publicly exposed acts of adultery—their own and others—in a direct confrontation with the oppressive, unjust laws of marriage. These radicals viewed consensual extramarital sex as not only necessary but also right when founded in love.

Victoria Woodhull's exposure of the Beecher-Tilton affair in her newspaper, *Woodhull and Claflin's Weekly,* was one moment in this larger campaign. Her newspaper also became the venue for spiritualist Moses Hull to announce and defend his open marriage. These attacks concluded with the civil trial of Henry Ward Beecher for criminal conversation, a sensational case that demonized free lovers, especially Stephen Pearl Andrews and Victoria Woodhull.[27]

Woodhull and her allies' arguments implied that sex outside of marriage, if sanctioned by love, might be a positive good and an act of resistance against unjust laws. By the end of the decade, such extreme views contributed to the temporary collapse of marriage reform. After the Beecher-Tilton trial, activists dropped the metaphor of adultery.

While their critique of marriage had been vilified, some of its aspects had also become normalized as marital orthodoxy. In one sense activists' conceptual critique of marriage disappeared because it had served its purpose. They redefined adultery as a betrayal of individual moral and physical integrity rather than a violation of church and state laws on marriage. In their view, only mutual love justified sexual intercourse. Scandalous in their time, they contributed to a larger acceptance of love as the foundation of marriage.

As their opponents rejoined, such arguments might excuse all sorts of illicit behavior. Americans might cite love as a rationale for pre- or extra-marital sex, or as an explanation for ending one marriage and entering another. And increasingly, Americans did just that. Nineteenth-century marriage reformers contributed to the decline of older forms of marriage based on familial, social, and economic stability, and helped establish American marriage as an institution dedicated to love and happiness.

*   *   *

Though they bridged different social movements and ideological perspectives, the marriage reformers discussed in this book came from similar backgrounds. This homogeneity influenced their views of marriage as well as their response to criticism from those who valued marriage as a bulwark against the dangers of free love.

Some of these marriage reformers are better known, including John Humphrey Noyes, the religious founder of the utopian experiment known as the Oneida Community, and Victoria Woodhull, the newspaper editor and suffragist who launched the Beecher-Tilton adultery scandal. Others will become familiar over the course of this book, including radical critics of marriage such as Oneida Community members Mary and George Cragin; communitarians like Stephen Pearl Andrews, Edward Underhill, Julia Branch, and Marie Howland; and spiritualists Moses, Elvira, and Mattie Hull. More moderate marriage reformers included spiritualists Mary Fenn and Andrew Jackson Davis; abolitionist poet Mary Booth and her lover, suffragist Mathilde Anneke; and clairvoyant and doctor Paschal Beverly Randolph.

Marriage reformers shared certain characteristics. Most of them were born and lived in northern states, though some moved to western states such as Wisconsin, and many traveled extensively throughout the United States and Europe. They came from comfortable, middling backgrounds, or they worked their way into the middle classes. They made their living as writers, journalists, and lecturers. Most were married. More female marriage reformers had divorced, however, indicating women's greater stake in new ideals of love, as well as their willingness to risk scandal to end unhappy marriages. Coming of age in a period of intense religious awakening in the United States, they left mainstream denominations for new spiritual movements or for no church at all. They all participated in at least one other social movement.

With the exception of spiritualist Paschal Beverly Randolph, a man of color from a multiethnic background, all of these activists were white. For most free, northern African Americans, fighting slavery and racial prejudice was the priority. Their legal marriages represented shared moral and civic values, providing a platform for inclusion in American society and politics. For those who had escaped from slavery, marriage was also a hard-won right.[28] African Americans may have been alienated by the arguments of marriage reformers, who viewed marriage as a more fundamental question of freedom. As spiritualist Andrew Jackson Davis wrote, "That is not Liberty which liberates the intellect, and enslaves the affections; that is not Liberty which emancipates the African from bondage, and refuses freedom to the unhappily married."[29] Other reformers also blithely dismissed the brutal realities of slavery and the significant differences between the institutions.

Indeed, white activists frequently compared marriage and slavery to highlight women's degradation and bondage. Once married, a woman became a legal nonentity, and her body and property belonged to her husband, who might exploit her labor as he pleased. Marriage reformers were particularly concerned with the wife's legal obligation to have sex with her husband, and they urged couples to give women power in the bedroom. Over the course of the nineteenth century, women's rights activists secured some property rights for married women, but the slavery metaphor indicated the extent of married women's dependence as well as the difficulty of escape. Though these laws applied to all married women, reformers directed their concern at the plight of white women.[30]

* * *

Nineteenth-century activists provoked a debate that anticipated broad changes in the ideal and practice of marriage. These reformers crossed and connected different social movements, from abolition and women's rights to spiritualism and communitarianism. In their writings, lectures, and personal lives, they argued for self-determination in love and marriage. The most radical among them believed that individuals should have the freedom to change partners when love disappeared. At a time when Americans judged women by their sexual virtue and maternal devotion, marriage reformers argued for women's sexual agency, believing that both women and men had a right to love. The adultery metaphor offered one way to protest the legal regime of marriage and construct a more liberating alternative.

CHAPTER 1

Adultery as a Sin and a Crime

"This is an adulterous and sinful generation," *McDowall's Journal* pro-claimed in 1833.[1] Its founder, the thirty-two-year-old Rev. John R. Mc-Dowall, was the former head of Manhattan's short-lived Magdalen Society, an institution devoted to reforming prostitutes. He intended his newspaper to publicize and prevent sexual immorality, and appealed to both "great and good men" and "pious and benevolent ladies" to join his crusade.[2] The response was immediate and overwhelming. Donations and letters of support arrived from around the country.

In addition to his newspaper, McDowall organized the American Soci-ety for Promoting the Observance of the Seventh Commandment, to halt "the progress of licentiousness, and to prevent the increase of adultery, fornication, and kindred crimes."[3] At the beginning of the 1830s, Mc-Dowall's views on adultery resonated with many Americans, who defined adultery as the enemy of marriage. The act of adultery caused divorces and civil suits, and most states also defined it as a crime. As evangelicals like McDowell saw it, however, adultery was both grievous and pervasive. They identified violations of the Seventh Commandment on city streets and their houses, slave plantations, and even in churches.

To remind all devout Americans of their duty, McDowall reprinted a sermon on "The Seventh Commandment-Lewdness" from the well-known divine Timothy Dwight (d. 1817), former president of Yale College. Its clear message was that a previous generation of American Protestants had been willing to enforce the commandment that "thou shalt not commit adul-tery," which, Dwight contended, prohibited *"impure thoughts," "all licen-tious words,"* and *"all licentious conduct."* This wickedness, warned Dwight, *"when it becomes extensive, overspreads a country with final ruin."*[4] Though Dwight set an all but impossible standard of sexual purity, a new generation of evangelicals embraced this vision for themselves and their communities. As another evangelical wrote, "To disregard the marriage institution, or to sanction anything that has a tendency to lessen its influence, or encourage its neglect, is directly supporting a system of concubinage, destructive to the peace and happiness of families, and the morals of the community."[5] Violations of the Seventh Commandment destroyed not only individual marriages but the very fabric of society.

Religious Americans had always viewed adultery as a sin, but in the 1830s McDowall and other evangelicals believed that they could banish such sins from the world. McDowall was writing and preaching at the height of the religious revivals known as the Second Great Awakening. The Awakening revitalized former Puritan denominations such as the Congregationalists and Presbyterians, and drew converts to the Methodists and Baptists. Over the next decade, new churches and religious movements emerged from this ferment, and devout Americans followed. Ministers and the faithful embraced the power of individuals to reject sin and shape their spiritual destiny. In 1832, evangelical businessman Lewis Tappan had lured the great preacher Charles Grandison Finney, who had led a series of wildly successful revivals in western New York, to Manhattan by transforming a rented theater into the Chatham Street Chapel.[6] Inspired by Finney, New York evangelicals like Tappan and McDowell distributed Bibles, published religious tracts, sponsored missionaries, established Sunday schools, and founded societies to fight the sins of intemperance, slavery, and, of course, licentiousness. They believed that Americans had previously neglected sexual immorality as a topic of reform because of fear of impropriety.

In New York City, evangelicals confronted a society that was more mobile, cosmopolitan, market-driven, and sin-ridden than their rural hometowns. Farmers, manufacturers, and merchants traveled to New York City to buy and sell goods. Young American men and women, as well as immigrants, moved to the city in search of jobs, opportunity, and excitement. After New York finally abolished slavery in 1827, the city became a destination for many African Americans. This movement of goods and people contributed to the growth of sexual commerce. In the early nineteenth century, prostitution expanded rapidly in New York and other cities. Evangelicals such as McDowall tried to combat this expansion by establishing Magdalen societies to rescue prostitutes. Following the sexual upheaval of the Revolutionary era, in which their fellow Americans had embraced

individual choice and happiness, evangelical and middle-class reformers
also emphasized marriage as the only appropriate venue for sexual love.[7]

McDowall attracted leading men to his campaign against sexual immorality, but he was far more successful at enlisting middle-class women. The
female members of Manhattan's Laight Street and Spring Street churches
immediately formed societies to support the cause. McDowall published a
sample constitution so women in other congregations and cities could follow their example. Based on this template, potential members pledged to
"do all that we can do to prevent licentiousness, and actions contrary to
the Ten Commandments, and to be chaste, and moral, and to persuade
others to be so too."[8]

In contrast to the reigning sexual double standard, McDowall believed
in holding both men and women accountable for adultery. McDowall
described moral reform as "A Work for Woman" in part because his definition of sin included both sexes, and because he believed that woman had
the power to influence male behavior: "If every female of worth and
respectability would frown on the seducer, it would effect much." When he
proposed a "general" female moral reform society in New York, women
organized the New York Female Moral Reform Society (NYFMRS) in 1834.[9]
Two years later, McDowall died after being suspended by the Third Presby-
tery for "unchristian and unministerial" conduct, a charge related to his
dramatic exposure of prostitution in New York as well as his mismanage-
ment of financial donations to the cause. The New York Female Moral
Reform Society transformed the "martyr" McDowall's newspaper into their
Advocate of Moral Reform.[10]

These women turned moral reform into a major social movement. In
1837, the NYFMRS reported 226 auxiliaries with 15,000 members. By the
early 1840s, they claimed over 500 auxiliaries and 40,000 members. Like
McDowall, female moral reformers believed that women had a particular
duty in this "war of extermination": "as *women*, we owe it to our sex; as
daughters, wives, and mothers, we owe it to society; and as *Christians*, we
owe it to our God, to adopt the most efficient measures in our power to
arrest the progress of licentiousness."[11] Middle-class women thus claimed a
new, and vast, field of influence as evangelical warriors. Their work started
in the home, with brothers, sons, and husbands, and extended to society.
Woman, they declared, must be the "guardian of her own virtue." Individu-
ally armed, women should unite their powers to "rebuke every impropriety
in men who keep their company, and banish from their company in public

and in private every man" who had "defiled the flesh." Female moral reformers vowed to shun the offenders, withdrawing their invitations, companionship, and affections from men who did not meet their standards of pre- and extra-marital chastity. The moral reform press dedicated itself to raising awareness of the wages of sexual sin, but also published the names of egregious sinners. Any woman who did not join them, the NYFMRS asserted, betrayed her sisters: "The woman who will not do it plays the traitor—sells the citadel of female virtue."[12]

Evangelical men followed women's lead, assuming leadership over the economic and political problems caused by prostitution, adultery, and licentiousness. In 1836, after the sensational murder of a prostitute named Helen Jewett, 1,500 men attended a meeting at Chatham Street Chapel to form a Men's Moral Reform Society, an auxiliary to McDowall's American Seventh Commandment Society. In their newspaper, the *Journal of Public Morals,* they renounced the privileges of the prevailing sexual double standard, and concluded that the presence of an estimated 75,000 prostitutes in the country depended on approximately 400,000 "male profligates." Like the Rev. Timothy Dwight, these male moral reformers viewed licentiousness as "*anti-social,*" filling the nation's poorhouses, prisons, and hospitals, and costing $45 million.[13] The moral reformer and abolitionist Beriah Greene argued that marriage should be the foundation of the nation's "free institutions": "*whatever goes to break up the arrangements of domestic life, goes to subvert the foundations of good government.*"[14]

As Greene's involvement indicates, evangelical movements against licentiousness and slavery found common cause. Abolitionists viewed the institution of slavery as contrary to sexual morality, or, as David Ruggles put it, "an Abrogation of the Seventh Commandment." Like the abolitionists who described slavery as a form of "legalized adultery, piracy, and murder," Ruggles criticized violations of the religious commandment against adultery.[15] Though he relied on the literal meaning of the term, his argument informed later metaphorical uses of adultery by identifying the illicit and immoral within the legal institution of slavery. In order to undermine slavery, abolitionists called attention to its sins and harms as a system endorsed and upheld by society, church, and state. Soon, critics of marriage would do the same.

In his 1835 pamphlet, Ruggles, the leader of the New York Vigilance Committee, which later aided Frederick Douglass's escape from slavery, asserted that "licentiousness of intercourse between the sexes, constant, incestuous, and universal" existed under American slavery. Baldly, he stated, *"purity is the exception, and dissoluteness the rule."*[16] Ruggles condemned the sexual double standard that enabled the sins of slaveholders: "All white men can habitually violate their nuptial vows and the law of chastity, if they please, without forfeiting their moral or Christian character." Undoubtedly anticipating a moral reform readership, he urged that slavery be fought with *"evangelical weapons."* American churches, he argued, "should no longer be a den of thieves and adulterers."[17] Citing 1 Corinthians 5:9–13 ("not to company with fornicators"), he invited northern women to rid their congregations of sinners. Ruggles excluded southern white women from this proposal, viewing them as complicit in the sexual misbehavior of their husbands and sons. Instead, he urged northern women to condemn slavery, and its violations of the Seventh Commandment, by signing a protest against visiting slaveholders who might occupy the pulpit or pews of their churches. If their warning was ignored, and a slaveholder appeared in the congregation, he advised all women to immediately exit the building.[18]

If northern women ostracized adulterous and fornicating slaveholders, Ruggles believed, slavery would lose its image as a respectable and Christian institution. He realized the potential of moral reform women to be enlisted against slavery: "Northern Christian ladies alone can eradicate the moral pestilence which destroys female purity and domestic comfort and endearments in the slaveholding states."[19]

Black and white women also saw the link between moral reform and antislavery. A former slave and preacher named Isabella Van Wagenen, later known as Sojourner Truth, worked with John R. McDowall and his allies to save prostitutes in the Five Points district of Manhattan. In 1835, following a lecture by McDowall, women in Van Wagenen's Zion Church—the African Methodist Episcopal Zion Church, the first black congregation in the city—formed a "(Colored)" Female Moral Reform Society. Two years later, they announced their membership had more than doubled to 138 members. Though they undoubtedly shared many of the same motivations as white women—religious faith, sexual morality, and a desire to help other women—African American women also confronted stereotypes of black female licentiousness. By organizing a moral reform society, free African American women demonstrated their sexual virtue to white allies.[20]

Yet as indicated by the *Advocate of Moral Reform*'s use of the modifier "colored," white moral reformers struggled with prejudice in their ranks.

At the New York Female Moral Reform Society's annual meeting in 1838, activists debated a resolution that the "*Advocate of Moral Reform* shall be open to the cry of our suffering colored sisters, and that we shall recognize them as *women*, whose dearest interests like our own are staked on the issue of this great question." Twenty-first-century readers may find it troubling that moral reformers needed a resolution to recognize African American women as *women*, with shared views and goals, but at a time when feminine respectability and purity was seen as a privilege of middle-class whiteness, this statement challenged the sexual and racial status quo. The resolution also raises intriguing questions about the identity of these "suffering colored sisters." Did the resolution refer to enslaved women? Or did it include free black women in their own city, such as those at Zion? To the NYFMRS's credit, the resolution passed with a "considerable majority."[21]

At the same 1838 meeting, the NYFMRS launched its campaign to criminalize adultery and seduction in New York State. Members approved a resolution that "petitions be prepared and circulated as extensively as possible, praying the legislatures of several states, to make the crime of seduction and adultery, offences punishable with imprisonment."[22] In their methods, moral reformers followed the lead of abolitionist women, who had flooded the U.S. Congress with hundreds of thousands of petitions asking for the abolition of slavery in the District of Columbia and the territories. In 1836, frustrated congressmen passed a "gag rule" preventing discussion of the divisive issue. Such petition campaigns not only sought a legal and political remedy to a social problem but they also raised awareness of the issue as a public matter.

To collect signatures, women had to talk to their friends, neighbors, and strangers, which also recruited new members to local moral reform societies. Still, it could be an uncomfortable task. Since their mission required speaking explicitly about sexual topics, including adultery and prostitution, women who circulated petitions needed to overcome shyness and embarrassment.

Borrowing from the abolitionist press, the *Advocate of Moral Reform* published a standard petition form that could be copied by local societies. Addressed to the (fill in the blank) state legislature, the petition declared "Seduction and Adultery" to be as destructive to "individuals, families, and society at large" as "theft, burglary, and arson." In addition to populating the state's almshouses and prisons, adultery and seduction broke "the hearts of fathers and mothers . . . causing considerable anguish to be felt through all the relations of life." As "Women of this State," the signers "respectfully and earnestly" pleaded with politicians to pass an act penalizing seducers and adulterers with a prison term. They believed "salutatory laws" would "greatly diminish this amount of human wo [*sic*]."[23]

As they planned a multistate campaign, New Yorkers learned from their colleagues in the New England Female Reform Society that adultery was already a crime in their states, including Massachusetts, where the penalty was up to three years in prison and a fine of up to $500. A majority of states and all of the New England states maintained such laws, in place since the "severe" colonial period, when the penalty might include whipping and/or the wearing of "two capital letters, viz A.D." In 1847, however, Vermont's punishment for adultery was a prison term of up to five years, and fines up to $1,000. In Virginia, North Carolina, and Mississippi, the punishment was fines between $20 and $500. In Georgia, an adultery conviction could bring a fine of up to $500 with a stint in jail up to 60 days. In New Jersey, the punishment was relatively mild: adulterers received a fine of $100, fornicators $14.[24]

One shocked former New Englander wrote upon moving to the Empire State that in New York "the prowling tiger" could encroach upon "the sanctity of female virtue," "disturb the peace and harmony of the conjugal relation," and destroy "the sacred enclosure of domestic happiness" and still retain all the privileges of a "free citizen."[25]

New York women fought for a criminal adultery statute on their own, but women in other states joined the petition campaign for laws against seduction. Pennsylvania passed an anti-seduction law in 1843. In 1849, soon after Wisconsin became a state, its laws included the following: "Any unmarried man who, under promise of marriage, or any married man who shall seduce and have illicit connection with any unmarried female of previous chaste character, shall be guilty of a misdemeanor." In 1846, however, Massachusetts activists failed to criminalize seduction.[26]

Just as adultery fed prostitution, moral reformers argued, so too did seduction. Despite contemporary evidence that most women became prostitutes for economic reasons, moral reformers believed that the wiles of a male seducer were the first step in a woman's fall from virtue.[27] In their view, innocent young women and girls fell prey to handsome, charming, amoral men, who with promises of love and marriage persuaded them to abandon their virginity. After a licentious man had seduced a naïve maiden, he abandoned her, alone, often pregnant, and cast out of polite society.

Moral reformers saw these women as victims, with no choice but to enter a life of prostitution. This view of female victimhood was one reason moral reformers emphasized a single standard of chastity for men and women, with similar consequences for any deviation. As their allies at the *Journal of Public Morals* proclaimed, the licentious man was *"no more entitled to respectability, or to the society of the virtuous, than the licentious female."*[28] The moral reform press published numerous stories of seduction, but these stories also captured the imagination of the flash press, newspapers that catered to young single urban men, interested in sports, theater, and women. In the guise of denouncing prostitution, the flash press advertised particular prostitutes, madams, and brothels. In one series, "Lives of the Nymphs," they retold the seduction tales (undoubtedly fictional) of their favorite women of the town.[29]

At first, the New York petition campaign received scant, slightly mocking attention from legislators.[30] The editor of *The Albany and New York Switch*, a paper specializing in the misdeeds of legislators and other Albany residents, did not hold out much hope: "Petitions are pouring in from every direction asking the legislature for the passage of a law for the suppression of this vice [licentiousness]; but whether they will meet with any better success than those of the last season remains to be seen," he wrote, as the present legislature contained about "as much morality" as the previous session. The editor then noted lawmakers' visits to the brothels on Denniston Street.[31]

By 1841, the New York Female Moral Reform Society had sent 40,000 petitions to the New York legislature. Two years later, they began to gain more "respectful attention" from Whig and urban representatives who viewed themselves as protectors of women. The Speaker pro tem of the House, Mr. Hathaway (probably Samuel G. Hathaway Jr., a Democrat from Chemung County), presented a petition signed by one thousand of his "fair constituency, among whom were the most virtuous and respectable of the city [Elmira]." Echoing the language of female moral reformers, he urged his fellow politicians that as "fathers, brothers, as Christians, we should remove this vile reproach upon our system of laws, and do something to satisfy the thousands that have year after year, implored our aid in vain."[32] Women's petitions had made an impact.

In 1847, the New York Senate's committee on grievances prepared a report and bill based on the thousands of petitions received from female "citizens." The Senate report included a brief history of anti-adultery laws since ancient Greece, noting that "*adultery*, has been deemed deserving of *punishment*, in almost all ages of the world" and in the "more enlightened, virtuous, and distinguished nations." Adultery, as the enemy of marriage, was a crime against society. The report provided a list of states that imposed fines or prison terms for the offenses of adultery and fornication. New York stood out in its "utter disregard" for this legal consensus as well as "the earnest wishes and deliberate judgment of a vast majority of her most enlightened, virtuous and philanthropic citizens." Though the state's legislators offered no explanation for changing the laws beyond the current, more educated views of the "nineteenth century of the Christian era," New York lawmakers had followed the lead of the English, who refused to prosecute adultery as a crime after the restoration of the monarchy in 1660.[33]

Moral reform tried to obliterate the sexual double standard in one sense—men were to be held just as socially accountable, and judged, as women—but it reinforced or created another kind of double standard in the cause of challenging the first: petitioners and politicians both presumed a male perpetrator and a female victim. The report referred to "his crime," and "his villainy and crime," a "debased and heartless offender," who performed "his hellish and disgusting work of sensuality and crime."[34] In the language of the report, lawmakers also re-created New York State as a female moral reformer, a guardian of her own virtue and that of her citizens.

The sweeping law proposed by the Senate committee included sections on seduction and abduction (enticing a chaste female into a house of ill fame)—which protected young, virginal women only—and sections on keeping a brothel. The law's section on adultery defined it inclusively as "sexual intercourse with the husband or wife of another person," which came with a fine of $500-$1,000, or a jail term of six to twelve months. By the committee's own admission, the penalties were "severe," but its members believed them necessary.[35] The section on adultery, like the section on keeping a house of ill repute, offered an indication that women too might be charged under this law. Whether due to its severity, politicians' self-interest, or male privilege, the proposed act failed. The following year, the legislature passed more circumscribed bills criminalizing seduction and abduction. Though these narrower laws passed by wide margins, one historian describes them as "virtually useless."[36]

Adultery did not become part of the New York State criminal code in the nineteenth century.[37] Agreeing that at least some forms of sex outside of marriage should be criminalized, legislators promised to shield pure young women from seduction and abduction, saving them for marriage. But New York politicians declined to define adultery as a public matter, seeing it as a private dispute between individuals. A cuckolded husband could sue his wife's lover for criminal conversation. Both wives and husbands could also seek a divorce on the grounds of adultery, the only fault possible in New York State. Criminalizing adultery would have created an extreme obstacle to these civil remedies. Of course, politicians might have acted out of sheer self-preservation, hoping to avoid prosecution under such a law.

*   *   *

Over the previous two decades, adultery had emerged as an issue of public and political significance. In the midst of the evangelical excitement of the Second Great Awakening, the act of adultery was not only a matter of individual sin but of social consequence. Moral reformers defined marriage as the foundation of both religion and society, and adultery, with seduction and prostitution, was a threat to the institution. The evangelicals who campaigned to criminalize adultery rejected the prevailing norm of the sexual double standard in order to buttress monogamous marriage. They also wanted to protect women, and they made common cause in both argument and methods with abolitionists, including David Ruggles and Sojourner Truth. While their campaign did not succeed in New York State, they established an evangelical, antislavery, and political consensus that adultery was the problem, and marriage the solution.

Moral reformers expected opposition from "flash" newspapers and other defenders of male sexual prerogatives, but a more insidious threat to this consensus came from within their evangelical ranks. In the 1830s and 1840s, a group known as perfectionists promoted different and troubling ideas about sin and its implications for sexual love. For two perfectionist couples, George and Mary Cragin, who had been involved in the NYFMRS, and Harriet and John Humphrey Noyes, the fact that New York did not have a criminal adultery statute would become very significant.

CHAPTER 2

Adultery as Freedom from Sin

Mary Johnson and George Cragin, like many residents, had moved to New York City from smaller communities. In 1815, when Mary was five years old, her family arrived from Portland, Maine, seeking a larger market for her father's bookstore. By some accounts, she became Charles Grandison Finney's first and most faithful convert in Manhattan. When she met George, Mary taught Sunday school at Union Church on Prince Street. In 1827, nineteen-year-old George had arrived in Manhattan from Douglas, Massachusetts, to work for a mercantile firm. After hearing Finney preach, he converted and formed a prayer group with other young single men at his business.[1]

George and Mary belonged to the same church and moved in the same evangelical circles, but they had never spoken. One Sunday, they met by chance in front of the notorious Bowery Theater, a gathering place for prostitutes and sporting men. Mary was with a four-year-old girl from her Sunday school class. The girl's parents had neglected to pick up their child, and Mary was desperately searching for them. Recognizing George, she conquered her "bashfulness and sense of female propriety, that would have deterred her from speaking to a young man in the streets," and told him her worries for the young girl. George suggested they walk back to the church, where they found the girl's mother waiting, confident that her daughter was safe with Mary.[2]

George recalled Mary as the perfect nineteenth-century woman: a vision of "female loveliness," with a beautiful smile and chaste, demure manner. He also admired her "good mind."[3] At first, Mary rejected his vows of love and proposals of marriage. She had decided not to marry in part because her father had become an alcoholic after his business failed. Mary told George, "I have too much regard for you to consent to disgrace your father's family by accepting your offer of marriage." This only made George love her more for her "benevolence and friendship," and he vowed to wait.[4] Taking her brother's advice, Mary finally agreed to wed.

After their marriage in 1833, the couple immersed themselves in evangelical reform. They taught Sunday school, led Bible classes, and visited the poor. When they found a family living in a dark, damp basement, they agreed to take in one of the children. After instructing the girl with "soap and catechisms," they found her a job in an umbrella factory.[5] George also left business to work as an agent, lecturer, and publisher for organizations such as the Maternal Association, the Female Benevolent Society, and its successor, the New York Female Moral Reform Society. In 1837, the *Advocate of Moral Reform* listed George as their agent. Mary served on the Board of Directors for the NYFMRS.[6]

But both George and Mary believed something was missing. They were pious and devoted their time and energy to moral reform. They loved each other, but, as George remembered, perhaps too much: "Our fondness for each other, however, savored too much of creature idolatry. We were childishly and unwisely absorbed in the intimacy offered to us by the marriage relation." Like many of their fellow Americans, the Cragins continued to be religious seekers, "hungering and thirsting after a better life."[7]

They found a spiritual guide in a Yale-educated minister named John Humphrey Noyes. In New Haven, he preached in an evangelical free church, which attracted worshippers from all denominations, and began to advocate perfectionism, or personal freedom from sin. In 1834, at age twenty-three, he went to New York City to consult with other perfectionists and evangelicals. These included Charles Weld, brother of the abolitionist Theodore Dwight Weld, and James Latourette, a prominent New York perfectionist and friend of the future Sojourner Truth. Noyes also called on Finney, who embraced a more socially acceptable, church-based form of perfectionism that Noyes called "Oberlin perfectionism," but, since Finney was out of town, the young minister prayed with Mrs. Finney instead.[8] Later, Noyes struggled for leadership with these individuals, but, for now, he hoped to prove the truth of perfectionism.

In New York City, Noyes embarked on a personal experiment with religious truth. He decided to test whether his faith in Christ would free him from death as well as sin. Over a three-week period, he prayed, experiencing first immense happiness, and then "a strange, murky atmosphere" and "darkness."[9] He felt like he was suffocating, and lay down on his bed to

Figure 1. John Humphrey Noyes, the perfectionist founder of the
Oneida Community, and of the theory and practice of complex
marriage. Courtesy of the Oneida Community Mansion House.

await death. When he did not die, Noyes stopped eating and sleeping, and
walked the streets of the city to the point of exhaustion. Like George and
Mary Cragin, Noyes traversed the "vilest" parts of Manhattan, descending
"into cellars where abandoned men and women were gathered," and talking
"familiarly with them about their ways of life, beseeching them to believe
in Christ, that they might be saved from their sins." He gave them Bibles
and some money, but claimed implausibly that he did not engage in their

sexual profligacy. The previously temperate Noyes also began drinking alcohol. This experience allowed him to differentiate between the "petty tyranny of fashionable morality" and a "new system of ethics" based on God alone. Struggling and defeating the evil he had brought into his life, Noyes emerged from this trial full of "confidence and peace."[10] The experiment confirmed Noyes's faith in himself: his personal victory over sin, his rejection of human laws and morality, and his direct obedience to God.

Perfectionists such as Noyes believed that an individual's acceptance of Christ led not only to salvation in heaven but also to freedom from sin on earth. In other words, they had achieved a state of spiritual purity, and no act or behavior could change that. Based on Matthew 5:48, "Therefore you are to be perfect, as your heavenly Father is perfect," they took the evangelical, reformist impulse to defeat sin to its logical conclusion.[11] Beyond this shared idea, perfectionists were a varied lot. Some, such as Charles Grandison Finney, defined the human potential for holiness as obedience to church teachings. These evangelical perfectionists continued to define extramarital sexuality as sinful.

Other perfectionists claimed greater knowledge of God's laws than the church. These radicals, including Noyes and then the Cragins, disputed the dominant view of marriage as a shield against sexual licentiousness. Instead, they viewed marriage, a worldly institution created by church and human laws, as itself sinful. Rejecting marriage as an institution of human rather than divine law, they defined an inclusive, open sexual love as a demonstration of their own perfection. In their view, the sin was not adultery, but rather the exclusivity of monogamous marriage. They raised the question: what if monogamous marriage itself was the problem?

Noyes's distinction between human and divine law, which identified marriage as a flawed, worldly institution, divided the Cragins' circle of Finneyites. In 1836, Harriet Cornelia Green, the Directoress of the New York Female Moral Reform Society, embraced perfectionism. Her husband, William Green Jr., a wealthy businessman, had helped found the Chatham Street Chapel, which brought Finney to New York. Green also worked with Lewis Tappan in the American Anti-Slavery Society. Despite their impeccable evangelical credentials, the Greens invited the already controversial Noyes to stay at their home on Prince Street. Writing after her conversion, Cornelia Green told Noyes of her subsequent resignation from the NYFMRS, her pity for her colleagues' "deadly" opposition to the truth, and, most important, her repudiation of moral reformers' view that marriage alone defined sexual morality. She asserted, "that which is now called purity will be seen to be utterly abominable in the eyes of God." Cornelia agreed with Noyes that the fashions of the world, including monogamous marriage, only interfered with relations between God and man: *every thing* ought to be under the leadings and guidance of the spirit, and *every relation* so far as it has a tendency to interfere with that Spirit, has the curse of God resting upon it."[12] Cornelia's husband moved more slowly and deliberately. William Green informed Noyes that "The Lord told me last fall, that the doctrines advanced by you were from hell." Green called him an "imposter." When he eventually realized that Noyes did not advocate licentiousness, however, William too declared his faith "in the truth you hold."[13]

The Greens' former colleagues in the New York Female Moral Reform Society rightly viewed Noyes's perfectionism as a threat to marriage. In an article in the *Advocate of Moral Reform*, they described perfectionism as "immoral and destructive," and a "dangerous and seductive heresy" that had already ensnared beloved colleagues (H. Cornelia Green). Moral reformers explained that perfectionists adhered to the biblical passage that in heaven, "they neither marry, nor are given in marriage" (Matthew 22:30). Claiming to have achieved a "resurrection state," perfectionists argued for the "abolition of the institution here." Moral reformers believed this doctrine would open "the floodgates to every species of licentiousness." The *Advocate* expressed shock and alarm "at the avowal of sentiments which seem to us, the very *refinement* of *licentiousness*." In their view, perfectionists had redefined sinful behavior—extramarital sex—as virtuous and pure. Just as they had shunned licentious men, members of the NYFMRS vowed to "refuse all fellowship" with perfectionists.[14]

Though the *Advocate* refused to publish it, Noyes wrote a reply that explained his evolving views on marriage. Noyes acknowledged that some perfectionists had used the doctrine as a "cloak of licentiousness," engaging in activities of which he disapproved, but he affirmed his belief that marriage did not exist in heaven. Noyes stated, "I believe that the will of God will be done on earth as it is done in heaven; consequently that a time will come when marriage will not exist on earth." According to Noyes, that time had not arrived. Instead, moral reformers had misrepresented his views and betrayed their trust "in written laws instead of the Holy Spirit."[15]

Noyes's view of marriage is also evident in his unromantic proposal to a wealthy perfectionist named Harriet Holton. In a letter dated June 11,

1838, Noyes disparaged marriage as limiting "the range of our affections." Instead, he envisioned marriage as one in which "my yoke-fellow will love all who love God . . . as freely as if she stood in no particular connection with me." Marriage should not, in his view, "monopolize or enslave" the heart, but encourage "the free fellowship of God's universal family." Harriet also rejected the marriage "fashion of this world," and accepted.[16]

The Cragins followed the Greens out of the New York Female Moral Reform Society and into the perfectionist fold. After reading some of Noyes's writings, Mary confessed that with Christ as her savior, "I shall never sin again." Noyes believed that being free of sin meant abandoning ego, possessiveness, and exclusive love. In accepting this scandalous doctrine of perfectionism, Mary showed her willingness to lose her husband, children, relatives, and friends for her beliefs. In November 1839, George also made his confession of faith. Thirty members of the NYFMRS held a meeting to judge him, producing as evidence Noyes's infamous *Battle-Axe* letter, named for the newspaper that published it without permission in 1837. In this private letter to a friend, Noyes argued that, "when the will of God is done on earth, as it is in heaven, *there will be no marriage.*" He also offered an example of such a heavenly marriage: "I call a certain woman my wife. She is yours, she is Christ's, and in him she is the bride of all saints. She is now in the hands of a stranger, and according to my promise to her I rejoice. My claim upon her cuts directly across the marriage covenant of this world, and God knows the end." George's response to this interrogation affirmed his belief that Noyes was "inspired by God" to "preach the true gospel of full salvation from sin." He speculated that "the letter in question referred to a future state of things, whether in this world or the next, I could not say; but with that state of things I had nothing to do at present." By the end of the meeting, George had lost his job and his social status, but now he and Mary shared the righteous confidence of true believers.[17]

As newly converted perfectionists, George and Mary had to reconsider the terms of their legal, worldly marriage. They needed to transform their exclusive love into an all-encompassing love, extending outward to the fictive family of perfectionists. George had the most difficulty. When perfectionists gathered at their home, he was jealous of other men, whom he thought were flirting with Mary. In retrospect, he realized he needed help with his "idolatrous love for his wife": "My wife and I were still babes in the school of faith—infants that required much nursing and correcting."

The Cragins trusted a fellow perfectionist, Abram C. Smith, a former Methodist preacher, who claimed "unity" and "partnership" with Noyes, to lead them out of their spiritual troubles.[18]

In 1840, the Cragins moved in with Abram Smith and his wife in Rondout, New York, blending households to defeat their monogamous, idolatrous love. Perfectionists viewed monogamy as creating false idols and the Cragins tried to purge themselves of this exclusive love with their sexual adventures. Mr. Smith and Mary Cragin began to spend more and more time together, often alone. George perceived a new coldness from Mary, and he began to despair. His wife was now the "ally" and "sweetheart" of another man, and he was in the "chains of self-condemnation" over his continued jealousy. "That in forsaking all for Christ as I claimed to have done, my wife was included," he remembered. "But my feelings, like willful, disobedient children, would listen to no such reasoning."[19]

Smith manipulated the situation to his advantage. Disappointed that George Cragin showed no interest in his wife, he forced Mrs. Smith to move in with relatives. Then, Smith secured George's permission to have Mary visit his bedchamber for "spiritual advice and relief." Realizing that the visit was "more of a carnal than a spiritual one," George wondered if this extreme act was really necessary to cure him of the "marriage spirit."[20]

Learning of the Cragins' marital experimentation in Rondout, sure to further taint perfectionism, Noyes intervened. He rebuked both Abram Smith and Mary Cragin for their "intimacy." Noyes also told George that his "claiming, legal spirit" was at fault, and so George "freely forgave" Abram and Mary. Smith's angry wife had an arrest warrant issued for her husband for kicking her out of her home, considered a breach of peace, and Noyes counseled Smith to leave town with him rather than stay and fight a mob. After returning to Rondout, however, Abram Smith persuaded Mary Cragin that Noyes approved of their relationship, and their "secret marriage" resumed. Mary later wrote to Noyes, "Guilty as I am, I have been miserably deluded by him." Wracked with doubt, she eventually confessed to George, and together they decided, "We will be brother and sister after this . . . as we don't seem to prosper in this warfare, as husband and wife." As brother and sister in Christ, they had no cause for jealousy. Everything but the legal fact of their marriage had ended.[21]

Cragin did not blame perfectionism for his wife's extramarital affair. Though Abram Smith had believed that Mary Cragin was his "spiritual

Figure 2. A later image of George Cragin, devoted and
jealous husband, and follower of John Humphrey Noyes.
Courtesy of the Oneida Community Mansion House.

wife and companion," Cragin assured readers that "no such spiritual wife-
ownership came to him through his acquaintance with Mr. Noyes or his
writings." Noyes's own response to the second affair indicated his more
nuanced understanding of adultery. During their first sexual relationship,
Smith and Mary might have (mistakenly) believed they were acting according to God's laws by shedding their worldly connections. After having
pledged to end their affair, however, Noyes declared that Smith and Mary
were "*adulterers,*" having transgressed "acknowledged obligations" to

himself and George. If he and George had approved, Noyes suggested, the sexual relationship between Abram and Mary might not be considered adultery. In theory, Noyes had redefined adultery, but, in practice, he had shifted the authority to judge from the law or church to himself. He responded swiftly, banishing Abram Smith from his company. Noyes treated the Cragins with more sympathy, inviting the family to Putney, Vermont, where he and his wife, Harriet, had established a small perfectionist community.[22]

In Putney, Mary Cragin underwent a five-year period of "rehabilitation," what Noyes and his followers would later call mutual criticism, which involved listening as community members noted one's failings. According to Noyes, Mary was so depressed that she attempted suicide. By 1845, he had facilitated a truce between the Cragins and Abram Smith. While Smith took the blame for deceiving George, Mary signed a statement that she was responsible for their sexual relationship: "I took the place of Eve in tempting and seducing the man. . . . I sincerely ask Mr. Smith's forgiveness for having dragged him down into sensuality."[23] Her statement indicates the goals of mutual criticism as well as Noyes's assumptions about the sexual weakness of women. Mary accepted this judgment of her actions. The thirty-five members of the Putney Community also struggled with the "irresponsible" freedom that had plagued the perfectionist household at Rondout. In addition to mutual criticism, Noyes decided that "subordination," or a hierarchical organization under his leadership, was essential to the success of perfectionist communities. Otherwise, he wrote, "our households might be turned into brothels."[24]

By 1846, not long after the Smith-Cragin adultery crisis had been resolved, Noyes had implemented both mutual criticism and subordination, and he was ready to "elevate love" and abolish "worldly restrictions on sexual union." The experiment began with the Noyeses and the Cragins. George Cragin expressed his love for Harriet Noyes as a "sister in Christ." Pleased, Harriet responded that her heart was drawn toward George. John Humphrey Noyes told Mary Cragin he loved her. Mary replied, "I had loved Mr. Noyes so much that I feared he would find it out; for I was not certain, my awe of him was such, that he wanted me to love him so much." After these declarations, they comprised a circle "which the Devil could not break," though they did not expect to act on their declarations of love, conforming "to the laws of this world until the time arrives for the consummation of our union." The time came when Mary Cragin and John

Figure 3. Mary Cragin, who embraced the perfectionist
criticism of monogamous marriage as sinful. Courtesy
of the Oneida Community Mansion House.

Humphrey Noyes went for a walk on a mild May evening. Noyes "yielded
to impulse" and "took some personal liberties." Afterward, they returned
home and confessed to their spouses, who gave their wholehearted approval. The Noyeses and Cragins combined their households.[25]

As the circle of initiates expanded, John Humphrey Noyes declared
that the Putney Community had attained the necessary state of grace to

disregard the customs, fashions, and laws of marriage. Noyes's sister Charlotte and her husband John Miller were the third couple to enter into what these perfectionists began to call complex marriage, or the rejection of monogamous marriage and domesticity in favor of communal love and life. John Miller had previously expressed his attraction for Mary Cragin, causing distress and pain to his wife. Mary now proposed a "partnership" with John Miller, provided that they make Noyes a "third party," teaching them "how to love each other in that way which would be the most improving to our characters and tend to make us the happiest."[26] Under Noyes's supervision, complex marriage became an expansive spiritual and sexual union of consenting men and women.

Finally, on June 1, 1847, John Humphrey Noyes declared that the kingdom of God had come. In his wisdom and goodness, God had created the Putney Community for a purpose. As Noyes reminded followers, "We have been able to cut our way through the isolation and selfishness in which the mass of men exist, and have attained a position in which before heaven and earth we trample under foot the domestic and pecuniary fashions of the world. Separate households, property exclusiveness have come to an end with us. Our Association is established on principles opposed at every point to the institutions of the world."[27] The act of adultery had become an expression of their freedom from sin.

Unsurprisingly, many citizens of Putney, Vermont, were unhappy about the marital principles and practices of Noyes's community. The state of Vermont had a criminal adultery statute, and in October 1847, John Miller was the first member of the Putney Community arrested under the law. To avoid arrest and the threat of a mob, Noyes left Putney for Brattleboro. Soon, the community learned that arrest warrants had been issued for George and Mary Cragin on charges of adultery. George Cragin and John Humphrey Noyes decided to flee to New York City. Noyes, as always, made the best of his flight, reminding his wife Harriet, "You know it is an old plan of ours to plant ourselves in that city."[28] Mary Cragin moved with her infant, Victor (possibly the child of John Humphrey Noyes) to Hamden, Connecticut, boarding with a family called the Tuttles. Mary reported that she was the subject of gossip: "Yesterday two women, our nearest neighbors, came and spent the afternoon. We had some intimations that they were intending to gratify their curiosity by having a look at me, and they did. They stared most unscrupulously and, I doubt not, to their heart's content." Mary also received a message from Noyes about Abram Smith, who was (predictably) receptive to Noyes's new system of complex marriage. Noyes advised Mary, "I think you and he will meet ere long under happier auspices than formerly, and that all offenses will be swallowed up in victory."[29]

Though a small cohort remained in Putney, John Humphrey Noyes needed more friendly ground on which to plant his utopian community. A group of perfectionists invited Noyes to Oneida, New York, and he determined to re-establish his community there. In the spring of 1848, members of the Putney Community began to arrive: George and Mary Cragin and their four sons, Charlotte and John Miller and their three children, brother George W. Noyes with his wife Helen and son, the Tuttles' daughter Louisa, and so on into the fall. Two individuals were notably absent: H. Cornelia and William Green Jr. After publicly proclaiming their faith in him, the Greens had apparently rejected Noyes's authority. As a result, Mary Cragin disparaged them as "Democratic perfectionists," or those unwilling to be subordinate to Noyes, identifying them with the "slippery, subtle character" of Satan.[30]

Following the policy begun in Putney, Noyes and his followers were open about their criticism of legal marriage. In Oneida, Noyes wrote and circulated his *Bible Argument*, which offered a strong condemnation of its wrongs: "The law of marriage 'worketh wrath.' 1. It provokes to secret adultery, actual or of the heart. 2. It ties together unmatched natures. 3. It sunders matched natures. 4. It gives to sexual appetite only a scanty and monotonous allowance."[31] Without monogamous marriage, Noyes believed there would be no desire or need for adultery, and thus no sin or crime. In the same pamphlet, Noyes also introduced the Oneida Community's system of complex marriage: "In the kingdom of heaven, the intimate union of life and interests, which in the world is limited to pairs, extends through the whole body of believers; i.e. *complex* marriage takes the place of simple."[32] The outside world might view the Oneida Community's sexual relations as adulterous, but Noyes believed that complex marriage banished the real sins of possessiveness and jealousy that characterized monogamous unions.

As the Oneida Community welcomed new members, they struggled to expand and regulate this system of complex marriage. They also continued to deal with the legal fallout from Putney, but they lived, at least for a few years, without fear of legal persecution. They were quite clear on their standing: their practices, considered adultery in Vermont, did not violate the criminal laws of New York State.

CHAPTER 3

"Two Kinds of Adultery"

In the new Oneida Community, John Humphrey Noyes struggled to put complex marriage into practice. His utopia was one small part of a larger American experiment with communal living, and needs to be seen in that broader context. During the 1840s, Noyes remembered, "sociological experimentation in America had reached an impassioned climax."[1] Some of the best-known communities included Brook Farm in Massachusetts, the North American Phalanx in New Jersey, and Ceresco in Wisconsin, but many more appeared, and then disappeared, over the next decade. All of these communities shared ownership and labor; only a few of them, such as the Oneida Community and Modern Times on Long Island, reorganized marital relations. Noyes's utopia was the most successful, but complex marriage was not an easy or stable practice. Noyes viewed his authority as a man and spiritual leader as essential to ensuring that communal sex, especially among female members, was not licentious.

✳   ✳   ✳

After resettling in the congenial legal environment of central New York, the Oneida Community turned to the daily operation of communal labor and family relations. The community eventually developed profitable industries in animal traps, silk thread, and, famously, tableware. All property and profits were jointly owned, and community members worked together to prepare meals, produce marketable goods, and write, print, and distribute newspapers and pamphlets that promoted their views. The Oneida Community eventually built a rambling brick mansion, modeled on an elegant Victorian home surrounded by gardens, so that the adults might live as one extended family.

By joining the community in complex marriage, men and women abandoned their legal pairings to share love and physical pleasure. Noyes and other community members assumed the heterosexuality of these liaisons. He also made clear that complex marriage should not be licentious, which he defined as any sex that occurred outside established lines of his authority, and prospective partners had to both consent to intercourse and gain the approval of community elders. After his wife Harriet experienced multiple miscarriages, Noyes became an early advocate of birth control. The Oneida Community practiced male continence, which relied on men suppressing their orgasm, and they strictly regulated the conception of any children. After the age of two, children resided apart from their parents in a separate communal house.[2]

In order to appease their neighbors' potential outrage over these unorthodox practices, the Oneida Community attracted some new recruits using legal marriage. This strategy was especially effective in the case of their first local convert, a twenty-one-year-old woman named Tryphena Hubbard, who had read Noyes's *Bible Argument*. Tryphena's parents and brother were unfriendly and suspicious, and it is not clear how much Tryphena told them about Noyes's views of sex and marriage. Sensing their distrust, Noyes sent another young convert, Henry J. Seymour, to sway the Hubbards.[3] Born in 1826 in Westmoreland, New York, Henry was no stranger to communitarian experiments. His whole family had supported the abolitionist John A. Collins, founder of a short-lived community in Skaneateles, New York, in 1843. Henry's brother lived in the colony, and Henry remembered the members engaged in a "dietetic furor," surviving entirely on "boiled wheat." Collins was temperamental, condescending, and lacked "good judgment." Soon Henry's mother became alarmed at reports of Collins's religious unorthodoxy.[4] Following the breakup of the Skaneateles colony in 1846, Henry was primed for Noyes's Christian communism.

The meeting between Henry Seymour and the Hubbards was a success. On August 29, 1848, Tryphena Hubbard married Henry Seymour and joined the Oneida Community.[5] Though the Seymours were not the only married couple among the communitarians, their legal bond, occurring so soon after Noyes announced the kingdom of heaven on earth and published his views in the *Bible Argument*, is striking. Certainly, their marriage reassured Tryphena's relatives and probably other locals as well. It provided a legal rationale for Tryphena to leave her parents' home. The two young people shared the fervor of conversion to Noyes's views, and their spiritual excitement may have contributed to their sexual and emotional attraction. Since original members like the Noyeses and Cragins had been legally married before embarking on complex marriage, perhaps they viewed it as a necessary training period. Or perhaps Henry and Tryphena were not ready to fully embrace complex marriage.

Whatever the motivations for their legal relationship, Henry and Tryphena's marriage disturbed the competing social foundations of their two communities. In Oneida County, they were husband and wife, with mutual legal, economic, and sexual obligations. In the Oneida Community, their loving relationship was no different from that of any other adult man and woman. This tension undermined the male authority inherent in both legal and complex marriage. Though Noyes and other leaders governed all sexual relations in the Oneida Community, Tryphena still had the right to reject her husband or choose another, more attractive partner. And Noyes had no official legal mechanism to enforce his spiritual power over Tryphena or other female members.

And Tryphena Hubbard Seymour proved difficult to control. The Oneida Community's descriptions of the unraveling of her marriage, compiled in an unofficial history, are deliberately vague. The community continued to face open hostility from Tryphena's family. With Henry's assistance, Noyes tried to win them over, and Tryphena's father, Noadiah, began attending an occasional meeting. But such reconciliations were short-lived. Though Tryphena was loyal to Noyes, her family threatened the colony, disrupted their meetings, and stole from their garden. Almost two years after her marriage, Tryphena was despondent and, it seems, unappreciative of the community's efforts on her behalf. By the end of 1850, she "had come under judgment for insubordination to the church and excessive egotism amounting to a kind of insanity."[6]

The following year, her "kind of insanity," for which she may have had a "tendency," grew more serious. Tryphena apparently wandered around the community at night, crying, "talking incoherently," and "raving." She frightened the community children, and the intervention of other adults came to nothing.[7]

Historian Lawrence Foster speculates that her insanity might have come from her own resistance to complex marriage, perhaps due to the opposition of her family. Another possibility, indicated by the Oneida Community's observation of her "egotism" and "insubordination," as well as her subsequent treatment, is that she enjoyed it too much to be governed by

Figure 4. Tryphena Hubbard Seymour, member of the Oneida
Community, disciplined by both legal and complex marriage.
Courtesy of the Oneida Community Mansion House.

Henry or Noyes. If so, she would not have been the only founding member
(male or female) to have sex with abandon. Noyes had defined complex
marriage in opposition to licentiousness, but defiance of his leadership on
sexual matters, especially from women, threatened this fine distinction.[8]

Despite differences in their views of marriage, the Oneida Community
and local officials agreed about the importance of male authority. In the
nineteenth century, wives were legally, physically, and materially dependent
on their husbands. Noyes transferred this patriarchal arrangement to complex marriage, placing himself at the head of an extended family. Noyes,
and seemingly the entire county, endorsed Henry's brutal method of disci-
plining Tryphena for her alleged egotism. In October 1851, the Oneida
Community recorded details of Henry's confession that he had whipped

Tryphena "with a rawhide every day for three weeks, that her back was in consequence as black as his pantaloons, and that one of her eyes was so badly injured that he was doubtful whether she would ever see out of it again." The Oneida Community had encouraged Henry's actions as the best approach to treating an unstable mind and body. In an indication of the broader social and legal acceptance of this treatment of wives and the insane, even Tryphena's family, the Hubbards, acknowledged Henry's "good intentions." Nevertheless, they charged him with assault and battery. Local politicians and businessmen rallied to support the Oneida Community, which had worked hard to establish good relations with neighboring authorities. Even the district attorney deplored the case, saying, "I should have no heart to punish [Henry]."[9]

This reassertion of husbandly power temporarily resolved the threat to the Oneida Community. Noyes resorted to the legal, literal, and conventional meanings of adultery when it challenged male—and, in particular, his—authority. A community founded by an individual who had seen marriage, not adultery, as the true sin now conceded that adultery was not only grounds for divorce but also, for women, a form of insanity. In a settlement with the Hubbards, the Oneida Community pledged to be responsible for Tryphena's support for her lifetime ($125 per year if she was healthy, $200 per year if she was mentally ill). They also offered to pay for a divorce, and in New York State, adultery was the only possible ground. Henry, who had offered to plead guilty to assault and battery, presumably volunteered to confess his own infidelity to save Tryphena's reputation. In the meantime, at the expense of the Oneida Community, Tryphena was admitted to the New York State Lunatic Asylum in nearby Utica.[10] Established in 1843, the Utica Asylum was dedicated to curing cases of temporary insanity. A state institution, the hospital admitted most patients through court order. They also accepted patients such as Tryphena, whose family requested, authorized, and paid for her treatment. The hospital emphasized a strict routine and physical labor as treatment. Though patients attended church on Sunday, the hospital staff viewed religious excess as a cause of insanity and guarded against it. Further, since many families committed their relatives for behaviors such as promiscuity and masturbation, the sexes were segregated. Tryphena's case was not unusual.[11]

The Seymours' divorce also forced the Oneida Community to abandon complex marriage. Tryphena's insubordination had threatened both Henry's and Noyes' authority. In addition, the evangelical *New York Observer and Chronicle* had recently published an exposé entitled "Perfectionism and Polygamy," which called Noyes the "founder of a disgusting order of adulterers." As the title suggests, the article compared the practices of the Oneida Community with the Mormons, and found Noyes's followers to be "even worse." Though the members of the Oneida Community professed to be "perfectly holy," the *Observer* charged them with "living in a state of vile concubinage." Their evidence was the community's own annual report, which contained the *Bible Argument*, widely and freely distributed by Noyes. The *Observer* was horrified to discover that members of the community had been upstanding members of "orthodox, evangelical churches," and concluded that the only remedy was holy matrimony, "the good old-fashioned morality of our mothers and fathers."[12] In March 1852, the Oneida Community announced that they had *"resumed the marriage morality of the world"*—in other words, given up complex marriage—as a "concession to public opinion."[13] The Oneida Community did not reject their previous views, but altered their practices to avoid further trouble.

John Humphrey Noyes viewed the cause of the public outcry to be "the nervous, irritable feeling which folks have about adultery." Noting that Christ forgave the woman in the temple (John 8: 1–11), he downplayed the seriousness of violations of the Seventh Commandment. American society had emphasized the sin of adultery at "variance" to God's wishes: "Here we have the gnat that public opinion makes a monstrous camel." Noyes argued that there were two types of adultery, "one referring to the human relation, and the other to the divine." While the public had charged the Oneida Community with violating lower, man-made proscriptions against marital infidelity, he accused his fellow Americans of a "higher adultery," betraying God's law of salvation from sin. Noyes vowed to "bring [the world] to trial before the bar of Christ."[14]

Although its members had vowed monogamy, the Oneida Community faced new legal charges of sexual licentiousness. Having dropped their assault and battery charge against Henry Seymour, the Hubbards now accused the Oneida Community of "seduction," illegal under New York State law since the 1848 campaign described earlier. The evangelical moral reformers who lobbied for this law might have been pleased. The Hubbards' rationale was that Noyes and the Oneida Community had misled Tryphena about their views. They had seduced her, in other words, by promising a true Christian marriage. The Hubbards also considered a charge of abduction, for luring Tryphena into a "house of ill fame."

Tryphena's father wanted $5,000 in damages. Neither the district attorney nor Timothy Jenkins, the local congressman, believed the Hubbards had a case on either charge. After all, Tryphena and Henry had been legally married, and Tryphena chose to remain a member of the Oneida Community. Further, the lawmakers were unwilling to characterize the Oneida Community as a brothel. In Tryphena's case, the community had demonstrated the same opposition to promiscuity and the same endorsement of male authority as their more conventional neighbors. By the end of July 1852, the Oneida Community had agreed on a new settlement. Noadiah Hubbard would receive $150, and an additional $150 if he used his influence in the neighborhood to prevent further trouble from hostile locals. Hubbard's response was that "he was glad on Tryphena's account, she would feel much better to know that we had settled and were good friends."[15]

*   *   *

Finally at peace with the Hubbards, the Oneida Community revived complex marriage after a five-month hiatus. They announced a new "Theocratic Platform," which included renewed pledges to the "sovereignty of Jesus Christ" and the "Resurrection of the Spirit," as well as "salvation from sin," the "Unity of All Believers," and the "Abandonment of the Entire Fashion of the World—especially marriage." With this triumphant return to complex marriage, the Oneida Community continued their "Cultivation of Free Love" and "Dwelling Together in Association." Their miniature kingdom of God had been restored.[16]

What did the return of complex marriage mean for Tryphena and Henry? After Tryphena's brief stay in the asylum, she regained her status as a consenting adult member of the Oneida Community. Yet is hard to imagine that her troubled marriage and divorce did not have an impact on her interactions with Henry. Some evidence suggests that they were estranged. By the early 1860s, Henry resided in Oneida, and Tryphena lived at the community's Wallingford, Connecticut, branch. Her letters from this period reveal a strong attraction to fellow member Marcus (or Marquis) LaFayette Worden, who had joined the Oneida Community in 1849. In December 1861, she told him "trust the Lord—he loves us & can we not trust Him to arrange *circumstances* that will promote our highest happiness?" The next month, she wrote, "I confess our union in Christ and hope we shall find each other in Him."[17] The couple waited for sanction from Noyes and other Oneida Community leaders, but it is unclear if the approval of their sexual union ever came.

This geographical separation did not end the sexual relationship between Tryphena and Henry. In 1863, fifteen years after their marriage and eleven years after their divorce, they had a daughter named Lucy. The Oneida Community successfully used male continence to control the number of children produced by complex marriage, so the pregnancy was probably not accidental. Henry and Tryphena also needed the permission of community leaders to procreate. These leaders may have encouraged the pregnancy to distract Tryphena from her romance with Worden. They might have endorsed this particular coupling because of the legal marriage or spiritual standing of Henry and Tryphena. In the Oneida Community, Tryphena had the right to decline, and she did not. Even so, their relationship must have been complicated. Lucy was their only child, and like other Oneida Community youngsters, she lived separately from her parents. Like exclusive love between husbands and wives, the Oneida Community discouraged special attachments between parents, especially mothers, and their children. Little Lucy lived in the Oneida Community until her early death in 1870. Marcus Worden, object of Tryphena's hopes for happiness, seceded (to use their language) from the Oneida Community in the same year. Still a faithful member, Tryphena died in 1876 at age forty-nine.

Henry Seymour became one of the stalwarts, and long after the Oneida Community dissolved, he clarified its sexual system for the public. He believed that the Oneida Community had improved upon marriage as well as solved all its problems. Seymour imagined the typical marriage with a short honeymoon period, followed by years of disillusionment and betrayal, which made the laws governing marriage "state prison laws" for a "sin-ridden world." In contrast, the Oneida Community members "believed that the Christianized human heart ha[d] infinite capabilities of love; that instead of being worn out by one honey-moon, such an experience gives it the better preparation to scale yet greater heights of human happiness." The Oneida Community, he argued, had also resolved the problem of women's subjection to their husbands' power. Oneida communists shared a love that was stronger and more sacred than a legal bond, and unlike sin-ridden marriages, left "no forsaken women and children by the way."[18] Henry Seymour probably comforted himself that he had done his best to help Tryphena, but this idealized portrait of complex marriage bore little resemblance to her experience. While the Oneida Community had not for-saken her, Tryphena's love life could not be described as an extended honeymoon. Instead, she found herself subject to the same legal and physi-cal restrictions as other American wives.

Women's power in the Oneida Community depended on their rela-tionship to John Humphrey Noyes. During the period of crisis with the Hubbards, Noyes mostly lived at the community's Brooklyn branch, but he also traveled to Niagara Falls with Mary Cragin for "a quiet opportu-nity of perfecting our union with each other."[19] Noyes considered Mrs. Cragin (not his legal wife, Harriet Noyes) as his female counterpart, though not his equal, in the Oneida Community, and "better qualified for that position than any other woman in the universe." While he dis-couraged exclusive love, Noyes was enraptured with Mary, writing that with her, "I have had the experience of love in all its beauty and har-mony."[20] But Mary Cragin's spiritual and sexual partnership with Noyes ended with her sudden death, which occurred in the midst of Henry and Tryphena's marital strife. Abram Smith, whose adulterous relationship with Mary had almost destroyed her a decade earlier, returned to play an unlikely part in this tragedy.

Abram Smith and his children had joined the Oneida Community in April 1849. His ornery wife did not accompany them. In addition to his willingness to accept complex marriage and Noyes's authority, Smith offered something else of value: his property. Smith gave (or gave up) his Brooklyn house to the community. He also captained, and may have pre-viously owned, the sloop *Rebecca Ford*, now owned by the Oneida Commu-nists as an additional money-making venture. Every month, the boat carried a cargo of limestone down the Hudson River from Kingston, New York, to Brooklyn.[21]

In July 1851, just months before Henry Seymour whipped Tryphena, he had worked as crew on the final journey of Captain Smith's boat. Joining Smith, Seymour, and the other members of the crew were two passengers, Mary Cragin and a recent convert named Eliza Allen. They sailed from Brooklyn and then, while the men loaded limestone in Kingston, Mrs. Cragin and Eliza went to look at the Rondout cottage where Mary and her husband had lived with the Smiths over ten years before. For Eliza's reli-gious edification, Mary probably recounted her struggles with monogamy, love, and religious faith. After the sloop had its cargo, the boat began the journey back down the Hudson. When they encountered a sudden storm, the crew reacted with confusion, and the ship dipped sharply, causing a load of limestone to crash into the hold. The *Rebecca Ford* sank in forty feet of water, with Mary Cragin and Eliza Allen trapped below deck. They were the only two to die. The men survived by holding onto floating pieces of the wreckage.[22]

Both George Cragin and Noyes were bereft. An anguished Cragin told Noyes that "My flesh is suffering and dying out." Noyes devoted his mental energy to overseeing the recovery of the bodies and the ship. It took nineteen days, and Noyes decided to sell the *Rebecca Ford* rather than repair it. At the end of the ordeal, he compared Mary's death to Christ's crucifixion: "This is a woman's dispensation . . . Mrs. Cragin's death is in this dispensation what the death of Christ was in the Jewish dispensation."[23] In Noyes's view, Mary's death would lead to the salvation of other women through acceptance of Christ's (and Noyes's) power.

Dabbling in a new religious movement known as spiritualism, Noyes also tried, unsuccessfully, to communicate with Mary in the afterlife. Just a few years earlier, spiritualism had emerged as a force in central New York, attracting believers from a variety of Protestant denominations. Mediums and clairvoyants helped grieving families contact dead friends and relatives, providing comfort as well as knowledge of the spirit world. When Abram Smith claimed to have succeeded in communicating with Mary, and that her spirit would lead them to pirate treasure, Noyes called him delusional. His battle for power with Noyes ongoing, Abram Smith seceded from the Oneida Community in 1857.[24]

To remember Mary Cragin's spiritual influence, the Oneida Community occasionally printed her writings in their newspaper the *Circular*, including "The Benefits of My First Confession," an article that alluded to her sexual affair with Abram Smith at Rondout. After Mary's first confession of Christ, her acceptance that he had saved her from sin, "I was prepared for any enthusiastic course of folly, under the impression that I could do no wrong." Her former colleagues in the moral reform movement had predicted nothing less from perfectionist doctrines. Mary called her involvement with Smith and its aftermath a "chasm of confusion and condemnation," but one that led to her "present redemption—that which led me out of sin." She had learned that salvation was not "instantaneous," and that temptation and suffering were part of it.[25] It was not that Mary Cragin stopped having sex with other men, but that she did so within the community of believers, out of obedience to the wishes of Noyes and God. In a short article that followed, H., probably Noyes's wife or sister Harriet, wrote that, "Mrs. C's visiting this particular scene [Rondout], just before her exit, was an incident of dramatic interest to those who knew her." She had left Rondout "in a state of unspeakable wretchedness," and "she returned forgiven, justified, perfected." For H., Mary Cragin's compassion for sinners had come from this experience. The author summed up Mary's life: "Exercise had made her adroit in *overcoming*."[26] Mary Cragin's power came from conquering her own desires and submitting to John Humphrey Noyes.

*   *   *

The same year that Congress passed the Compromise of 1850, which included the notorious Fugitive Slave Act, Noyes had published a small pamphlet titled *Slavery and Marriage: A Dialogue*, which compared the two institutions and condemned both. Always attuned to the press, Noyes chose as a setting for this dialogue, "Newspaperdom," and in the Brooklyn branch of the Oneida Community, Noyes had positioned himself near its center. Noyes criticized the nation's newspapers for emphasizing the political issue of slavery over marriage, which he viewed as the more pressing issue facing the country. In the national debate over slavery, however, both abolitionists and their pro-slavery opponents viewed marital morality as key to their arguments. Pro-slavery forces argued that slavery was institutional kin to marriage—a natural hierarchy—while abolitionists denounced slavery as corrupting the marriages of whites and destroying those of African Americans.[27] His pamphlet invoked these arguments for his own end: to prove the superiority of complex marriage. In contrast to moral reformers, but with many other communitarians, he was not interested in abolition or racial equality. The membership of the Oneida Community was exclusively white. Though they interacted with abolitionists such as their wealthy neighbor Gerrit Smith, and undoubtedly knew of his assistance to fugitives, Noyes's criticism of marriage as a form of slavery did not lead them to empathize with slaves. Despite his challenges to conventional marriage, Noyes accepted inequalities of sex and race.[28]

Noyes's pamphlet begins with a conversation between two characters, Judge North and Major South, over the nature of slavery. Judge North argues that slavery is arbitrary, cruel, and "contrary to natural liberty." Major South replies that slavery is a "*natural*" institution, with happy slaves and benevolent masters. While North suggests that *"liberty breeds virtue,"* South believes that emancipation will lead to murder of whites. At this point, a character named "Mr. Free Church" intervenes, telling Judge North, "I hold the same opinion about Marriage that you do of slavery, that it is an arbitrary institution, and contrary to natural liberty. What do you say to this opinion?"[29] North responds with the same arguments that South has been using to defend slavery: marriage is natural and examples of its cruelty exceptional.

Free Church argues that "Marriage gives man *the power of ownership* over woman," and this power is as wrong in marriage as it is in slavery. Judge North turns to a biblical defense: " 'Thou shalt not commit adultery' is one of the Ten Commandments." Free Church replies that this endorsement is a negative one, and, quoting Matthew 22:30, argues that the Bible's sanction of the institution is only temporary. Instead, Free Church describes marriage as contrary to religion, "a huge Bastille of *spiritual tyranny; where men and women have the power to debar each other from their rights of conscience, and the enjoyment of their religious faith.*"[30]

Just as Major South argued the end of slavery would lead to murder, Judge North fears the end of marriage would lead to "unbridled licentiousness." Free Church returns to Judge North's argument that liberty breeds virtue: "free-love, or complex marriage, combined with community of property, would annihilate the very sources of adultery, whoredom, and all sexual abuse." The "compulsory abstinence" of monogamy caused these "crimes." If men and women experienced sexual plenty, Free Church asserted, "chastity and self-control" would be the result.

Judge North admits defeat, his own arguments against slavery utilized against marriage: "I must either let Slavery alone, or go for a revolution of society at the north as well as the south." Free Church does not envision revolution, but an expansive love. In the kingdom of God, Free Church responds, "love works righteousness in *freedom.*"[31] Noyes rested his case that complex marriage solved the problem of licentiousness.

Although he was not alone in comparing marriage to slavery, Noyes differed from other marriage critics in his failure to argue for women's equality. As the experiences of Tryphena Hubbard and Mary Cragin indicate, Noyes was no feminist. He criticized marriage without attacking patriarchy or male sexual privilege. Though he railed against marriage laws that defined women as the property of their husbands, in the Oneida Community's formative years Noyes also relied on the laws of marriage to control

women's sexual behavior. His interest in women's rights did not extend
beyond their reproductive rights, such as their right to consent to sexual
intercourse, and their right to choose when to have children.[32] But other
communitarians were beginning to criticize the institution as a violation of
the individual rights of women as well as men.

CHAPTER 4

"Legalized Adultery"

Throughout his career, John Humphrey Noyes took a great interest in other utopian experiments, exchanging visits and publications, and eventually writing his own *History of American Socialisms* (1870). Noyes criticized these communitarians, particularly followers of the French socialist Charles Fourier, for focusing on "external conditions" such as the structure of work and the extended household, leaving the pressing questions of "our relation to God and the relation of the sexes" for later.[1] But it was really in the "relation to God" that these communitarians differed from Noyes. Fourierists, including Stephen Pearl Andrews and Mary Gove Nichols, rejected his religious redefinition of adultery in favor of a more secular justification of their freedom to love. This included a more explicit commitment to women's rights and sexual autonomy. They turned to the metaphor of adultery to criticize loveless marriages as a violation of individual desire and moral agency.[2]

At the end of 1852, Americans reading the *New York Tribune*, the newspaper with the largest circulation in the country, encountered a shocking debate over the institution of marriage. Henry James Sr. had started the debate with the mild suggestion that more liberal divorce laws would contribute to happier marriages. He did not question the benefits or value of the institution. The reform-minded editor Horace Greeley was deeply interested in communitarian experiments, including the Oneida Community. Though he had praised Noyes's *Slavery and Marriage*, Greeley situated himself as an ardent defender the "sanctity, integrity, and perpetuity" of marriage.[3]

The most scandalous argument came from Stephen Pearl Andrews, founder of a Long Island utopian community called Modern Times, who responded that marriage was an "arbitrary and artificial institution." In its place, he advocated the "complete emancipation and self-ownership" of the individual. Like Noyes, Andrews believed that both men and women had the right to choose their lovers, in and outside of marriage. Unlike Noyes, Andrews did not base his views on the Bible. Andrews declared, "A mere handful of individuals, along with myself, do now, for the first time in the world, accept and announce the sovereignty of the individual, with all its consequences, as the principle of order as well as of liberty and happiness among men."[4] This "handful of individuals" were among the first to use adultery as a metaphor for unhappy legal marriages.

Andrews and his coworkers were a different kind of communitarian— secular, with little use for Christianity. Influenced by Fourier, they wanted to create a more equitable, harmonious society for men and women. In 1842, the reformer and translator Albert Brisbane had introduced Americans to Fourier in the pages of the *New York Tribune*. Aspiring to create a society free of social and economic conflict, Fourier advocated small communities, or phalanxes, in which individuals could pursue their own "passional attractions," including love, ambition, family, and pleasure. For Fourier, communal living was more efficient than the "isolated household," thus allowing men and women greater time for their spiritual and physical development.[5] Communitarians also argued that shared labor eased the burdens of childrearing and homemaking for women, suggesting that only those with an "affinity" would take on the responsibilities of childcare.[6]

Though one Fourierist, Marx Edgeworth Lazarus, described monogamy as "social sleep," most of Fourier's American followers downplayed the sexual implications of his theories to focus on the pragmatic reform of labor and households. These followers included Warren Chase, a veteran of the Wisconsin Phalanx, who remembered "the great advantages and economies of combined labor and living," noting that the community in Ceresco "never had a case of licentiousness, nor a complaint of immoral conduct." As in Fourier's original plan, Ceresco and other American experiments relied on rich investors. With thirty phalanxes formed in the first ten years, Fourierism was much more popular than Noyes's Christian communism, but none of these phalanxes lasted as long as the Oneida Community.[7]

Stephen Pearl Andrews diverged from many Fourierists in his outspoken opposition to marriage. Born in 1812 and raised in New Hampshire, Andrews was the son of the Baptist minister Elisha Andrews and his wife, Wealthy Ann Lathrop. Named after a hero of the War of 1812, he later reveled in his connections to the elite Lathrop family. In many ways he was an entirely self-created character, perhaps not as brilliant as he imagined himself to be, but magnetic, brazen, and a bit of an oddball. His biographer aptly describes him as a humorless egomaniac.[8] Andrews rejected his father's Baptist religion for grander schemes to save humanity.

Andrews developed his contrarian view of marriage from boyhood. In an unpublished autobiography, he recalled, "I had noticed the terrible results of [marriage] in putting an end to the romance of love and substituting instead the stern realities of strife . . . and I conceived a dread of marriage." Andrews felt more sadness at marriages than at funerals, as he watched young couples moving toward that "fatal end." Cutting short his education at Amherst College, he went to Louisiana to teach at the Jackson Female Seminary, a school run by his widowed sister-in-law, Jane Andrews. The students were the daughters of wealthy planters, and approximately twenty slaves lived and worked at the seminary. Andrews described the oppressive atmosphere of slavery as a "tomb," and he vowed never to marry a "slave-holding heiress," but that did not stop him from enjoying the company of the planters' daughters. One of the students was Louisa Tyson, who was apparently one-eighth Creek. She was his brother Thomas's fiancée, "a dazzlingly beautiful woman," a "brunette" with "flashing dark eyes" and a modest and graceful blush.[9]

Andrews left teaching to study law with Thomas in Clinton, Louisiana, where he again confronted the insidious influence of slavery. His brother's antislavery views came to the attention of local regulators, a "volunteer body of spies and cutthroats enlisted on behalf of 'public order,'" composed of planters' sons and "corrupt" northerners. After one attack, Andrews recalled that he and his brother were "armed to the teeth." Thomas eventually married Louisa Tyson, but for Stephen Pearl, the relationship raised the metaphorical comparison between marriage and slavery. The young couple's love could not and did not survive either institution. First, the privileged Louisa proved to be an incompetent housekeeper, and their household became even more disorderly when she had four children in succession. Further, Thomas and Louisa had attempted to free their slaves and provide new homes for them in Illinois, but they died of malaria soon after their move to the north. In Stephen Pearl Andrews's view, his married brother had become "the slave of slavery which was endless, hopeless, and inexorable."[10] This endless, hopeless bond was not chattel slavery, but legal marriage, which bound man and wife in an exploitative, degrading economic knot. Upon his marriage, Thomas had become the owner of slaves. Andrews acknowledged his brother's attempt to free enslaved African Americans, but he saw the master-slave relationship continued in his sister-in-law's household labor and reproduction.

After his relatively staid career in the 1830s, Andrews's reputation as a radical grew when he moved his legal practice to Texas. Despite his strong opposition to wedlock, Andrews had married a former student, a Connecticut native named Mary Ann Gordon, a fact that he neglected to mention in his unpublished autobiography, which ends abruptly in 1835. Their son later described her as "largely in sympathy" with Andrews's "freedom loving propensities."[11]

In Texas, Andrews conceived a proposal to abolish slavery by convincing the British government to take over the territory in order to negotiate the compensated emancipation of all its slaves, a plan he floated to prominent abolitionists in both the United States and England. This proposal made him wildly unpopular in Texas, and, during heightened tensions with Great Britain over the Oregon territory, horrified U.S. officials. They assured their English counterparts that they had not authorized Andrews to visit London. Instead of freeing Texas slaves, Andrews's actions contributed to President Tyler's ultimate decision to outmaneuver the British and annex Texas in 1845.[12]

With this failure, Andrews seized on a new technology—shorthand—becoming the first American "teacher, author, and propagandist" of Isaac Pitman's system of phonography. Based on his own interest in linguistics, Andrews saw phonography as an art "for the people," a better path to literacy than the "present false and barbarous orthography and cumbersome hand-writing."[13] In 1844, he started a phonographic school in Boston and published *The Complete Phonographic Class-Book*. Andrews showcased the democratic power of phonography by teaching four illiterate African American men to read before a large audience. But phonography spread most rapidly among young, upwardly mobile white men, and some women.

These young Americans embraced the potential of the "new phonetic gospel" with religious zeal. Andrews's courses sometimes enrolled up to five hundred students, as "thousands of teachers and others all over the country essayed the new study, and did something with it."[14] Phonography opened new career paths, but for a variety of Americans, including marriage reformers, workers, and communitarians, it also promised to transform communication. The Oneida Community offered classes in phonography, as did Brook Farm. A young Lowell, Massachusetts, mill employee named

Marie Stevens also studied the art in her spare time, later becoming a radical utopian. Phonography had strong ties to Fourierism, with phonographic reporters such as Andrews, Theron C. Leland, and Henry M. Parkhurst affiliated with the Boston Union of Fourierists and other groups.[15] Newspapers like the *New York Tribune*, which eventually hired Andrews and many of his followers, used phonography to quickly and accurately report on speeches by reformers, politicians, and courtroom lawyers.

The early career of Edward Fitch Underhill, a future disciple of Stephen Pearl Andrews, shows how phonography spread through central and western New York, home to the Oneida Community. Born in 1830 in Wayne County, Underhill began work in a woolen factory in Waterloo, New York, at age sixteen. This factory was probably the Waterloo Woolen Mills, owned by Richard P. Hunt, at whose home the Seneca Falls women's rights convention was first conceived. Though Edward Underhill was not a member of the Society of Friends, his Quaker relatives may have provided the contact to Hunt. After only one week at the factory, Underhill had a terrible accident, losing the fingers on his left hand. In early 1848, he began to take stenography classes with Theron C. Leland, a leading "missionary" of both Fourierism and phonography.[16]

Underhill's simultaneous introduction to Fourierism and phonography led to his participation in the first American women's rights convention. In July 1848, Underhill and his aunt Martha Maria Barker Underhill attended the gathering in Seneca Falls, New York. Both aunt and nephew signed the convention's Declaration of Sentiments, which, in addition to declaring women's fundamental equality, harshly criticized marriage laws. The declaration stated that married women were "civilly dead." In marriage, the husband became the "master" of the woman, with rights to her property, her wages, and her children. Further, man had "so framed the laws of divorce, as to what shall be the proper causes of divorce."[17] After signing this document, Underhill moved west to become a reporter for the *St. Louis Reveille*, but by 1853, he and his new wife, Mary S. Post, were living in New York City, where he worked for the *New York Times* and then the *Tribune*.

Stephen Pearl Andrews had already relocated to the hub of American publishing, and in 1851 he and the anarchist Josiah Warren established their own experiment called Modern Times in the Pine Barrens of Long Island, later the town of Brentwood. The organizing principles of this association were Andrews's theory of "individual sovereignty," or the self-ownership of every man and woman, and Warren's concept of "cost the limit of price," or the idea that the price of goods should be based on how much they cost to produce, with no profit factored in. As a student of Fourier, Andrews believed these doctrines usefully compromised between cooperation and individualism. Modern Times was distinct among American utopias in its embrace of private property. Community members were individuals in "property relations, in business, in responsibilities, in modes of thought, opinion, and action," only bartering for goods and exchanging labor. Due to this more "equitable commerce," residents could afford to buy property and build homes within a two-hour train ride of New York City. The town included 220 lots, organized into a rectangular grid, at a reasonable price of $20 per acre. Though they did not settle in Modern Times, the first investors included Andrews's wife, Mary Ann, and his philosophical opponent Horace Greeley, who remained an avid follower of socialist utopias. Andrews's close friends, the phonographer Theron C. Leland and the marriage reformers Mary Gove and Thomas L. Nichols, lived at Modern Times. By 1855, the community had 85 residents, all of them white.[18]

When Andrews published his views of marriage in the *New York Tribune*, he encouraged an association between individual sovereignty and free love that continued to plague Modern Times. Rumors of unorthodox marital relations had already started to circulate, and they grew after the arrival of the Nicholses in 1853. In 1855, James A. Clay, in jail for adultery in Maine, imagined Modern Times as a more welcoming residence and purchased two lots. Two years later, a visitor confirmed these reports of Modern Times, "The arrangements of marriage were, of course, left entirely to the men and women themselves. They could be married formally or otherwise, live in the same or separate houses, and have their relation known or unknown to the rest of the village. The relation could be dissolved at pleasure without any formulas."[19] While residents clearly tolerated extramarital sex, as well as nudism and vegetarianism, the historian Roger Wunderlich believes it was only a "vanguard of sexual radicals," such as Andrews and the Nicholses, who contributed to the scandalous reputation of Modern Times.[20]

There is no evidence that Stephen Pearl Andrews himself committed adultery, but his exchange with Greeley and James, which he published in book form, declared his (theoretical) opposition to marriage. The debate began when Andrews took exception to a review of *Love vs. Marriage*, by Marx Edgeworth Lazarus, a proponent of Fourier's social theory of attraction. As his title suggested, Lazarus prioritized love over the institution of marriage, writing, "Love, it is life; love, it is force; love, it is power; love, it is liberty!" He also defined adultery as a "reassertion" of "personal liberty," a reaction to the "paralyzing marriage form." According to Andrews, the author of the book review, Henry James Sr., had resorted to "rampant and ferocious moralism." Though the *Tribune* editor Horace Greeley called Andrews's views "eminently detestable," he agreed to print them.[21]

Andrews asserted that individual sovereignty was "the most important principle of social and political order" "ever discovered." Believing this doctrine to be a natural outgrowth of American political values, he stated, "The right of self-government means with me the right of every individual to govern himself or it means nothing." Andrews extended the right of self-government to sexual relations, claiming, "The most stupendous mistake that this world of ours has ever made is that of erecting an abstraction, the State, the Church, Public Morality . . . and making it paramount to the will and happiness of the individual."[22] For Andrews, marriage was a political, legal, and religious construction that hindered the romantic freedom of men and women. Greeley called Andrews's vision "bestial pandemonium."[23]

Andrews redefined adultery as an essential part of his criticism of marriage and "public morality." Greeley and most other Americans defined adultery as "breach of a legal bond." Even Lazarus had defined it as a (understandable) betrayal of the marriage vow. In contrast, Andrews described adultery as any "sexual union" that did not grow from "mutual love," whether it was in a legal marriage or not. If love, and the "amative conjunction" it inspired, was the only true basis for sexual intimacy, as Andrews believed, nine-tenths of married couples committed adultery "not out of, but within the limits of, their marriage bonds."[24] If love died, men and women had an obligation to end the relationship. Individual sovereigns, including women, must be true to themselves and not to this arbitrary institution. While he was not the first to use the adultery metaphor, Andrews introduced it to a wider audience of readers when he collected and expanded the *Tribune* debate into a book in 1853. He built on the arguments of abolitionists and perfectionists that identified a legal institution as the container for sins and crimes. By the time of the *Tribune* debate, a few spiritualists and communitarians had also begun to use the phrase to denounce obligatory sexual relations within a loveless marital bond. Its use grew over the next decade.[25]

Andrews's identification of loveless marital sexual relations as adulterous must have confounded nineteenth-century Americans. For most readers, the word "adultery" meant a violation of a marriage law or promise. Andrews's use of the term pointed to a violation or betrayal of the individual, and offered a different criticism than the slavery metaphor. When individuals had sex with a spouse they did not love or desire, he defined it as a violation of their personal and physical integrity. Individuals had a right to choose the person they loved, and love alone determined the morality of the sexual relationship.

Rejecting Greeley's fear of sexual chaos, Andrews offered the provocative suggestion that all men, including Greeley, had a right to determine "what woman (or women) you love well enough or purely enough to live with, or how many you are capable of loving." Andrews advocated a new standard of sexual morality, based on love alone. Importantly, Andrews believed women had the same right. Rather than attack the sexual double standard by defining adultery as equally bad for both wives and husbands, Andrews asserted that adultery, in effect, was equally good for both—if literal adultery meant escape from a loveless, and therefore metaphorically adulterous, legal marriage. Andrews quoted his confidante Mary Gove Nichols as saying the "truly emancipated" woman "needs no human law for the protection of her chastity." A free woman's decisions, Nichols asserted, would always be pure. Rather than a shield, she saw marriage as an obstacle to women's pursuit of virtue. Like Andrews, Nichols believed that "it is not fidelity to a legal bond, where there is no love." She also referred to marriage as " 'lawful' whoredom," "where there is force on one side and fear on the other," underlining the economic as well as moral coercion in unhappy marriages.[26] It is not surprising that Greeley refused to print this part of Andrews's argument in his newspaper.

John Humphrey Noyes followed the *Tribune* exchange, and the subsequent publication of Stephen Pearl Andrews's book, with interest. He praised Andrews for his "clearness, consistency, and precision," "straightforward Yankee meaning," and for producing a truly "American" theory. Noyes also reminded his followers that sexual freedom required "loyalty to the Bible," mutual criticism, and distinguishing between intercourse for pleasure and reproduction. In the *Circular*, he placed his comments on the James-Greeley-Andrews exchange immediately above a short article about Amelia Bloomer's feminist newspaper *The Lily*. The Oneida Community congratulated itself on the female editors and printers of their own newspaper. "As women are precluded from preaching," they wrote unquestioningly, "it is no more than fair that we should give them the press."[27]

In his *History of American Socialisms,* Noyes called Modern Times "the mother of Free Love," this feminine metaphor perhaps a deliberate contrast between his own patriarchal views, and Andrews's feminist philosophizing.[28] Unlike Noyes, Andrews and his free-love allies supported a broad platform of women's rights. In an unpublished manuscript titled "Love, Marriage, and the Condition of Women," Andrews described women's status as one that "deteriorates" from "marriage until death." Separated from the world in their "isolated households," women were the "domestic slaves" of "petty princes." Andrews believed that women had the same rights as men to education, financial and professional independence, and self-improvement, but he did not think women were the same as men. Instead, in the "right conditions," women and men complemented and influenced each other. Rather condescendingly, he viewed woman as "the natural queen in the whole sphere and realm of the affections" and man as "living in the domain of intellect." Andrews called for woman to be the "sovereign legislator and arbitress of all that relates in life to the domain of the heart."[29]

Andrews believed that the organized women's rights movement was "a forerunner" of women's emancipation, but he described it as "still excessively frivolous." He asserted that the women who had met at the Seneca Falls, Worcester, and Syracuse conventions were misguided in their focus on political and property rights. Though feminists critiqued marriage, they did not go as far as Andrews, who thought all other rights meaningless when women themselves were "confiscated," or owned by others. Viewing marriage as an obstacle to women's liberation, he argued that the ultimate goal should be for woman to "control her own person," including her body.[30] Andrews called loveless marriage "involuntary confinement," and "the most filthy, the most debasing, the most infernal of all the influences which pervade a corrupted humanity." These relationships, "called marriage in the world," were nothing more than "legalized adultery." The solution was for men and women to love whomever they chose.[31]

* * *

Stephen Pearl Andrews's own marriages suggest he was more conservative in his personal life. His first wife died in 1855. The next year, he married Esther B. Hussey, "a regularly graduated physician" and a spiritualist medium with "extraordinary powers of mind." She also shared Andrews's belief that women's rights meant "full possession of herself, her soul and its affections, her body and its desires," though we do not know what this meant for, or in, their marriage.[32] His personal papers contain little evidence about either woman, and certainly no insight into their relationship with a notorious free lover. His son William S. Andrews recalled that his father never uttered a harsh word to his wives or children. He also described both Mary Ann and Esther as "devoted" spouses, with great "confidence" in their husband. Stephen Pearl Andrews may have been monogamous. Perhaps his marriages were models of true sexual love, achieving the right balance of the "material" (physical) and "spiritual." Or perhaps the fact of his marriages, and the presence of his wives, did not hinder his personal freedom.[33]

After the *New York Tribune* debate, Andrews continued to promote individual sovereignty as the basis for human relationships. As one of the chief theorists of free love, which criticized marriage as an oppressive institution, and advocated individual freedom in its stead, Andrews had an important influence on American attitudes toward sexual love, often from behind the scenes. He recruited new followers to the free-love movement, some of who became more famous than their mentor.

Many Americans in the mainstream, to recall Noyes, had "nervous, irritable feelings" about adultery. Many also believed that marriage, prescriptively, should be about love. But both Andrews and Noyes believed that only love made a marriage authentic, and sexual intercourse was only legitimate when guided by love, not law. Noyes relied on the sovereignty of Christ and his own authority to sanctify sexual relationships out of wedlock, and his marriage radicalism ended up reproducing sexual hierarchy. In contrast, Andrews argued for individual rights, including those of women. The only justification he required was mutual love. Rather than a violation of the marriage vow, Andrews and other marriage reformers transformed adultery into a metaphor for any sexual encounter, even those sanctioned by church and state, without love. In Andrews's view, such sexual acts violated individual sexual and moral autonomy.

The sexual prescriptions of Noyes and Andrews proved more difficult in practice. In the Oneida Community, women had very different experiences of complex marriage. For Mary Cragin, who was willing to submit to Noyes's spiritual authority, complex marriage expanded and enhanced God's love. Others, like Tryphena Hubbard, were frustrated and chastened in their desires.

In Modern Times, free love may have been more theory than reality. Even Andrews seemed to remain faithful to his marriage vows. Still, these free lovers argued for women's right to choose her sexual partners, which, in combination with the alleged marital fluidity of individual sovereigns, brought scandal and opprobrium. Their ideas were scandalous, but they also gradually infiltrated more mainstream, prescriptive texts on marriage ideals, which preserved the institution but imagined it transformed, sometimes in the image of free lovers.

CHAPTER 5

True vs. False Marriage

On November 25, 1856, Mrs. Mary Fenn Davis spoke at her first national women's rights convention at the Broadway Tabernacle in New York City. To a large audience of one thousand people, Davis reviewed the history of women to the present day and shared her belief that laws giving a husband the right "to the person of his wife" thwarted their potential in the "spiritual and artistic realms." This patriarchal right, Davis continued, was "one of the most prolific causes of woman's woes." She described the case of a beautiful wife and mother who had committed suicide. Despite her wealth, Davis argued, "the marble halls in which she lived were a prison to her, and her silken robes were chains that bound her to a tyrant's lust." For Davis, men's authority over the sexual relationship in marriage led to "physical and moral pollution." She imagined a time when women "would be able to love without self-annihilation." Like Stephen Pearl Andrews, Davis urged the audience to "give her [woman] supreme control of her most sacred function."[1]

To all appearances, Davis herself had achieved both marital bliss and control over her person. Mary had ended an unhappy marriage and wed the well-known clairvoyant Andrew Jackson Davis, who shared her view that women must rule in matters of love. Reformers such as Fenn and Davis modeled a newer, more egalitarian form of marriage based on true love, which they defined as a transcendent spiritual connection. The Davises prioritized their emotional over their physical relationship, and mutual love and consent governed the frequency and timing of intercourse. Such views not only allowed women to limit conception, but also fundamentally shifted power within a marriage. Andrew Jackson Davis and other reform-minded men willingly relinquished some of their legal rights.

In the 1840s and 1850s, Mary Fenn Davis and other marriage reformers made some of the same critiques as Stephen Pearl Andrews and John

Figure 5. Mary Fenn Davis, feminist, spiritualist, and divorcée, who argued for women's control over their bodies. Courtesy of the Special Collections Research Center, Syracuse University Libraries.

Humphrey Noyes. All of them identified infidelity, prostitution, boorish husbands, and delicate and dependent wives as problems in marriage. But unlike Andrews and Noyes, the Davises agreed with evangelical reformers and most other Americans that marriage was an unbreakable spiritual and material bond between man and woman.[2] Their goal was to redeem the institution—not to reject it—by promoting true love and happiness as fundamental to marriage. To this end, these moderate reformers advised husbands to contain their sexual urges and continue to woo their wives. They emphasized the importance of mutual desire (or reciprocal love and consent) in marital sexual relations.

The metaphor of adultery also helped these more moderate reformers define the ideal marriage. Though he spurned any connection to Stephen Pearl Andrews's individual sovereignty, Andrew Jackson Davis too identified false marriages, which he described as "ephemeral" and "superficial," as "legalized adulteries."[3] In this new marital ideal, sex with anyone other than one's true love was a form of adultery. Any sexual act that was not mutual was adulterous. This idea developed and circulated among both free lovers and more mainstream reformers. Even as they distanced themselves from free love, and defended the inviolability of true marriages, the Davises and other moderates partially embraced sex radicals' redefinition of adultery.

*   *   *

Six years earlier, in 1850, twenty-six year-old Mary Fenn Robinson Love appeared to be a happy wife and mother. She and her husband, a teacher named Samuel Gurley Love, lived in the village of Randolph in Cattaraugus County, New York, with their two young children, Frances, age three, and Charles, age one. The couple also shared a religious faith, having embraced spiritualism, a fast-growing, nondenominational religious movement that emphasized the connection between the living and the dead. In 1848, two sisters, Kate and Margaret Fox, who lived in nearby Rochester, had sparked the movement by claiming to communicate with spirits through knocking noises. Spiritualism attracted a wide array of American Protestants. Even Noyes and other members of the Oneida Community experimented with spiritualism to reach the much-mourned Mary Cragin. Moreover, as the historian Ann Braude writes, spiritualists became a strongly progressive force, and their broad platform included both women's rights and criticism of marriage. Their critics warned that spiritualists' ideas contributed to the dissolution of marriages, as spouses left to search for their perfect partners. But spiritualists were not free lovers. Although they advocated equal rights for women within marriage, spiritualists nevertheless believed the union should be monogamous, mutual, and eternal.[4]

As a student of the nascent women's rights movement, Mary Fenn Love also absorbed feminist critiques of marriage laws. At the Seneca Falls Convention, signers of the Declaration of Sentiments agreed that marriage meant civil death for women. Women's rights activists regularly cited the eighteenth-century British legal theorist William Blackstone's view that "The very being and legal existence of woman is suspended during marriage—incorporated or consolidated into that of her husband, under whose protection and cover she performs every thing."[5] The free lovers Mary Gove and Thomas L. Nichols concluded that there was "abundant evidence that the Woman's Rights Movement is an attack upon the marriage institution."[6]

Still, many feminists remained cautious, worried about associating their movement with Stephen Pearl Andrews and individual sovereignty. Elizabeth Cady Stanton believed that "this whole question of woman's rights turns on the pivot of the marriage relation," yet she did not want to "hurry" the question or "avoid it." Lucy Stone argued that "husband's rights" in marriage led to "appalling" "abuse," but, as to calling for more liberal divorce laws at women's rights conventions, it was not "*time* to strike."[7] Like spiritualists, feminists shared free lovers' criticism of marriage as an oppressive legal and religious institution. While they highlighted the wrongs of married women at their conventions, most feminists were reluctant to discuss marital sex or advocate liberal divorce. As Stone's letter indicates, they disagreed among themselves. They also worried about the inevitable public condemnation to follow.

By 1854, Mary and Samuel Love concluded that their marriage was "false" and loveless.[8] In Rochester, at the home of the radical abolitionists and spiritualists Isaac and Amy Post, the couple consulted with the "seer of Poughkeepsie," Andrew Jackson Davis, called Jackson by family and friends, whose remarkable rise from uneducated, wayward youth to clairvoyant healer had made him famous. In his autobiography, Davis recalled this conversation about the relative importance of individual principles or American marriage policies. He advised Mary and Samuel to act on principle, describing marriage without love as a "crime against the 'higher law' of your own soul, the penalty of which is disastrous and inevitable." He believed that "all intercourse not prompted by mutual love, is positive adultery; and that the sanction of priest or passion or statute-law, is no source of justification, and can not render the private vice a public virtue."[9] The Loves accepted his advice, and Mary traveled to Indiana, the state with the most liberal divorce laws in the country, to end her marriage.

If the state of New York had one of the most restrictive divorce statutes, Indiana had one of the most liberal. The state allowed judges to determine whether a plaintiff had a legitimate cause for divorce, expanding the possible causes from adultery to abandonment, failure to support, impotency, physical abuse, and drunkenness. Other states had this "omnibus" clause as well. In 1852, however, Indiana had passed a law that set no time requirements for state residency. Only later did Indiana amend its laws to require a one-year residency, and then amended them again to mandate a two-year stay. Mary secured her divorce by spending a summer in the state.[10]

Though Mary was not the only women's rights activist to divorce, it was a radicalizing experience for her. As she wrote Davis, her marriage and its end gave her life new purpose: "I will do something toward shaking our selfish law-makers from their posts—unless they will give us statutes that more fully meet the wants of humanity."[11] Mary proposed to raise awareness of the problems of legal marriage and to create political momentum to liberalize divorce laws. Though she did not succeed in altering New York's strict law, Mary became a popular speaker in her home state and across the northeast. She was an attractive yet modest woman, with long, dark hair. Despite the potential scandal of her divorce, she managed to project an image of female respectability while lecturing on controversial topics such as marriage and reproduction. Her second marriage also contributed to her relatively pure reputation.

The end of the Loves' marriage brought new romantic possibilities. Mary and Samuel had separated with "mutual good-will," and Mary planned to live with her children, former husband, and his new wife. While Mary was in Indiana, however, Davis had a vision that she was his soul mate. His previous wife, his benefactress, Catherine (whom he called Katie or Silona) DeWolf Dodge, had died the previous year. Davis had believed his union with Katie to be a "true marriage" and thus "indissoluble," but her spirit informed him that their marriage "could not extend beyond the tomb."[12] This barrier overcome, Mary and Jackson had to face her family's disapproval. Though she had received legal advice from her brother-in-law Charles Plumb, other family members viewed Jackson and his beliefs as "immoral and dangerous." Mary's brother implied that Jackson was the cause of her divorce from Samuel, a charge they would confront again. Her father, a Baptist and "temperance man," believed Mary had made "a shipwreck of religion and a shipwreck of marriage." He advised her to remain single and support herself through teaching.[13]

Figure 6. Andrew Jackson Davis, spiritualist advocate of
true, monogamous, eternal marriage. Courtesy of the Special
Collections Research Center, Syracuse University Libraries.

Jackson Davis informed his friend William Green Jr. that he was undeterred by this religious and familial opposition. He had met the perfectionist businessman and his wife, Cornelia, who had briefly aligned themselves
with John Humphrey Noyes, in 1848. For the rest of their lives, the Greens
placed their faith (and money) in Andrew Jackson Davis. In a trance state,
Davis claimed to have learned medicine from the spirit of ancient Greek
physician Galen, and he served as the Greens' personal homeopath. The
Greens also embraced Jackson's version of spiritualism, known as harmonialism, which he adapted from Emanuel Swedenborg, an eighteenth-century

Swedish theologian who had visions of the afterlife. Due to Davis's own mystical powers, the two seers were able to converse directly in the spirit world. Swedenborg's writings about "conjugal love," and its opposite "false marriage," also influenced a number of marriage reformers. As Swedenborg's disciple, Davis argued for the ultimate harmony of the universe, and marriage was one example of its "infinite conjugalities." As he wrote, men and women were complementary parts of a harmonious whole: "heart and head, soul and body; sun and earth; light and heat; right and left; attraction and repulsion; expansion and contraction; positive and negative; male and female; intellect and love."[14]

Davis assured William Green of the growing acceptance of spiritual pairings. "The public mind is moved greatly by our Harmonial Philosophy," he wrote.[15] In February 1855, he told his friend Green that he and Mary would be "married," putting the word in quotations to show his disdain for this worldly, legalistic necessity. True love did not need the law. He described Mary as "a healthy, loving, intelligent, companionable *woman.*" Since Davis viewed men and women as different, their marriage would be the "*perfect union.*"[16]

On May 15, 1855, Mary and Jackson wed. Before their marriage, Jackson asked Mary to consider the following question: " '*Can I, in obedience to my highest attractions and noblest impulses and purest aspirations, yield to Jackson all my affections and confidence forever?*' " He assured her that her "personal, spiritual, and social liberty" was of utmost importance to him. He did not want to confine her to a "*second bondage.*" Mary's answer to his question was positive: he was her "soul's companion."[17] Her second wedding did not come without sacrifice. Her children stayed with Samuel Love "according to the tyrannical laws of the state of New York." In addition, believing their Indiana divorce invalid, Samuel filed for divorce (again) in New York State so that he could remarry. Since adultery was the only possible grounds, the petition cited her relationship with Jackson. As Davis wrote in his autobiography, he did not blame Mr. Love for charging Mary with infidelity, as he "was compelled to do as he did by the absurd and inhuman laws of the Empire State."[18] Concerned about scandal, Jackson wrote that he had "a certified copy of Mary's previous divorce decree . . . recorded in the Erie County clerk's office," thus correcting the record in her home state.[19]

Fittingly, the same year as his marriage, Andrew Jackson Davis also published the fourth volume of his grand philosophy, *The Great Harmonia,* which focused on conjugal love. His statement of purpose on the title page read: "absolute purity of heart and life is the richest human possession; and perfect obedience to the highest attractions of the soul is the only means of its attainment." In other words, individuals must be true to themselves in love and marriage. The attainable goal was to join another in "endless" marriage; he defined a true marriage as one based on "a harmony between outward attractions," "a harmony between love and wisdom," and "*a blending of two souls* so absolutely" that nothing could interfere with their "*internal* attraction."[20]

But Davis acknowledged the reality of unhappy couples, or those who suffered "constitutional inadaptedness." Divorce, he believed, should be granted at the mutual request of the couple. If the law required a "*crime*," Davis suggested applying the metaphorical definition of adultery: if a woman married someone whom she did not love, they had committed "*adultery*." He also expanded on the adultery metaphor. If a woman no longer loved her spouse, and loved another but did not marry him, "she is then guilty of being both a prostitute," with her husband, "and an adulteress," unfaithful to herself and her true love. Even in the face of law and social convention, he believed, women's moral autonomy was paramount. Like Mary Fenn, women must act on their highest attractions, noblest impulses, and purest aspirations. Though he used a feminine example, Davis argued the same "moral law," that love was the only basis for sexual relations, applied equally to men. In advocating this law of love, he unwittingly echoed the free lover Stephen Pearl Andrews.[21]

After their marriage, Mary and Jackson set out upon the "Field of Reform."[22] Their non-traditional relationship included Jackson's friend and supporter William Green Jr. Even before they met, Mary wrote the now-widowed William, "my soul secretly blessed you for your devoted friendship, your noble liberality and your faithful adherence to the sublime principles which like the golden rays of a newly created sun are penetrating the labyrinths of mind." She promised to be William's sister, cheering his "heart by the ministrations of affection" and sharing his "immortal aspirations."[23] When they were not with Green, the Davises spent the early years of their marriage traveling and lecturing. Jackson reported to William that he and Mary worked well together, and "her lectures are even more acceptable to the people than mine." In 1855, Mary lectured to a Utica audience of one thousand. A year later, almost three thousand heard her speak in the same upstate city. By 1857, the couple earned $40 per lecture.[24]

Their relationship became a public example of an ideal spiritualist marriage. In 1857, Andrew Jackson Davis published his autobiography *The Magic Staff*, devoting the final chapters to his courtship of Mary. Their earthly ceremony only confirmed what the spirits had endorsed. Theirs was a *"true marriage," "the consecration of one man to one woman."*[25] As her speech at the national women's rights convention indicated, Mary lectured on marriage as well as spiritualism. At one progressive gathering, she addressed "the oppressive bearing and the unhappy effects upon woman, of the *legal* marriage bond."[26] Her critique of marriage laws resonated with some feminists such as Susan B. Anthony, who praised her for "lifting the curtain from the pollution & prostitution of all that is sacred in the marriage relation."[27]

For Mary, as for other spiritualists, the law was the problem. A true marriage transcended the material world, and it could never be oppressive because it was entered willingly and with love. The Davises believed they had achieved the ideal: a lasting, harmonious, monogamous union. In contrast to their own true marriage, they saw most legal marriages as false, unsanctified by love, and thus adulterous in character. As Jackson Davis also acknowledged, their falseness contributed to (literal) adultery as individuals sought their true loves outside of marriage.

*   *   *

If Americans could not attend lectures by Mary and Jackson, they might read Davis's books or other treatises on marriage. In this period, diverse reformers—including socialists, evangelicals, phrenologists, abolitionists, and spiritualists—published advice on finding a life-long companion and achieving a higher form of marriage. The shared goal of these writers was to improve the experience of monogamous love.[28] They were intent on reforming marriage from the inside, as well as within the boundaries of law, but their writings show that they offered reformulations of adultery, love, and legal marriage similar to those of free lovers. With the Davises, they emphasized mutual desire and women's right to control her body. In practice, they assumed women to be less passionate than men and interpreted "mutual" to mean male self-control. These writers rejected a legalistic definition of both marriage and adultery, and thus ventured toward free love—at the same time, they also reinforced marriage as a natural, sacred, and lasting institution. They suggest how more moderate discourses absorbed and promoted radical views of marriage.

An early reformist view of marriage came from Robert Dale Owen, whose career began at his father's utopian community in New Harmony, Indiana, and whose booklet *Moral Physiology* became the straw man for later marriage writers. First published in 1830, Owen's tract was controversial for its advocacy of birth control, but one of his main concerns was "happiness" in marriage. Without birth control, early marriages led to regular pregnancies, ruining women's health and dooming couples to poverty. Owen agreed with the Oneida Community founder John Humphrey Noyes that sex should be for pleasure and procreation.[29] He also viewed marriage as an institution with both personal and public dimensions. In addition to promoting birth control, Owen put his ideas into practice as a state legislator, further liberalizing Indiana's divorce laws by including alcoholism as cause, and fighting for married women's property rights.[30]

On the opposite end of the reform spectrum, Sarah Jackson, who became the second wife of the evangelical abolitionist Lewis Tappan in 1853, offered the moral reform view of marriage. From her perspective, marriage was not an option for women, but the ultimate end, "and no movement in life is fraught with more serious consequences." Jackson defined marriage as "intimate and permanent." Since women's autonomy stopped at marriage, she focused on the importance of choosing the right spouse in the first place, before a woman's irrevocable lot was cast. In contrast to Andrew Jackson Davis, she did not view a woman's attractions as the most relevant guide to this decision. Rather, she insisted that women seek the Lord's permission. Most important, this desire to obey God must be shared by the future husband: "If the ruling desire of your heart is to please God, you will not allow your affections to be placed on one who does not sympathize in this desire." Jackson's worry was that young women wanted to marry for love, and attraction might lead them to choose an "impenitent" man in hopes of converting him. She described Christian women married to unconverted men as "sad and weary-hearted," unable to be a moral influence in their families.[31] Jackson did not challenge women's subordination in marriage, so she viewed a common religious faith as essential.

In service of reconciling newer standards of marital love and authenticity to the old parameters of legal and conventional marriage, phrenologists offered more concrete advice on choosing the right partner. An early form of psychology, phrenology analyzed individual character through the shape of the head. Many notable Americans had their heads studied, including John Humphrey Noyes and women's rights activist Lucretia Mott. Scottish reformer George Combe had popularized the pseudoscience on his 1838–40 tour of the United States. The leading American phrenologists, the brothers Orson and Lorenzo Fowler, published numerous works that applied phrenology to courtship, marriage, and reproduction.[32] The Fowlers advised readers to study their own phrenological organization as well as that of their intended for telltale physical signs of compatibility in sentiments, tastes, desires, and other qualities.

The Fowlers urged phrenological mate selection in order to preserve the institution of marriage. Like many commentators, Orson Squire Fowler viewed love as "the most sacred element of man's nature," but he ventured into dangerous advocacy of free love (or, as he called it after Robert Dale Owen, Owenism) when he proclaimed, "*Love constitutes matrimony*. Marriage does not exist in its *legal ceremony*, nor in any sanction thrown around it *by law*." Fowler's resolution of the tension, and his defense, was that phrenology revealed a natural law, one that merged love and the conventions of marriage: "love and marry once, and *but* once."[33] Lorenzo Fowler echoed his brother's advice, describing "perfect love" as "a true union of two in marriage." Perfect love had both physical and spiritual dimensions, and comprised "union of sentiment and affection which no external defects can dissolve." His definition preceded that of Andrew Jackson Davis, who simply transliterated Fowler's perfect marriage into his "harmonial" one. Yet the Fowlers believed their scientific approach had the potential to solve the "evils" of the current system, frequent "social and domestic disarrangements, quarrels, separations, and divorces," rather than subverting or upending them.[34]

The Fowlers' definition of marriage as a lasting bond of perfect love led to some contradictory views of adultery. On the one hand, they shared the metaphorical redefinition of Stephen Pearl Andrews, Andrew Jackson Davis, and other reformers that loveless marriages were a form of adultery. As Orson Fowler declared, there should be no "marriage without love, and no love without marriage," so "Intercourse without Love is Double Adultery." He explained that the adulterer betrayed the spiritual and physical components of perfect love: "All males and females who love one but marry another, or marry one they do not love, perpetrate both spiritual adultery with their lover against their legal companion, and personal adultery with their legal partner against their lover."[35]

On the other hand, rather than seeing divorce or literal adultery as a solution to loveless marriages, Orson Fowler was in the reformist camp. He agreed with the views of lawmakers in New York, who defined adultery as the betrayal of legal marriage. "Infidelity Deserves Divorce," he announced. The Fowlers believed that sex outside of marriage caused disease—both venereal disease and inflammation of phrenological organs—and was thus "unpardonable."[36]

The Fowlers were not alone in their overriding concern about the dangers of sexual excess, which informed much of the marriage debate during this time. In her speeches, Mary Fenn Davis described women who had been debilitated by the erotic demands of their husbands. She cited books by abolitionist Henry Clarke Wright, the reformer most associated with the idea of sexual self-control in marriage, including *The Unwelcome Child*. Wright was unhappily married to an older woman, and, either through impotence or by choice, practiced celibacy. He had many intimate, flirtatious, platonic relationships with antislavery women in the United States and England, and from them developed his critique of a husband's rights. Preaching male sexual restraint, he offered couples a way to achieve greater emotional intimacy. His definition of marriage was similar to that of Davis and the Fowlers: "a mutual love between one man and one woman, which unites the soul of each to that of the other, leaving neither an independent existence in any of the interests of life: and fidelity to that love." He recommended that couples discuss their sexual expectations before marriage. When sex was a mutual expression of love, he advised, the child created would be healthy and happy. But Wright and other reformers warned that unwanted sex produced diseased children.[37]

With similar views on marriage, Henry Clarke Wright and Andrew Jackson Davis developed something of a mutual admiration society. Wright praised Davis for guiding "the unmarried, in entering into the conjugal relations" and "husbands and wives in their treatment of each other and their offspring."[38] In return, Davis hailed Wright's *Marriage and Parentage* (1854), writing "my soul is in practical sympathy with the principles it inculcates, makes me think of the Pure, the Just, the Self-Harmonized." He noted Wright's principles as first, "*the right use of the Reproductive Element in Man, as a means to his elevation and happiness*," and second, "ONE ONLY AND TRUE MARRIAGE FOR ETERNITY." The two men believed in monogamous and eternal love, allowing both men and women the opportunity to develop their full spiritual potential in marriage.[39]

The Fowlers also warned of "excessive and abusive exercise of the sexual feelings," with its threat to the health of the married couple and their children. As an example, Lorenzo Fowler made the remarkable claim that children born during the French Revolution were "to a vast proportion, idiots and insane."[40] In his manual *Love and Parentage*, Orson Fowler recommended that marital sex be "spiritual" rather than sensual, and woman, as the "*personification*" of love, must be the "umpire": "On *her* verdict, rests the issue" of the frequency of intercourse. He believed women had a smaller organ of passion than men, and did not desire sex except for procreation. Fowler believed this self-imposed abstinence would both increase "the sum total of enjoyment" and produce better offspring.[41]

Reformers also advocated sexual restraint because it resulted in fewer children. For the sake of propriety, none of these authors supported the available birth control methods advocated by Owen, including withdrawal, condoms, sponges, and douching, nor did they embrace Noyes's practice of male continence, or withholding male orgasm. But they were well aware of the reasons couples wanted to limit reproduction. The Davises, Wright, and Fowler argued that the wife, who risked a potentially life-threatening pregnancy, should decide when to have sex.

*   *   *

A prominent mixed-race clairvoyant named Paschal Beverly Randolph offered a useful guideline for sexual frequency: every two weeks, preferably on a Sunday morning. As he explained, married couples were too tired to have sex at night, and children conceived in daylight had "better forms, fuller Minds, keener Intellects, profounder judgment, clearer Perceptions, nobler Aspirations." On Sunday morning, husband and wife were rested and "filled with bright and joyous hopes." Randolph recommended every two weeks because weekly intercourse was "dangerous to domestic peace," and "oftener than that—it ceases to be human, and sinks below the level of the brutes."[42]

Though most marital advice was written by and for whites, P. B. Randolph relied on his "conglomerate" background for authority on sex and health. Self-described as "tawny" or "sallow" skinned, with black hair and a mustache, he became an unusual and "distinguished Spiritual Medium," delivering over three thousand lectures before renouncing spiritualism.[43] Randolph eventually wrote multiple books on sex and marriage, but on his early publications he collaborated with his first wife. The 1850 census listed Paschal and Mary Jane Randolph as "mulatto," and at different points in his career, he identified as African American. In 1860, the same year the Randolphs published their pamphlet *Human Love,* however, they were categorized as American Indians. The Randolphs may have self-identified to the census enumerator, as the authors described themselves as an "Indian Physician and Scrofula Curer" and an "Indian Doctress, Midwife."[44]

At other times, P. B. referred to himself as "the most perfect specimen of the composite" man. Though he staunchly denied any "drop" of African ancestry, he claimed his mother was the daughter of a Madagascar "queen," apparently placing greater emphasis on the island's South Asian connections. She also had "French, Spanish, Indian, and Oriental blood." From his white father, allegedly William Beverly Randolph of Virginia, he was "English, Celtic, Cymrian, Teutonic, and Moorish."[45] In *Human Love,* Randolph asserted the superior health and wisdom of Native Americans to support his scientific discovery that love took physical, fluid form that connected men and women. With this discovery, he believed that obedience to the laws of love would produce "vigor, beauty, nobility of character and manhood of every person in the world." Ignorance of these laws infected and poisoned this fluid.[46]

Aside from this discovery, Randolph's marriage advice did not differ from that of other moderate reformers. He believed married couples should have sex only when both were willing and healthy.[47] Randolph's goal was "true love" or "perfect love," and he believed "perfect health was perfect love." He advised cleanliness, cold water, exercise, fresh air, and proper food. He defined faithfulness as *"truth to a genuine love,"* and adultery as impossible if the "heart and affections are right."[48] Like the Fowlers, he believed unhappy couples could follow his advice and rediscover their love, but he also argued that divorce should be an option.

Randolph expressed the same disdain for the law as other marriage reformers. As he wrote: "It is sheer folly to expect or attempt to make people love each other by statute law. God makes marriages if any are made, and all others are sheer frauds, counterfeits, and not worth the paper upon which the certificates are written." Like his colleagues, Randolph believed legal marriages could be adulterous, and that love alone justified intercourse.[49]

The adultery metaphor infiltrated the writings even of reformers such as Randolph, who distinguished his views from those of both radical free

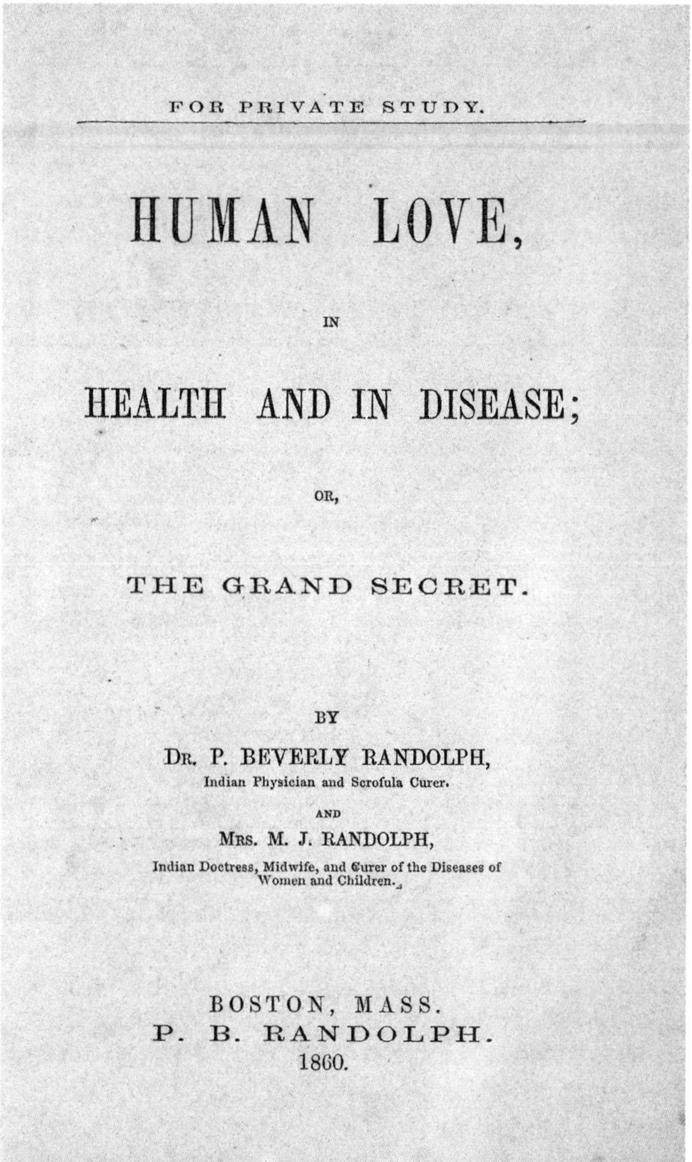

FOR PRIVATE STUDY.

HUMAN LOVE,

IN

HEALTH AND IN DISEASE;

OR,

THE GRAND SECRET.

BY

DR. P. BEVERLY RANDOLPH,

Indian Physician and Scrofula Curer.

AND

MRS. M. J. RANDOLPH,

Indian Doctress, Midwife, and Curer of the Diseases of Women and Children.

BOSTON, MASS.

P. B. RANDOLPH.

1860.

Figure 7. Title page of *Human Love* (1860), by Paschal Beverly Randolph and Mary Jane Randolph. Though Paschal Randolph identified as mixed-race or black at other points, here he and his first wife present themselves as Native American to promote their unique wisdom on the topics of sexual love and health. Courtesy of the American Antiquarian Society.

lovers and moderate spiritualists. In part, he judged their advice as faulty, writing, for example, that phrenologists were "mistaken" in matters of love. Of the Oneida Community, Randolph scoffed, "Just think of promiscuity being divine! Divinity in a brothel!" He called free lovers "passion-mad" and "pitiable monomaniacs." Doubtless, Randolph criticized other reformers to promote his own comparative expertise, but his strong denunciations also emerged out of his negative experiences among white spiritualists. Acknowledging the concerns of their other detractors, he accused these spiritualist "pretenders" of contributing to "thousands of desertion and divorce suits" by informing people that they were "improperly married; that your wife or husband—as the case may be—is not *adapted* to you; that there's no affinity."[50] Randolph's attacks on spiritualists frequently named Andrew Jackson Davis as a dangerous purveyor of this "mad philosophy." He also condemned Davis for racism and hypocrisy, quoting Davis as stating that "even 'Niggers'" had immortal souls and then recanting. Though he expressed more concern for Davis's theology, Randolph's reference to this slur indicated the racism and condescension he had experienced as a person of color in a mostly white movement.[51]

Randolph's public criticisms of spiritualism established his independent moral authority on love and marriage. He ultimately turned his status as a "SANG MÊLÉE" into an asset, a morally superior position from which to defend the value of monogamous, legal marriage against those (white) reformers who threatened it. He also claimed its privileges for himself and other people of color. Later in his career, he advanced the possibility that marriage could be an interracial institution. Like romantic racialists, northern liberal thinkers who attributed different character traits to blacks and whites, he viewed the race or ethnicity of the sexual partners not as impediments to, but as ingredients in their union. The end goal remained a true marriage.[52]

Though the Davises, Fowlers, Wright, and Randolph all denied it, their views of marriage strongly resembled free love. These free-love ideas pervaded and linked different reform movements. More moderate reformers agreed with free lovers that women should govern the sexual relationship. Likewise, they believed that a legal contract did not make a marriage, and that adultery could occur within as well as outside a marriage. Free lovers like Mary Gove Nichols and Thomas L. Nichols, Stephen Pearl Andrews's colleagues who had lived at Modern Times, argued that adultery was not a civil, criminal, or biblical offense. Instead, they stated its metaphorical definition, of "sexual commerce unsanctified by mutual love." In their book *Marriage*, the Nicholses joined other writers in citing their devotion to "Truth" "Purity" and "Holiness" in the "marriage relation." They described their own union as filled with "uninterrupted happiness."[53]

The Nicholses differed in their emphasis on freedom. They criticized the one true monogamous love, expounded by Davis, Wright, and others, as "dogmatized Duality." Instead, they advocated "fidelity to one's self." As the Nicholses wrote in *Marriage*, "The society that we want, is men and women, living in freedom, sustaining themselves by their own industry, dealing with each other in equity, respecting each other's sovereignty, and governed by their attractions; no one presuming to interfere in the delicate, the private, and personal matters of the affections."[54] Love was a matter of individual choice, and should therefore be free from interference from the church, state, or social norms.

The Nicholses wrote *Marriage* as a political statement, but Thomas offered practical tips for couples in his book *Esoteric Anthropology*. Perhaps unsurprisingly, the free lover recommended weekly intercourse. Aside from this relative frequency, Thomas Nichols warned against early marriages, believing that both individuals must have reached the "full development of their powers, physical and intellectual." Of course, couples should only have sex "with all the attraction and charm of mutual love." They should also be healthy. He advised a vegetarian diet, plenty of cold water, baths, fresh air, exercise, and sleep. Nichols wanted all children to be conceived in love, and he recommended birth control if couples did not want children. In addition to abstinence, he noted two weeks of every menstrual cycle during which women could not get pregnant (unfortunately, they were the wrong two weeks, falling between periods), as well as other methods like withdrawal, condoms, and douching. Nichols also considered abortion an option, the only one of these marriage writers to do so, and he offered different ways to procure one. Even though he viewed birth control and abortion as unnatural, Nichols stated, he saw no reason for "legal interference." As with love, such decisions should be left to the individual.[55]

* * *

Midcentury marriage reformers defined love as central to the human experience. They imagined love as a sacred, transcendent, and joyful union of a man and woman. As they studied American society, they perceived the reality of marriage to be far different: a legal prison condemning two unhappy people to a life sentence. For these different writers, such "adulterous" marriages caused social problems like disease, poverty, crime, and drunkenness. While moderate marriage reformers shared free lovers' use of the adultery metaphor, and its criticism of false, inauthentic marriages, they did not share their ends. Their solution was to reconcile the legal standards and reform ideals of marriage by leading couples to mutual and lasting love through God, phrenological or harmonial study, and obedience to the higher laws of health and affection.

Like evangelical moral reformers, many of these more moderate writers perceived women as the chief victims of the marriage bond. While radical free lovers like Stephen Pearl Andrews and the Nicholses argued that women were individual sovereigns who had the right to choose the father of their children—married or not—moderate reformers believed that husbands should cede control over sexual relations to their wives as a way to improve and fortify the institution of marriage. Many feminists agreed with these reformers' challenge to the sexual double standard. It remained to be seen if their ideas worked in real marriages, and, when these real marriages erupted in scandal, as we will see, both the influence and the limits of these marriage reform ideals became clear.

CHAPTER 6

"His Adultery Is Proved So Clear"

Reform couples wanted to achieve wedded happiness. Their commitments to abolition, spiritualism, women's rights, and other movements, however, involved time, travel, and exposure to new ideas and people, including members of the other sex.[1] Some legal marriages suffered under the pressure, leading to accusations of infidelity and abandonment from the jilted spouse. For example, former slave and abolitionist William Wells Brown returned from a lecture tour to find his wife, Elizabeth, with another man. When the Browns separated, she took her grievances against William public, accusing him of desertion. Ohioan Charles S. S. Griffing contacted a fellow activist to express his outrage over his wife Josephine's antislavery speaking tours with reformer Parker Pillsbury. His suspicion of their extramarital affair contributed to the Griffings' divorce.[2]

The marriage of abolitionist Sherman Booth to Mary H. Corss began as a model of true love. Sherman's subsequent public betrayal of their vows exposed the difficulty of maintaining this high standard, or navigating relationships by reformist ideals of love, which could inspire the creation and the demise of a marriage alike. The Booth marriage also demonstrates the quick and thorough adoption of new ideals of marriage in reform circles. Moderate reformers such as spiritualists and phrenologists had transformed notions of romantic love into a higher calling, essential to human happiness and spiritual development. These reformers might criticize loveless marriages as "legalized adultery," yet, unlike some free lovers, they also condemned individual, literal acts of adultery and responded with shock, anger, and pain when such instances occurred in their own true marriages.

* * *

Sherman Booth was a well-known abolitionist, and Mary, a poet, shared his antislavery commitments. She was also immersed in the speeches and writings of phrenologists, spiritualists, and feminists. At the beginning of their relationship, they both believed in true love, and they relied on marriage reformers' conception of love to justify and explain their scandalous marriage. In November 1849, eighteen-year-old Mary Corss and thirty-six-year-old Sherman Booth married against the wishes of her family. At the time, Mary was living apart from her mother in Milwaukee, Wisconsin. She had relatives in the city, and she may have seized an opportunity to teach. In her free time, Mary took art lessons and wrote poetry. She also socialized with the "very first of people" of Milwaukee, and received attention from several eligible young men.[3] At the end of September, Mary wrote her first letter to her mother, Adaline Corss, in Connecticut about "Mr. Booth," a recent widow, describing him as "devotedly religious" and "perfection personified." Like Mary, Sherman was a new arrival in Milwaukee, having moved to the city in 1848. As an undergraduate at Yale College, he had tutored the *Amistad* captives, and thereafter made a career of antislavery newspapers and politics. Soon after they met, Mary had told Sherman that she loved him, and he responded, "Mary, my heart leaps joyously to meet thine." Sherman romanced her by claiming "a chord of holy sympathy like a chain of electric fire links my soul to thine."[4]

Worried about Mary's "indecorous" speedy courtship with an older man, her family acted swiftly to prevent further damage to her reputation as a virtuous young woman.[5] They asked a couple named Mr. and Mrs. Sabin to protect Mary by confining her in their home, which they did. Sherman protested that "were [Mary] *insane* she could not have been placed under stricter surveillance." Mary later wrote, "You cannot know what I suffered while there." She was ill and the Sabins mistreated her. Further, Sherman viewed the Sabins as dangerously immoral. He described Mr. Sabin as "very passionate, & one of the most profane men," and Mrs. Sabin as a "gross, coarse, sensual-looking, heartless, selfish woman." Sherman accused Mr. Sabin of using indecent language in front of Mary, "fit only for the class of the abandoned" (or prostitutes), and Mrs. Sabin had laughed. In Sherman's view, Mary's virtue depended on leaving the Sabins' home. He had no recourse but to save her.[6]

Once she was freed from the Sabins' questionable guardianship, Mary and Sherman faced another question of decorum. Booth had brought her back to his home, but living with an unmarried man was not proper under any circumstances. Mr. Sabin appeared at Sherman's house to demand that Mary return to her family. Sherman declared her too ill to travel, and decided that the solution was to marry. Within days of leaving the Sabins' house, Mary and Sherman wed, with the hapless Mr. Sabin as a witness. As Mary wrote to her mother, "It is not right that we should be married so soon, but what could we do—How could we help it?"[7]

With expediency as one justification for their marriage, Mary and Sherman both wrote rapturous letters explaining the strength and nobility of their love. Mary claimed their "only crime" was "loving each other. *That* I do not consider a great sin." Sherman reminded Mary's mother that she had taught her daughter to marry for love. He proclaimed, "My reasons, conscience, & I believe, my Father in heaven, approve the choice my heart has made, & I have no regrets to cherish & no apologies to make for my course." In part to prove that he had not acted from "passion," Sherman and Mary did not have intercourse. After two weeks of marriage, Sherman reported that Mary was "still a *virgin*," informing Adaline that "she is innocent as a very child." Mary echoed his language, writing "Mr. Booth appreciates all my feelings, and regards me a child, as I am—He is tender of me as you would be of a flower." Neither Sherman nor Mary considered it odd or improper to compare a husband's relationship to his wife to an adult and child. They used the term to indicate her sexual virtue and relative inexperience. And, in many ways, as women's rights activists complained, women had a similar status to children under the law.[8]

The Booths also shared marriage reformers' commitment to emotional over sexual intimacy, and her childlike innocence enabled this higher love. Invoking the arguments of spiritualists and, perhaps inadvertently, free lovers, Mary explained to her mother that their love was of the "*Spirit*" rather than "earthly." She declared, "I believe that no two persons ever loved so purely as we love." Sex would be part of their relationship only when she was ready.[9]

With his private rights in Mary's hands, Sherman Booth claimed his public rights as a husband. He pointed out that eighteen-year-old Mary was of "legal age" to make her own decisions. In addition, he wrote to Mary's mother, "no one can *compel* her to leave me." He declared that Mary belonged to him by "every right human & Divine," and he promised to "take the *appropriate legal* measures to enforce my *right*." As if to soften these threats, Sherman wrote that he understood Mrs. Corss's concerns about "our course being unusual, & contrary to established custom & all that." But, he explained, it was a matter of custom yielding to "common sense & the common good."[10] He was willing to defy social custom for love, but he relied on the law to defend his marriage.

Soon, Mary's family relented, and she and Sherman settled into a conventional reform marriage. Sherman supported the family as editor of the antislavery newspapers *American Freeman* and *Daily Free Democrat*. He was also active in abolitionist party politics. In 1854, he became nationally famous for his part in the liberation of Joshua Glover, who had been arrested under the Fugitive Slave Act. As the alleged instigator of the mob that freed Glover from jail, Sherman Booth struggled with the legal repercussions for years.[11]

At home, Sherman's daughter from his first marriage died, and he and Mary had three daughters, though only Mary Ella and Lillian survived infancy. Mary also took an interest in reform. When Orson Fowler lectured in Milwaukee, she attended and allowed him to analyze her head. Fowler declared she was a perfect woman and "exquisitely organized." He also observed that Mary was devoted to her husband, who "could mould her at his will & make her what he pleased."[12] During their appearances in Milwaukee, Mary Fenn and Andrew Jackson Davis visited the Booths' home, where Jackson became obsessed by one of Mary's other guests, the German revolutionary writer and feminist Mathilde Anneke.[13]

Anneke had "enraptured" Mary Booth at one of her lectures at Treat's Hall. By 1858, they were giving each other language lessons (with Milwaukee's large German-speaking population, Mary also enrolled her daughters in a German-English school). She identified Anneke to her mother as "the most talented German lady authoress & speaker in America." Mary also described her as a "beautiful" woman, who had been "in battle, like 'Joan of Arc.'" This brief summary was accurate. In 1849, Anneke and her husband, Fritz, had immigrated to the United States after their participation in Germany's failed democratic revolution. In addition to publishing a revolutionary newspaper, Mathilde had followed her husband onto the battlefield. Once in the United States, Mathilde started the *German Women's Newspaper*, and, in 1853, she addressed her first national women's rights convention in New York City. In 1859, Fritz left to find work in Switzerland, and Mathilde and her children moved in with the Booths.[14] Mathilde was present when Mary's marriage went into crisis, providing much needed emotional and financial support.

On February 28, 1859, Sherman Booth was in the house alone with his two daughters, aged eight and four, and a fourteen-year-old friend and neighbor, Caroline Cook. Mrs. Booth, who was out of town, had invited Carrie to spend the night, presumably to help entertain her daughters. According to Carrie's testimony, before she went to bed, Booth had kissed her and asked her to come to his room. She refused. While Carrie slept, Sherman entered the bedroom, undressed, and "put his hand on my bosom; he then got on me; he said nothing to me before he got on me; he said nothing to me while he was on me; he took his hand and put it *in* me; he penetrated the private parts of my body with the private parts of his own." According to Carrie, he had sex with her twice in that room, where his daughters also slept, and then took her to his bed and had sex with her again. The following morning, he apparently asked her if she had begun to menstruate. Carrie had been "unwell," as she put it, but Booth did not impregnate her. At some point, Mary Booth found out what happened and told Carrie's father. Mr. Cook immediately sought an arrest warrant, and a grand jury indicted Sherman Booth for seduction in April 1859.[15]

The new state of Wisconsin had passed its seduction statute in 1849, one year after moral reformers finally passed the law through the New York legislature. At a time when the crime of rape was largely conceived as a violent, overpowering assault by a stranger, seduction laws opened new opportunities to charge men who violated sexual boundaries. The prosecutors believed that Booth's actions did not constitute rape, but, as moral reformers intended, the Milwaukee district attorney believed the seduction statute "was designed to protect the chastity of the female." The language of the law, a matter of intense debate during the trial, read: "Any unmarried man who, under promise of marriage, or any married man who shall seduce and have illicit connection with any unmarried female of previous chaste character, shall be guilty of a misdemeanor." If convicted, Sherman faced up to one year in prison. Since the facts that the "female is unmarried and that the defendant is married" were not "controverted," the issues in the case were their illicit connection, Carrie's previous chastity, and Booth's seduction.[16]

Sherman Booth's defense depended on attacking the sexual reputation of fourteen-year-old Carrie. His defense lawyers questioned whether or not Sherman had penetrated Carrie Cook, and they also attacked her virtue, arguing that chastity meant purity of both body and mind. One of Booth's defense attorneys, M. H. Carpenter, noted that "If there was any blemish

Figure 8. Sherman Booth, abolitionist and husband, who embraced
reform ideals of marriage, was tried for seducing his fourteen-year-old
neighbor. Image WHi-9485, courtesy of the Wisconsin Historical Society.

whatever upon *her reputation*, it is sufficient." He also pointed out that
seduction was a relatively new term in criminal law and it had no "technical
definition." Did Booth's single proposition constitute seduction? Carpenter
said no because "a woman is not to be seduced in a day." For Booth's
lawyer, seduction was a longer-term project designed to "ensnare" a virtuous woman by appealing to her desire for love and marriage.[17]

This exposure of Sherman's sexual transgression illuminated the
uncomfortable reality of Mary Booth's perfect marriage. Despite Fowler's

diagnosis of her malleability, Mary's tolerance for submissive devotion required true love, so when she learned of her husband's sexual betrayal, she instigated the destruction of her marriage. Well aware of her husband's guilt, she did not testify or attend the trial. Mary still shared his home and children, however, and she noted that "everybody blames me for living with him, now that his *adultery* is proved so clear." Her language indicated that the incident was not isolated. Though Mary described the evidence against Carrie as "all a lie," she also wrote that Carrie, "poor thing, dare not tell all." Mary wrote that Sherman spent all his money on lawyers, and had even hired someone to manufacture evidence of Carrie's wantonness. Highlighting another of Sherman's failures as a husband, she noted they would starve without Mathilde's financial help.[18] While she detailed Sherman's failings as a husband, he criticized her weaknesses as a wife. Mary observed that Sherman had gained public sympathy because some people believed "he was *driven* to it." Even Sherman came to accept this interpretation: "He says all the time that I have brought it all upon him." Both Sherman and Mary wanted to separate, but she ultimately refused a divorce, worried that he would somehow "outwit" her in the ensuing legal battle and win custody of their daughters.[19]

Sherman's ability to blame Mary was a sign of his conceit, but it also suggests how reformers' ideal of true love contributed to their marital troubles. At the beginning of their marriage, the Booths followed the advice of phrenologists and spiritualists to practice abstinence. They probably continued to exercise self-control in order to avoid pregnancy and prioritize their emotional bond. These same marriage reformers had appointed women as sexual umpires, and it is likely that Mary refused to have sex on occasion. Mathilde Anneke, who observed the couple closely, blamed Sherman's "sexual drive" for his treatment of the "innocent" Carrie. Indeed, Anneke may have had her own unwanted encounter with Sherman, writing to Fritz that "I have taken—without any further provocation—a more determinate posture. *He was not allowed in my room, that stayed locked.*"[20] In public, Sherman was a model of reform virtue; in private, he lacked the necessary self-restraint.

Sherman's view of Mary as virtuous and innocent had also changed. Their marriage occurred when Mary was relatively young, and Sherman clearly associated youth with purity, beauty, and submissiveness. Despite his reform credentials, he also held on to older notions of male privilege and the sexual double standard. At the end of their marriage, he disparaged Mary by telling her that she "*used* to be *pure*."[21] Mary and Carrie Cook may not have been the only objects of his desire. At the beginning of his marriage, Sherman wrote an inappropriate, flirtatious letter to Mary's sixteen-year-old sister, Jane, describing eighteen-year-old Mary as "too old" for him. Though he dismissed it as mere "playfulness," it is possible that Sherman had a sexual or emotional relationship with Mary's sister. In 1859, Jane was institutionalized for insanity caused by "years of suffering endured for her sister" as well as Sherman's "sudden unlooked for and overwhelming cruelty." One friend wondered how Jane would react to the "horrible disclosures" of the Cook case.[22]

If Sherman Booth defined female purity only by youthful virginity, Mary's romantic fantasies echoed reformers' construction of sensitive, self-controlled manhood. Disappointed in her husband, Mary embarked on a love affair with a German immigrant whom she probably met through the Annekes. Identified only by last name in her surviving correspondence, "Biedermann" was probably Julius Biedermann, a thirty-two-year-old musician, who had arrived in the United States in 1847, and became a naturalized citizen in Milwaukee in 1858. Mary focused her hopes on Biedermann as another devoted savior. Just as Booth rescued her from the Sabins, Mary hoped Biedermann could rescue her from her failed marriage. Like Booth, he proved to be a disappointment. When Mary informed him that she would be penniless if she divorced Sherman, Biedermann responded that he had stopped loving her, and "could not marry her."[23]

Unwilling to relinquish her true love ideal, Mary Booth turned to race to explain her recent fall from virtue. She never questioned the innocence of Carrie Cook or her friend Mathilde Anneke, but she did identify a flaw in herself. One evening, Mary revealed to Mathilde that she was "the descendent of a native Indian." Her great-grandmother was the "Daughter of the Forest; one of the last Mohicans." Mary had never told anyone else because "her origins have given her so much sorrow her whole life long." For Mary, this hidden bloodline held an explanatory power: "Everything angry in her is blamed . . . as inheritance of the Indians." But race also offered the potential for liberation. With her marriage all but over, Mary embraced an Indian identity as a way to rebel against social expectations for middle-class women. As Mathilde reported, "she makes herself an Indian outfit, she has sewed a dress totally on her own."[24] Mary Booth was preparing to shed her marriage and other trappings of sexual respectability.

As the trial closed, Sherman Booth was optimistic about the outcome. With his defense focused on attacking Carrie's character, he did not testify,

and spoke only once during the proceedings. E. G. Ryan, one of the prose-
cuting attorneys, had accused Booth of delighting in persecution. As an
abolitionist, Ryan argued, "persecution is profitable to him, politically and
pecuniarily." Booth cried, "That's a lie!" He quickly apologized for his out-
burst. In his instructions to the jury, the judge rejected the defense's argument that chastity meant something besides virginity, but he accepted their
definition of seduction as implying a feat of art, strategy, and persuasion.
Still, Sherman had been overly confident. The jury returned, unable to
make a decision in the case. Seven jurors had voted to convict, and five to
acquit. The Booths prepared for another trial.[25]

Sherman Booth's case was never retried. In March 1860, he was arrested
in connection with the now six-year-old Joshua Glover fugitive slave case,
and jailed in the Custom House, postponing another trial for Carrie Cook's
seduction. Abolitionists made several attempts to free Sherman, but he was
still in prison on July 4, when he addressed a crowd outside his cell window,
rallying support for the Republican cause. The following year, on March 11,
1861, President Buchanan pardoned Booth.[26] Meanwhile, the seduction case
evaporated, possibly due to heightened sectional tensions and the onset of
war, or possibly due to the reluctance of Carrie and her family to allow her
chastity to be further questioned.

Even as they visited Sherman in prison, Mary and Mathilde planned
their own escape from the miserable remains of the Booth marriage. In July
1860, the same month Sherman addressed supporters from his window,
Mathilde took Mary and the Booths' younger daughter, Lillian, to Zurich.
Mary had sent her older daughter, Mary Ella, to live with her mother during
the trial.

Before marrying Sherman Booth, Mary had viewed true love as pure and
noble. Her marriage disabused her of this notion. In Zurich, Switzerland,
where she and Mathilde Anneke lived from September 1860 to July 1864, the
two women formed a loving union that soon supplanted their legal marriages, with Mathilde as the "foolish head" of their "foolish family."[27] Mary's
descriptor "foolish" indicated their radical, unexpected departure from social
and sexual convention. The two women had moved to Switzerland for practical reasons, and their unusual household developed as much from circum-
stance as intent. Unlike the Booth marriage, which had begun with high ideals
and devolved into compromising reality, this relationship began in reality
and evolved into something closer to reformers' definition of true or authentic love. Mary and Mathilde shared an intense emotional and physical bond,

Figure 9. Mary Booth *(seated)* with feminist Mathilde Anneke.
The marital troubles of the Booths led Mary and Mathilde to
forge an alternative form of true love in Switzerland. Image
WHi-72188, courtesy of the Wisconsin Historical Society.

and they engaged in a romantic experiment that fueled their creativity. They
supported themselves by writing antislavery and pro-Union articles for American and European newspapers. Mary also wrote multiple poems about love,
many of them later published in her volume, *Wayside Blossoms* (1865). None
of her poems associated love with purity, virtue, or spirituality, but neither
did she consider her relationship with Mathilde to be adulterous or illicit.
Mary Booth's poems were a sensual and grounded exploration of love in the
dramatic setting of the Alps.[28]

Though Mary had succeeded in isolating herself geographically, she remained legally, financially, and emotionally connected to her husband. By 1861, Sherman had been freed from prison and started a newspaper, the *Daily Life*. With little hope, Mary asked Sherman to send money to Hartford to support Mary Ella and to Zurich to support Lillian. Out of frustration at his failures, she agreed to write for Sherman's journal in order to be able to send money to her mother and daughter. These practical exchanges brought back the pain of the seduction trial. Mary complained to her mother that Sherman wrote her "love trash" and "glorified" his actions toward her. Mary vowed, "I shall never live as a wife again with that man if I die first—never!"[29] Sherman filled other letters with vitriol, charging Mary with having an affair with "Mr. Anneke" or speculating that she had made an "*unvirtuous* connexion" among other "unprincipled people in Europe."[30] Even though Mary lived with Mathilde, neither Sherman nor their contemporaries imagined their relationship as anything more than friendship, a fact that allowed the two women to commit the legal act of adultery.

Mary viewed Mathilde Anneke as both her chivalrous protector and talented lover. When Sherman Booth's "awful" letters made Mary physically ill, Mathilde ordered him to stop. Mary told her mother that Mathilde wanted to provide a comfortable home for them, and was frustrated that she could not. Mathilde's masculine role emanated from her larger size as well as her actions. As Mary wrote, "her heart and soul are as a great as her body." But Mary also insisted on Mathilde's feminine power, calling her a "Queen."[31] In one love letter, Mary described Mathilde as a life-giving sun: "You are the morning star of my soul, the beautiful auroral glow of my heart." In this same letter, she also turned to erotic floral metaphors to describe their relationship, telling Mathilde that she was "the saintly lily of my dream, the deep dark rosebud unfolding in my bosom day by day, sweetening my life with your ethereal fragrance—*dearest*, you are the *reality* of my dreams, *my life*, my *love*." Her letters confirmed that Mathilde was part of her nights as well as her days. When visiting a spa for her health, Mary assured Mathilde that "I think about you every *night*," extending the sentiment to what seems to be a kinky sexual reference to "the *bell-rope*, & all."[32]

Though her responses to Mary have not survived, Mathilde saved Mary's love poems and letters. One handwritten poem is identified as being composed by the side of a brook in Zurich, and describes the physiological response to a lover's name, "Throbbing and sobbing, a name—a name/Is pulsing forever through brain and blood. . . . But rushes in flushes and blushes of red. . . . And all this sweet tumult in soul and in form/Is made by the sound in my heart of a name." Another poem expressed Mary's sense of being subsumed by her love for Mathilde: "Words come not up through love's overwhelming tide/I turned away to let my heart oer'fill/And drown in rapture which it sought to hide." Two of the poems that Mathilde kept also appeared in Mary's *Wayside Blossoms*. Both "Coming, Love" and "For F. M." (Mary called Mathilde "Franziska Maria"), renamed "Beat to the Pulses Sweet" for the volume, describe the couple's pleasure in being together. In "Coming, Love" Mary describes the anticipation of reuniting with her love: "And we were all the world, mine own/Its joy and melody and moan." "For F. M." is a lullaby about a woman's décolletage in the moonlight. The first words of each line, "Beat" "Creep," "Blow," "Come," "Float," "Faint," "Meet," and "Rest" could describe foreplay, sex, and orgasm.[33]

"Alpine Lovers," another poem from *Wayside Blossoms,* captures the isolation and experimentation of Mary and Mathilde's home in Zurich. The poem observed that the two lovers, a "gentle maid" and a hunter, existed outside of social expectations: "She never heard, of what the world calls 'fashion'/ And never thought of what the world might say/ Yet loving deeds, of beautiful compassion/Flowered on her mountain way." Their world was limited to the mountains, and even more so, to their bed:

> She never knew that music needed teachers,
>   But learned her warblings of the singing rills;
> She thought God's mountains, his divinest preachers,
>   His holiest shrines, His hills!
>
> The incense of her loving heart's devotion,
>   Rose little higher than her hunter's cot;
> She thought the spring of love's auroral ocean,
>   Welled from one mountain spot.[34]

The lovers in the poem learned from each other and from the natural environment around them. Love, in their case, as in Mary and Mathilde's, did not involve laws, religious ceremonies, marriage experts, or other worldly trappings.

When Mary left Zurich in the summer of 1864, she broke her Swiss idyll with Mathilde, though she did so reluctantly and out of "duty" to her older daughter. Back in the United States, Mary wrote frequent letters to Mathilde, but months went by—an "eternity" in Mary's view—before she got a response. Mary pleaded with Mathilde not to doubt her love, "though you often *seemed* to do so toward the last—but of that time, I will not speak." She assured Mathilde that her feelings had not changed: "*love* you *I do*, with all the old truth and reverence—think you that anything on Earth could, or can ever fill your place in my *heart*?" Mary flirted with Mathilde by demanding that she read her letters before Fritz Anneke's. In one letter, for example, Mary referred to their shared secret of her alleged Indian ancestry, by noting that her "tomahawk is sharpened" in the event that Mathilde prioritized her husband's letters.[35]

Despite her hopes to return to Switzerland, Mary began to build a new life in bohemian New York City. With both daughters now living with her mother in Hartford, Mary moved into a boarding house at 159 East Fifty-First Street. She worried that people might gossip about her marriage to Sherman, but she found support from old acquaintances such as the publisher Charles M. Plumb, brother-in-law of Andrew Jackson Davis, and the abolitionist Gerrit Smith, who had visited Mary and Mathilde in Zurich. Mary wrote a poem for Smith that appeared in newspapers as well as *Wayside Blossoms*, describing him as "the world's most loving brother." She also made new friends, including Theodore Tilton, editor of the *New York Independent*, who promised a good review of her forthcoming book of poems. One friend aroused Mathilde's jealousy, a twenty-two-year-old German artist named Louis Wust, a fellow boarder who worked for *Frank Leslie's Illustrated Newspaper*. He painted Mary as well as more famous subjects like the pianist Louis M. Gottschalk, lover of actress Ada Clare. Mary described Wust as looking more French than German, with black eyes and thick black hair. In one letter, Mary called him her "lover," but it might be more accurate to say he was an attentive and devoted friend. Mathilde disliked him on principle, and pointedly asked Mary if she had heard from her old boyfriend Julius Biedermann (she had not).[36]

By early 1865, Mary's health began to deteriorate. She had experienced health problems in Zurich, at one point writing that "the *inside* of me has not been just *right for a long time*."[37] In Manhattan, a homeopathic physician named Greves operated her boardinghouse, and she consulted a number of doctors, male and female, who tried clairvoyance, magnetism, and "the new movement cure." Andrew Jackson Davis prescribed massage oil from a recipe he had received in a trance. Louis Wust brought her food and sat with her through the night. Mary described herself as "dreadful old & sick."[38] When she started a spotty menstruation, the doctors speculated that Mary was going through menopause. She had trouble breathing and walking. Mary diagnosed her problem as emotional as well as physical, writing to Mathilde that "I do not know, my sweet bird, if I shall ever get well—there is not much to do for a broken heart." Mary might have referred to Sherman, Biedermann, or Mathilde, or perhaps to all of them. Her self-diagnosis was acute. Mary Booth, aged thirty-four, died of heart disease on April 11, 1865.[39]

The European experiment of Mary Booth and Mathilde Anneke had provided a brief "oasis" from their legal marriages and their troubled country, mired in the Civil War.[40] For a time, they achieved the ideal that all marriage reformers advocated: a mutual partnership based on a love that existed above and beyond the law. Since these reformers advocated heterosexual love, Mary and Mathilde abandoned their theories in favor of practice, free of legal or cultural definitions of adultery. Mary was head-over-heels in love with Mathilde, whom she regarded as her idol, defender, and the head of their household. Mathilde, who castigated Sherman, expressed jealousy when they were apart, and saved Mary's letters and poems, likely reciprocated her passionate devotion. Inevitably, the harsh reality of money and family intruded, and their experiment came to an end. Before she left Switzerland, Mary had predicted that she would die without Mathilde, and she did.

When Mary Booth lived in Switzerland, she and Mathilde Anneke created a love that defied legal or gendered definitions. Perhaps, her experience suggested, only two women could achieve a true marriage, unencumbered by legal and social expectations. But Booth's criticism, evidenced only in a sweet, sentimental volume by a lesser female poet, had little impact.

*   *   *

In retrospect, the ideas of moderate marriage reformers, which informed the initial romance of Mary and Sherman Booth, as well as the love between Mary and Mathilde Anneke, seem uncontroversial. Spiritualists, phrenologists, women's rights activists, and abolitionists agreed that love was the only basis for marriage. Within marriage, they wanted to empower women to control their own bodies and determine the frequency of intercourse. They believed in one perfect love, so they viewed marriage as monogamous and everlasting. But their arguments bordered on free love when they defined the legal bond as irrelevant to true love.

At the time, many Americans viewed their ideas as dangerous, undermining the social and gender stability made possible by the institution of marriage. These critics may have had a point. True love had proved impossible to control, justifying the impulsive, scandalous, and short-lived marriage of Mary Corss and Sherman Booth. Reformers had adopted the metaphor of adultery to create a new ideal of marriage, but its literal, legal meaning proved just as applicable in reform marriages. At the end of the 1850s, many of these moderate reformers became embroiled in a national controversy over free love.

CHAPTER 7

Adultery Among the Free Lovers

In 1849, Stephen Pearl Andrews moved to New York City to further spread the gospel of phonography, or Pitman's shorthand. Since giving up phonography for utopianism, he defined his profession as "rare scientific and philosophical investigations—some efforts towards social reorganization."[1] When Edward Fitch Underhill, a signer of the Seneca Falls Declaration of Sentiments, moved to Manhattan, he was already knowledgeable about phonography and Fourierism from his time in central New York, and quickly became Andrews's devotee.

In October 1853, Underhill proclaimed his fealty to the principles of Modern Times: individual sovereignty and cost the limit of price. Underhill also declared "the law" to be "one of the greatest encroachers on individual rights."[2] He joined the Progressive Union Club, which Andrews founded in 1853 as an extension of Modern Times in New York City. The League, as it was also called, included a Grand Order of Recreation to provide uplifting entertainment to working people. In 1855, it moved to 555 Broadway, above Taylor's Saloon. Though the newspapers disparaged it as the Free Love Club, the League's goal was to offer affordable, twice-weekly meetings featuring amusing, wholesome, and educational activities. Andrews, Underhill, and friends also frequented the well-known bar and restaurant Pfaff's Cellar.[3]

Those who sought the Free Love Club's brand of conversation considered themselves to be cosmopolitan intellectuals. Employed in various capacities by the city's newspapers, they were an interconnected group of journalists, socialists, free lovers, and spiritualists. They shared a broad interest in radical politics, as well as a willingness to challenge the sexual mores of the larger society, both in private and in print. These friends were less religious, more international, and more working-class than other marriage reformers. This bohemian subculture of male writers and activists included a few white, female free lovers, like Marie Stevens and Julia Branch, who were willing to risk their sexual respectability.

Jane Cunningham (later Croly), better known as the writer Jennie June, was the Free Love Club's English-born "mistress of ceremonies and wore a handsome badge of office."[4] She may have been the woman interviewed by a female reporter for the *New York Tribune*. On a visit to the Free Love Club, the journalist found two hundred participants, of whom one-third were women. These included "bright and intelligent" women as well as those "whose external appearance bore witness to a life of sensual indulgence." A respectable woman with an official role as a floor manager— possibly Jennie June—defended the mixed crowd, arguing in favor of democracy. "What we desire," she explained, "is to furnish the means for social and intellectual enjoyment, and then bring these people together to act and react upon each other." This woman also proclaimed her belief in the "freedom of the affections," which, like John Humphrey Noyes, she saw as leading to chastity rather than licentiousness.[5] The journalist, poet, and stockbroker Edmund Clarence Stedman went to the Free Love Club a few times, and later wrote that he "took no harm" from the experience.[6]

Marie Stevens, a former Lowell mill girl turned schoolteacher, met her future husband at the Free Love Club. She described Lyman (also known as Leon) Case, a lawyer who had briefly flirted with the priesthood, as a "real radical socialist."[7] After their marriage, Case brought Marie to the meetings of the "Revolutionary Committee of all nations," a group of "cosmopolite revolutionists," who staged torchlight demonstrations in honor of the "martyrs" Orsini and Pierri, Italian nationalists executed for attempting to assassinate Napoleon III. He also escorted Marie to a socialist banquet celebrating the anniversary of the 1848 French Revolution.[8]

Two years after its founding, the Free Love Club came to a dramatic end. Motivated by frenzied coverage in the city's newspapers, the mayor ordered police to raid 555 Broadway; among those arrested was socialist Albert Brisbane, who had introduced Fourierism to American reformers. In the midst of addressing the assembled men and women on the prevalence of prostitution in New York City, Brisbane had allegedly called New York "nothing else than a Great Free-Love Club!" His remarks did not violate any laws, but the *New York Times* still expressed dismay that a "large number of ladies were present," assuming them to be "strong minded women who came to reason philosophically and found to their sorrow that philosophy did not work." As the women exited the saloon, "like a flock of frightened sheep chased by wolves," the crowd apparently cried, "Let us see 'em" and "Hoo-ray for the Free-Lovers."[9] Underhill, who had managed to escape arrest, sought legal advice and funds. Although the charges were dropped, the Free Love Club shut its doors.

*   *   *

With the demise of their club, free lovers turned to another, highly anticipated project, the opening of the Unitary Home on May 1, 1858. Originally located on Stuyvesant Street, this communal brownstone housed approximately twenty-five individuals. In families or as individuals, they slept privately in apartments, but shared the common living and dining rooms. The residents also shared expenses, which Underhill estimated at $3.44 per adult per week, a third less than what they would spend living in isolated households. As proprietor, Underhill paid the annual rent on the building and managed the shared purchasing and hiring decisions.[10]

Unitary Home members further fueled the free love crisis. Underhill defended the Unitary Home from accusations of free love by scandal-hungry newspapers, describing residents as "persons of refinement and culture." His personal convictions were another matter. Though married, Underhill declared himself to be "a *free* lover, and not a slave lover," who believed that "the institution of civilized marriage" was "at variance with the instincts of human nature" and the "principles of Christianity." Like other marriage reformers, Underhill prioritized his cause over slavery. Observing the growing sectional conflict, Underhill stated, "it is an extraordinary fact that while free speech, free press, free conscience, free soil, and free men, which in their time have been violently abused, and are now the ruling ideas, at least in the north, Love is the only thing which public opinion wants enslaved."[11]

Despite, or perhaps because of, the negative attention it received from New York City newspapers, the Unitary Home became a hub for journalists. In his apartment, Underhill and a team of assistants worked day and night preparing their phonographic reports for publication. Anna Ballard, a reporter for the *New York Sun*, was a founding member. Other residents included the city editor of the *Evening Post*, Alfred C. Hills, and Charles Tabor Congdon of the *New York Times*. Congdon, another resident recalled, "lived the life of a hermit," an unlikely characterization for a resident of a

Figure 10. Edward F. Underhill, phonographer, signer of the
Seneca Falls Declaration of Sentiments, and free-love manager
of the Unitary Home. Possession of the author.

commune. Henry Clapp Jr., editor of the *Saturday Press*, and better known
as the "King of Bohemia," was a frequent visitor. And, with his interest in
the power of print as well as communitarianism, John Humphrey Noyes of
the Oneida Community also paid a "jovial" call.[12]

The Unitary Home attracted its share of unusual characters. Marx
Edgeworth Lazarus, author of *Love vs. Marriage*, the book that had
launched Stephen Pearl Andrews's debate with Horace Greeley, lived on
the top floor. One resident remembered this thin, long-haired, "well-born

former Israelite" as an "inoffensive citizen, chaste to asceticism, a worshipper of the eternal feminine, chivalrous, and courteous in discourse." His book offers one reason Lazarus may have been the only celibate resident of the Unitary Home. He identified woman as the "queen of harmony," and the fount of love, but he viewed maternal rather than romantic love as its highest form.[13]

Another eccentric was Giancinto Achilli, an ex-priest who now assailed the Catholic Church, who moved in temporarily. When Achilli lived in England, he had won a libel suit against Cardinal John Henry Newman, a convert to Catholicism, who had accused Achilli of seduction, fornication, and adultery with many women dating back to his years as a priest in Italy.[14] After leaving the Unitary Home, Achilli, with his pregnant "wife" and their son, traveled to the Oneida Community. Before they could admit the family as members, the Oneida Community investigated and discovered that Achilli was married, but not to his female companion. Indeed, he had served a jail term in New Jersey for adultery. Thus discovered, Achilli departed for the train station and was never heard from again. The community's *Circular* speculated that he had committed suicide. His lover, Josephine Bogue, returned to England, but their two sons, Frank and Ittilio, both lived at the Oneida Community for a time.[15]

Despite the masculine atmosphere, Underhill believed that the Unitary Home's system of organization contributed to women's emancipation. He criticized the "isolated household" as both expensive and undesirable for women. The Unitary Home, in contrast, offered shared domestic harmony. With the woman freed from "the monotonous drudgery and never-ceasing cares of the isolated home," he wrote, "man and woman find in the social enjoyment of the parlor—in music, in conversation and in reading, a pleasing contrast to the misanthropy of our present household system."[16] Underhill argued that most women spent their lives at the "the cooking-stove, the wash-tub, the cradle, the needle, and the broom-handle," and, as a result, "their growth in true womanhood is dwarfed." Fourierists and free lovers alike focused on re-creating relations between men and women; everything else, they believed, followed. In contrast to other Americans, they did not value women primarily as mothers. The Unitary Home allowed women to explore "every avenue of learning and usefulness to which she may aspire."[17]

As in many utopian communities, the theory may have been more appealing than the practice. Underhill did not offer the perspective of his wife, Mary Post Underhill, who hosted many parties at the Unitary Home, but he did mention that a "lady" served as the housekeeper. A female resident later remembered this individual as the "very competent" Mrs. Chambers. Other female servants helped her run the large household, so only some women had been liberated from the cook-stove and wash-tub.[18]

As at Modern Times, marriage coexisted with "romances and jealousies." In addition to Edward and Mary Underhill, other married residents included *New York Herald* reporter Leonard Hendricks and his wife, and Edmund Clarence Stedman and his wife, Laura, who shared their three private rooms with their two children, a maid, and Edmund's brother. Stedman remembered fondly the public dances on Wednesday and Saturday nights, and the Fourierist mantra that there were no "evil passions." In retrospect, however, he claimed no involvement in the more risqué aspects of communal living, and Laura, he wrote protectively, "kept to her room" and "never heard discussion on dangerous points, nor would she have understood them."[19] Stedman protested a little too much. He had some kind of romantic encounter, described as "a cluster of perfect hours" and "a symphony of such pure and profound delight," with married resident Marie Stevens Case.[20]

Stedman's career as a financier and member of the literary establishment depended on his respectability, but youthful (or even current) indiscretions were tolerated among men. The same was not true for Laura Stedman. Even many years after the fact, an affiliation with this revived free-love club had the potential to damage her social standing and reputation as a virtuous lady.

Marie Case was one of the few women who willingly flouted society's expectations of sexual purity and put her reputation in jeopardy. The Case marriage itself was a sort of social experiment. Lyman Case's love interests followed his radical politics. In addition to studying for the priesthood, Case had also enrolled in Wesleyan University and Union College before deciding on the law. In 1849, he married Mary Harriett Boudinot, a graduate of Mount Holyoke College and one of the daughters of the Cherokee leader Elias Boudinot and his European-American wife, Harriet Gold. Mary Harriett died in 1853.[21] Four years later, Case's marriage to Marie Stevens transgressed class rather than racial lines, and he took it upon himself to educate her. As Marie remembered of their Pygmalion relationship, Case coached her in "speech, manners, movements, etc. etc. & I was very grateful for the pains he took." She concluded, "I owe much to the training of Mr.

Case. He put me through the course of logic of the Fordham school for priests, using a Latin text book when I did not know a hundred words in Latin." She remembered Lyman as "magnanimous," but "full of *little* criticisms."[22]

Lyman Case's generosity extended to other men. Although a twice-married man, he was an opponent of the institution. According to another habitué of the Unitary Home, Case "not only did not believe in marriage as an institution, but professed to be entirely free from the selfishness which prompts men to claim the exclusive right of the affection and person of the women they love."[23] When Henry Clapp Jr. brought his *Saturday Press* partner Edward Howland—a southerner, former cotton merchant, and a Harvard man—to the Unitary Home, Marie was smitten. After Edward and Marie danced, Lyman told her "Marie, you have met your destiny." When she responded, "I thought I had met my destiny," he replied, "No lying, Marie. You have met the man of all men whom you need."[24]

Not everyone remembered Case's treatment of Marie so positively. In a later attempt to undermine Case's reputation, William S. Andrews, Stephen Pearl's son, wrote that Case made a mockery of his marriage. To prove his "extreme liberality," Case invited the teenage William "to sleep with his wife, in her presence, and told her that she must initiate me into the delights and mysteries of love (or words to that effect)." William Andrews did not take him up on the offer, and Marie apparently told him that "Mr. Case did not mean what he said. . . . he desired to lead her into some indiscretion that would enable him to obtain a divorce." Case, William Andrews concluded, "was utterly devoid of moral sense."[25]

Given Marie's warm memories of Lyman Case, William Andrews's record of this exchange, particularly Lyman's intent to manufacture grounds for divorce, is questionable. Marie and Lyman did divorce, but his benevolence was evident in this act as well. The Cases' marriage ended in New York on July 11, 1865. With adultery the only possible cause, Marie's complaint detailed her husband's disregard for the "solemnity of the marriage vow" and charged him with having "carnal connections" with "several persons to this plaintiff unknown" as well as with a prostitute named Antoinette Muller. Two attorneys investigated this charge, interviewing Muller and a man named Leon Whiting, who had apparently accompanied Lyman Case to the brothel. The open marriages at the Unitary Home should have provided ample evidence for adultery, so it is likely that Lyman Case cooperated in constructing this particular incident. He often used the name

"Leon"—indeed that is how Marie referred to him—and no Leon Whiting has been found in city or census records. Antoinette Muller undoubtedly provided her affidavit in exchange for payment.[26]

Soon after her divorce from Case was finalized, Marie married Edward Howland. With Case's blessing, they had been a couple since they first met at the Unitary Home, but they too had an open relationship. She and Edward patronized Pfaff's restaurant, where they socialized with a literary and theatrical crowd. The actress and writer Ada Clare (pronounced "I declare"), a southerner born Ada Jane McElhenney, was the "queen" of these bohemians. One writer described Ada Clare's rooms on Forty-Second Street as a gathering place for "intellectual pleasure-seekers, who were not bound by conventional rules, nor fettered by the rigidity of custom, but harmonized by fine feeling." Although Clare was "crazily enamored" of the Jewish pianist Louis Gottschalk, and had a child after their sexual relationship, she was "never without a woman companion." Marie became one of these female companions, spending every Saturday night at Ada Clare's home, and sharing her bed. Only occasionally did Edward accompany her.[27]

In addition to Unitary Home residents' sexual experimentation, members harnessed their literary connections to publicly criticize the current state of marriage. Poet Edmund Clarence Stedman remembered his compatriots as "free-lances, news gatherers, or when items fell short, *making news*, and selling it as best they could."[28] In 1859, Stedman himself made news with his poem "The Diamond Wedding," which mocked the society marriage of Frances Amelia Bartlett to a wealthy Cuban, Marquis Don Estaban de Santa Cruz de Oviedo, who was "three times her age" and in the "Autumn of life."[29] For Stedman and other residents of the Unitary Home, now in a larger location on Fourteenth Street, such matches proved that marriage was far from sanctified. Idealizing pure, romantic love, Stedman's verses pointed out the mercenary nature of modern marriage: "But now, True Love, you're growing old/Bought and sold, with silver and gold."[30]

The bride's father, who lived on the same street as the Unitary Home, took offense at Stedman's suggestion that he had sold his daughter to the highest bidder, and challenged him to a duel. The Unitary Home was in a "delightful expectancy," with one resident as his second, and the others defending him in the press. Ultimately, Bartlett withdrew his challenge, citing Stedman's inferior social status.[31]

Not all the journalists, bohemians, and free lovers who took up residence at the Unitary Home were free lovers, but they had to be tolerant of or intrigued by its possibilities. Rejecting the staid respectability of the larger society, the men and women of the Unitary Home created an open, fun-loving environment, a site of social and marital experimentation, and combination dance and lecture hall. In this context, women such as Marie Case may not have been equals, but they had a taste of sexual freedom.

*   *   *

From the Unitary Home, free lovers orchestrated a national movement against marriage. Though Stephen Pearl Andrews did not live in the Unitary Home, he was a constant presence. His coworker Mary Gove Nichols, who had lived at Modern Times, had since converted to Catholicism, but not before publishing a scandalous memoir in 1855. Written in the form of a novel, *Mary Lyndon* recounted her unhappy first marriage, divorce, and subsequent romance with journalist and free lover Thomas Nichols. Some Unitary Home residents, including Marx Edgeworth Lazarus, appeared as supporting characters. More important, the book portrayed Gove Nichols's first husband as "ignorant, jealous, and a tyrant," who claimed his legal right to have sex with her. This experience, she wrote, led to her conviction that "marriage without love was legalized adultery."[32]

The new "female leader of the Free-Lovers" was Julia Branch, another resident of the Unitary Home. Born in 1827 in Rhode Island, she was the daughter of Elisha and Eliza Peckham. The details of her marriage to Mr. Branch are unknown, but by 1855 she was widowed or divorced. One disgruntled gentleman gossiped that Julia had "left two husbands" to live with the free lovers, but her friends affirmed that she had "suffered" in marriage. The *New York Times* described Branch as an attractive, curly-haired brunette with "literary tendencies; writes for some of the Sunday papers in New-York; is a poetess and is very well known." She also associated with spiritualists, and may have worked as a trance medium.[33] In her headline-grabbing speeches, Branch further developed Mary Gove Nichols's argument that loveless legal marriage deprived women of virtue by forcing them to have sex with their husbands.. The bonds of marriage, they agreed, violated women's own conscience and right to self-determination.

These radical marriage reformers further improvised the metaphor of adultery, and refined it in ways that would become more prominent after the Civil War. They criticized loveless marriages as providing a veneer of respectability, an exchange of sex not only for economic support (the prostitution metaphor) but a virtuous reputation (the adultery metaphor), limiting women's moral capacity and autonomy.

On reading *Mary Lyndon*, a horrified Henry Blackwell, the husband of Lucy Stone, wrote, "I trust these 'free lovers' will not thrust their immoralities before the public in the 'Womans Rights' disguise which they are trying to assume." He suspected a "plan of that kind."[34] Blackwell was right to be worried.

CHAPTER 8

Feminists and the Marriage Question

On May 13, 1858, less than two weeks after the Unitary Home opened, Stephen Pearl Andrews and Julia Branch attended the annual women's rights convention in New York City. To the increasing dismay of feminists, free lovers were, indeed, bringing their theory of individual sovereignty to women's rights conventions. Andrews had long considered equal political and civil rights to be mere distractions, but he caused a sensation when he informed activists that women's right to maternity—to decide when and, more significantly, with whom they conceived—was more important than any other right. To the consternation of the organizers, newspapers reported that he had demanded women's "right to be unchaste" with no opposition from the gathered women.[1] Offstage, Branch confronted Lucy Stone, asking, "How can [woman] have the right to vote when she has not even the right to her name in the marriage bonds?" Stone responded that women did have the right to their names: "I have not given up mine, and no law can compel me to." While Stone understood the question literally, Branch had meant the "good name"—integrity or reputation—given by the husband's surname. Whether Lucy used Stone or her husband's name, Blackwell, Branch replied that common knowledge of their legal marriage protected her sexual respectability.[2]

Lucy Stone had approached her own marriage, and its personal and legal implications, with caution. During their courtship, Stone gave Henry Blackwell a copy of Henry C. Wright's *Marriage and Parentage*, which advocated sexual restraint. In May 1855, when they finally wed, Stone and Blackwell issued a protest against the institution. Their marriage, the couple stated, was a public acknowledgment of their "mutual affection," but implied "no sanction of, nor promise of obedience to such of the present laws of marriage, as refuse to recognize the wife as an independent, rational being." These laws included those that granted the husband "the custody of the wife's person." The newlyweds agreed that theirs should be "an equal and permanent partnership." Accordingly, Blackwell ceded control of their sexual relationship to Lucy. Though she wanted to have a child, Lucy expressed some nervousness about as well as aversion to intercourse. The couple did not consummate their union on their wedding night, and they may have abstained for several months.[3]

Despite Stone's open criticism of the laws of marriage, women's rights activists feared any association with free love. Among themselves, feminists debated whether and how to address women's inequality in marriage. Those feminists who addressed the topic of marital rights, such as Lucy Stone or Mary Fenn Davis, did so in defense of the institution. Still, even when they offered the mildest criticism, newspapers charged the women's movement with undermining family, church, and country. As historian Lori Ginzberg observes, "free love" became an epithet, designed to mislead, misinterpret, and otherwise undermine the women's movement. Though feminists tried to distance themselves from free lovers, the different metaphors of adultery, prostitution, and slavery inflected feminists' debate over the marriage question.[4]

In 1855, pioneering feminist Sarah Grimké rejected recent accusations from the *New York Times* that the women's rights movement embraced free love principles. "On the contrary," she stated, "our great desire is to purify and exalt the marriage relation." Equal rights, Grimké argued, was the only solution to the "legalized licentiousness"—a broader metaphor that encompassed both adultery and prostitution—of loveless marriages. But even in cases of "false marriage," she believed couples must "abide by the consequences" and should not divorce. The couple might live separately, but they had to be celibate and "keep themselves pure."[5] While not all feminists agreed with the unmarried Grimké's staunch opposition to divorce, they shared her desire to separate women's rights from free-love radicalism. Women's rights activists believed their movement depended on their outward commitment to marital respectability.

As a result, the appearance of Andrews and Branch at the 1858 women's rights convention caused an internal crisis. Elizabeth Neall Gay wrote to Susan B. Anthony that she was "shocked" that Anthony, as president of the convention, had allowed Andrews to speak. Others also complained, but Anthony had merely adhered to their policy of a "free platform." While Gay worried about the movement's reputation, other activists viewed the topic as personal rather than political. Martha Coffin Wright wrote Anthony that she was "sorry for all that was said about 'unwilling maternity' because that is a subject that no Conventional or Legislative action can ever reach, & therefore it is better let alone." Vaguely, Wright hoped that as "people become more enlightened, all those evils that have arisen from that source may be avoided."[6]

Free lovers continued to challenge feminists to take a public stand on women's sexual and reproductive agency. Their next stop was a series of so-called "free" conventions. At the first convention in Rutland, Vermont, which met from June 25–27, 1858, "a curious gathering" of "all sorts of queer people" debated slavery, free trade, and spiritualism, as well as women's rights, marriage, and maternity.[7] Julia Branch's speech, however, inspired the nickname "free love convention" in the press.[8] She spoke against the convention's resolution on marriage, which stated, "That the only true and natural marriage is an exclusive conjugal love between one man and one woman." Further, this rather innocuous resolution named the "isolated home" as the only appropriate site for true love. Spiritualists Mary Fenn and Andrew Jackson Davis addressed the convention, and this resolution implicitly endorsed their idealized view of "true," monogamous marriage at the expense of the unnamed practices of radical free lovers, communitarians, and Mormon polygamists.[9]

In opposing the resolution, Branch's provocative goal was to establish women's independent moral as well as legal standing. She described women as garnering meager benefits from marriage, including the "privilege to become Mrs. Brown, instead of Miss Smith," and "the right to bear children." Though she did not use the phrase "legalized adultery," her speech contained the same criticism that monogamous marriage provided a polite cover for immorality. According to Branch, society judged a woman's character by her marital status rather than her individual worth. The only purpose of marriage, in Branch's view, was "to keep woman virtuous and respectable." She asked, "Has [woman] no nature that may not be proscribed and estimated by man-law-makers? Has she no inborn right that belongs to herself? As she stands now before the world, she has none." As she argued for women's autonomy, Branch's language indicated her embrace of Stephen Pearl Andrews's notion of individual sovereignty. She asserted that a woman should have the right to love "when she will, where she will, and who she will." Branch also proposed her own resolution to replace the convention's ode to true marriage: "Resolved, That the slavery and degradation of woman proceeds from the institution of marriage; that by the marriage contract she loses the control of her name, her person, her property, her labor, her affections, her children and her freedom."[10] In Branch's formulation, legal marriage not only exploited women's labor, it debased her true self.

Like John Humphrey Noyes, Edmund Clarence Stedman, and other marriage critics, Branch compared marriage to slavery. She asserted that, "Women are bought and paid for, as the negro slave is. She is educated as a thing of barter, for a man counts the cost of his intended wife as deliberately as if he thought of keeping a cow, a dog, or a pig."[11] Unlike the adultery metaphor, the slavery metaphor emphasized wives' status as forced labor for their husbands. Though it was extreme, abolitionists at the convention were sympathetic to this comparison, which offered the possibility that marriage might be reformed and improved. Abolitionists differed from Branch in identifying slavery itself as "the sin and crime of our country," the nation's most pressing cause.[12] And for those concerned with licentiousness, reformer Henry C. Wright reminded audiences that chattel slavery protected and promulgated "adultery . . . pollutions, and incests."[13]

Reaction to Branch's speech was immediate, as reformers rushed to denounce free love. After she finished speaking, abolitionist Stephen S. Foster and spiritualist Joel Tiffany "sprang to their feet" to limit the impact of her remarks. Foster, noting his happy marriage to Abby Kelley, asked, "Is not the remedy worse than the disease?" Tiffany, who believed that true marriage transcended all earthly institutions, worried that "people couldn't see the difference between Free-Love and Free-Lust."[14] Feminist Ernestine Rose agreed with Tiffany's portrayal of "a true and genuine conjugal love" as an "affinity of mind and soul and spirit" and not "a matter of money." But, she pointed out, "facts are stubborn things, and we have only to look at and investigate [not] what ought to be, but what is." Rose concluded by arguing for women's economic, legal, and political equality as the only way to reform marriage.[15]

As an advocate of true marriage, Mary Fenn Davis joined in this more tempered, reformist criticism of the institution. She and her husband were already on record as advocating liberal divorce laws. At Rutland, Mary argued that women should not be "driven into marriage" out of economic or moral necessity (such as an unplanned pregnancy) by the "power of society." The only true basis for marriage, she believed, was love, which gave women as well as men the power to choose their mate. She did not go as far as Branch and other free lovers, who used the adultery metaphor to argue that only love was necessary to legitimate sexual intercourse. As she had in previous speeches, Davis deplored marriage laws that gave the husband rights "to the person of his wife," calling this a system of "legalized prostitution." Together with the slavery metaphor, the prostitution metaphor offered a critique of women's economic dependence in marriage, exchanging sex and housework for financial support. Though she agreed with the convention's resolution on monogamous, loving marriage, she urged women to "resist" all "oppressive statutes" for the sake of their own purity and that of their children.[16]

Other speeches at the Rutland convention also highlighted the uncomfortable similarities between feminist and free love arguments about marriage, which variously compared marriage to slavery, prostitution, and, of course, adultery. Even if they did not use it explicitly, some feminists engaged the conceptual critique provided by adultery: that women did not need legal marriage to make virtuous choices. Like Branch, Mary Fenn Davis had attended the women's rights convention in May, as had her fellow spiritualist Eliza Farnham, a writer, lecturer, and prison reformer. Farnham believed that women were "organically" as well as "spiritually" superior to men, a theory that most women's rights activists treated with some skepticism. At Rutland, Farnham classified "the marriage question" as "nothing alarming or disorderly," but the natural result of "the spirit of freedom, entering into the hearts of men and women, [producing] rebellion against the chains of slavery."[17] She also scandalized the audience with the following example of women's superiority: "I could go into the Five Points in New York, and take a class of women,—the lowest I could find,—capable of becoming mothers, and so educate them that they should never, after the day they had seen me, bring such children into the world as they had before." In other words, any woman, even a prostitute, had the capability to be a "free" and "wise" mother. Farnham asserted that womanhood, not chastity or marriage, endowed these imaginary Five Points residents with moral authority. Julia Branch likely agreed.[18]

Henry C. Wright spoke in defense of "conjugal love," but his speech also echoed that of Stephen Pearl Andrews at the women's rights convention. True marriages, Wright argued, were not about the law, but "exclusiveness" and "love." "The first law of marriage, as fixed by nature," he explained, "is monogamy, or one man to one woman, and one woman to one man." He called polygamists "moral monsters," and labeled sexual intercourse outside of true marriage as "prostitution, licensed or unli-censed" (or metaphorical and actual). While his support for monogamy may have assuaged opponents of free love, he also promoted his belief, shared by Andrews, that "Of all woman's rights, her right to decide for herself how often and under what circumstances she shall assume the responsibility and endure the sufferings of maternity is the most sacred and important."[19] Most feminists saw such proposals for women's right to determine sexual relations, espoused in different ways by Branch, Davis, Farnham, and Wright at the Rutland convention, as impractical and more important, dangerous to their cause rather than the cause itself.

Feminists and abolitionists moved to limit the damage. Ernestine Rose, who had supported the stubborn facts in Julia Branch's speech, published a correction to the *New York Times* report that described her as "free love on principle." Rose stated, "This I most emphatically deny." She described Branch as a "stranger." Instead, Rose stated that she supported Stephen Foster's amendment to the marriage resolution, that "exclusive conjugal love," or monogamous marriage, should be "based on perfect equality between one man and one woman."[20] Abolitionists Elizabeth Neall Gay, James Miller McKim, and William Goodell complained of the "ultra free love people"—lumping together Branch and Andrews with Farnham and Wright—to the Quaker activist Lucretia Mott, a respectable mother and grandmother, and asked her to use her influence against them. McKim described Branch's speech as intended to "shock the instinct of Modesty in the love & marriage & maternal" realm, catering to "prurient curiosity." Mott considered their proposal "ungracious," as she too had suffered from misrepresentations by her opponents. Instead, Mott suggested, "Let each & all expound their own creed & then let us judge."[21]

The second free convention, also known as the "Philanthropic Conven-tion," held that September in Utica, New York, was the brainchild of Mary Fenn and Andrew Jackson Davis. Though the press considered it another free-love event, the Davises wanted it to be a platform for their eternal vision of true marriage. The official theme of the convention was "over-coming evil with good." Mary Fenn Davis argued that women, as mothers, were central to this project: "Woman is an artist par excellence. . . . The woman who brought into existence the first child, did more than the most gifted artist ever can do, by giving life and being to an immortal soul." She offered resolutions on women's equality, but she went further than most feminists by arguing for the necessity of divorce for "false" marriages. Davis also asserted the importance of married women's control over sexual inter-course: "she should be free to select her own surroundings, and to specify her own time for assuming this great artistic work of reproduction."[22] One newspaper approved her language as "chaste," but another scoffed at her attempt to disguise "open and undisguised sensuality" as art.[23]

Again, Julia Branch dissented from this idealized portrayal of marriage in favor of women's independence. She refused to retract any part of her scandalous speech at Rutland, further describing marriage as the "slavery and degradation" of women. Branch also argued for this institution's nega-tive impact on children: "Society should abolish all ties of uncongeniality as an outrage upon its morals, as a preventative of the accumulated evils in the shape of half-formed, undeveloped and perverted children." To prevent the harm of loveless marriages, women must have an "absolute right" to say "when, where, and how" they bear children. She proposed a resolution that "all children born under any circumstances within any State, shall be declared by the State legitimate."[24] The resolution expressed her outrage that women's moral standing as mothers depended on their relationship to men. While moderate reformers like Davis wanted women to be able to decide when to have sex in the context of marriage, Branch advocated a woman's right to determine her reproductive destiny regardless of marital status.

Primed by the Rutland convention, Branch's speech at the Utica con-vention unleashed another journalistic outcry. In an article titled "The Free Lovers Again," the *New York Herald* portrayed the speeches by Julia Branch and Mary Fenn Davis as an attempt to "drag" women to the "depths of indecency."[25] The *Herald* had a point. As a free lover, Branch, and to a lesser extent spiritualist and divorcée Davis, had rejected the sexual respect-ability and protection of marriage. In their words and actions, they deliber-ately blurred the lines between themselves, adulterers, and prostitutes. One newspaper even characterized Branch's speech as "on prostitution." Another expressed their moral disapproval by describing the women of the Utica convention as "homely," "repulsive," "brazen-faced, bold and disagreeable."[26]

*   *   *

It was in this charged context that Paschal Beverly Randolph, the mixed-race author, announced his break from white spiritualists, and joined the

newspapers in identifying Davis's brand of feminist spiritualism with free
love. The newspapers described Randolph as "half white" and a "colored
gentleman," but he declared that "single handed and alone, and black at
that, he would tell these reformers they were wrong." In Utica, Randolph
identified as black in order to expose the narrow, exclusive doctrines advocated by white reformers. He argued that Branch's resolution "must not go
out into the world uncontradicted, to encourage prostitution and profligacy." In contrast, Randolph wanted his sisters, black women, "to hold up
their heads before the world pure and virtuous."[27]

His remarks indicated the racial divide on the issue of marriage. White
women like Branch criticized the institution from a position of privilege.
As a white woman, her audiences might assume her sexual respectability—
that is, until she opened her mouth. Fighting negative stereotypes of their
licentiousness, African American women did not have the same luxury.
With racism limiting black women's ability or desire to criticize marriage,
Randolph seized on the issue of free love to challenge white Americans'
claims of sexual morality.

As sectional tensions over slavery intensified, Randolph also used the
platform to confront white abolitionists. He argued that the antislavery
movement "had done more to degrade the slave than all the slave owners
in existence." With white abolitionists Parker Pillsbury and Stephen S. Foster in the audience, he criticized the American Anti-Slavery Society's advocacy of disunion, or the severing of all political and economic ties with
slavery, and thus slaveholding states. He asserted that "this union is the
impregnable fortress against despotism, the only home of pure and liberal
sentiments." In his mind, white abolitionism and spiritualistic free love
both disregarded religion, which alone could reform the world. The men
and women who had spoken at the Utica convention, he stated, ignored
"the existence of God."[28]

After the convention, Randolph carried his criticism of free love-
spiritualism to larger audiences. In November, the *New York Tribune* covered his "recantation" speech at Clinton Hall in New York City, in which
Randolph declared that spiritualism was a form of slavery "worse than
southern bondage" and an "enemy of God, morals, and religion. . . . the
most seductive, hence most dangerous, form of sensualism." He believed
spiritualism had destroyed his mind and body, and blamed Andrew Jackson
Davis's anti-Christian harmonialism.[29] Two years later, in *The Unveiling, or
What I Think of Spiritualism*, he described Davis as bringing bad spirits, or

vampires, into the world, responsible for all the "adulteries and fornications, affinity business, and home desertions" in the spiritualist movement. He urged readers to "assert your manhood" and "NEVER part with consciousness, as ere long they may part with conscience, through the PARALYSIS OF THE WILL."[30] Randolph turned Davis and his followers into evil temptresses, whose feminine wiles could be resisted only by exerting masculine self-control and following his path to spiritual enlightenment and physical health.

As the Utica convention's organizer, Andrew Jackson Davis was undeterred by the contempt of Randolph or the press. Despite the newspaper coverage that concluded "Evil Not to Be Eradicated Just at Present," he planned another philanthropic convention to be held the next year in Buffalo.[31] In August 1859, he wrote to William Green Jr. of his plans to use the convention to establish an "American Harmonial Institute" and "A publishing House." The next month, Davis declared the Buffalo convention to be "*best* meeting I ever attended." The nation's newspapers did not agree, and ignored the event.[32]

For several years, free lovers' campaign against marriage achieved at least one of its goals, as reports of the Free Love Club, the Unitary Home, as well as Edward Underhill, Julia Branch, Stephen Pearl Andrews, and their scandalous remarks on marriage and maternity dominated American newspapers. Indeed, with their many connections to journalism, they could generate their own positive and negative publicity. This free-love crisis enveloped women's rights activists and other moderate marriage reformers, like Mary Fenn Davis and Henry C. Wright, who advocated true love as the only basis for marriage. After the Utica convention, however, the press coverage suddenly declined. Randolph's remarks on abolition indicate why. With a national crisis looming, most Americans lost interest in those who perceived marriage to be a greater social problem than slavery, and the free-love crisis ended abruptly.

* * *

Participants in the marriage debate took different lessons from the scandal. A celebrity after the Rutland and Utica conventions, Julia Branch proposed to "take the field as a lecturer" with the subject of "that ubiquitous female 'Mrs. Grundy,'" a fictional stand-in for a prudish, judgmental neighbor, and her "penchant for interfering in other people's affairs." The *New York*

Tribune speculated that "Mrs. Branch has a personal grudge against Mrs. Grundy which she desires to settle by making her the theme of a lecture."[33] Several months later, however, Julia Branch married James L. Crosby, a phonographer associated with the *New York Tribune*. The couple probably met at the Unitary Home. "So much for free-love doctrines," one newspaper commented.[34]

Branch disappeared from public view, but women's rights activists continued to struggle with the marriage question. At the annual woman's rights Convention in May 1860, Stanton delivered a long-planned, controversial speech on divorce, in which she described marriage as "legalized prostitution," compelling women to have sex with men they did not love in order to survive. Indebted both to free lovers' concept of individual autonomy as well as to moderate reformers' definition of true love, she argued that happiness was an "inalienable right." She proposed a resolution that, "any constitution, compact, or covenant between human beings, that failed to produce or promote human happiness, could not, in the nature of things, be of any force or authority;—and it would be not only a right but a duty to abolish it." In another interpretation of the adultery metaphor, Stanton echoed the concerns of spiritualists and free-love advocates with the children of such loveless marriages: "Children born in these unhappy and unhallowed connections, are, in the most solemn sense, of unlawful birth."[35] In her view, then, love and happiness legitimated reproduction as well as intercourse. Stanton's radical speech provoked opposition from the floor as well as hostility from newspapers. Though her resolutions were not erased from the convention proceedings, as some feminists wanted, the subsequent discussion exposed a divide between the small number of women's rights activists willing to question the current state of marriage, including Stanton and Mary Fenn Davis, and the majority who considered the topic untouchable.

Shortly after the women's rights convention met in New York City, the *New York Tribune* announced the "demise" of the Unitary Home. According to Edward F. Underhill, the experiment was in the "full tide of its success," but his career had overtaken his responsibilities to the cooperative.[36] The Unitary Home had provided a space for marriage critics to test their theories about love and sex, and created a free-love crisis in the women's rights movement. Free lovers challenged feminists to address women's moral autonomy, or the ability to decide when and with whom to have sex.

Although they publicly disagreed over what to do about marriage, free lovers, spiritualists, and feminists alike criticized the legal bond that compelled a woman to have sex. They all compared monogamous, legal marriage to prostitution, prison, slavery, and adultery. Each metaphor offered a different critique of the institution. Feminists preferred "legalized prostitution," which highlighted the contractual exchange of sex for economic support. The adultery metaphor, by contrast, offered a moral and emotional critique of marriage by suggesting that loveless marital sex itself was an immoral act, and a violation of individual conscience. As Stanton's speech shows, free love ideas infiltrated and shaped feminists' arguments, even as feminists worked to distinguish their own views as reformist rather than revolutionary.

*   *   *

For most marriages activists, the Civil War was a disruption rather than a transformative moment. For example, in 1861, Warren Chase, a spiritualist and former resident of the Wisconsin Phalanx at Ceresco, published a treatise entitled *The Fugitive Wife*. With the national debate over slavery erupting into war, Chase's title evoked the political and violent conflict fueled by the 1850 Fugitive Slave Law, which facilitated slaveholders' pursuit and capture of escaped slaves in the north. But Chase had little interest in the fate of enslaved women. With most northerners agreeing that the Fugitive Slave Law was "cruel" and "unjust," Chase asserted the greater cruelty of "fugitive-wife laws," which forced (white) women back into the sexual slavery of their marriage beds. While acknowledging the harmony of some relationships, Chase argued that three-quarters of "legal" marriages were unhappy, with more wives committing suicide than slaves. To save the institution of marriage, Chase proposed that "we must protect the wife, as we do the unmarried woman, against the passions of man, and give the husband no more control over the person, body or soul, of the woman, after marriage than before."[37]

Chase relied on the familiar comparison of marriage to slavery to condemn the "ownership of persons" within the institution. He advocated the liberation of women and men from their legal and ecclesiastical bonds. Only "love," this free lover argued, should unite couples. Chase also employed the metaphor of adultery to criticize the institution, writing, "adultery is a crime against nature, not against the statute." In his view, any sexual relationship based on love was by definition virtuous: "Lust commits adultery;—love never can."[38] But these metaphors neither resonated nor agitated as they had before because Americans at this time, unlike Chase, had the literal enslavement of African Americans as their urgent priority.

Chase's views of marriage came in part from experience. In his auto-biography, *The Life-line of the Lone One* (1857), which he wrote in the third person, identifying himself only as the "Lone One," Chase bemoaned Americans' lack of education in diet, physiology, and "moral and mental science," all essential to individual health and happiness. After reading Thomas Nichols's *Esoteric Anthropology* and Andrew Jackson Davis's *Great Harmonia*, he described a "new fountain of feeling . . . higher, holier, purer, and more devoted, than he had ever felt or knew before." This feeling restrained his "animal and passional impulses" in favor of the "purely spiri-tual and affectional." But his wife, Mary, with whom he had three children, was not "congenial."[39] Describing himself as a "ladies' man" and the "ladies' advocate," Chase got along well with other female reformers due to his support for women's rights. Though he characterized his relationships with these women as "chaste" and "delicate," his opponents circulated rumors about his unfaithfulness to his wife. She also judged her husband for spend-ing time with these other women. It was only after she had a similar spiri-tual awakening, and became a medium, that their relationship moved beyond the "scorn-storm of jealousy, prejudice, and envy" to the "plane of mutual love, mutual confidence, mutual purity, and mutual interest."[40]

Marriage reformers such as Chase had mixed responses to the Civil War. Some participated directly or indirectly. Chase spent the war touring as a spiritualist lecturer, but his son served as a surgeon in the Sixth Michi-gan Volunteer Infantry.[41] Stephen Pearl Andrews's protégé Edward F. Underhill worked as a war correspondent for the *New York Times*. He was captured by the Confederate general Stonewall Jackson, tried as a spy, and held as a prisoner of war.[42] Paschal Beverly Randolph, who had ended his marriage to his co-author, Mary Jane Randolph, recruited African Ameri-can troops for the Union army, and by 1864 he was aiding in reconstruction efforts in Louisiana and teaching in freedmen's schools. In Louisiana, he was briefly married to a mixed-race woman named Martha McMaster. Ran-dolph also joined the Republican Party.[43]

The women's rights movement suspended its conventions for the dura-tion of the conflict, and feminists formed the Women's National Loyal League to petition for emancipation.[44] After helping organize the Loyal League, Eliza Farnham nursed the wounded at Gettysburg, and wrote two books before her untimely death in 1864. The first explained her ideas of women's moral superiority, and the second applied them to a fictional love story between a virtuous woman and a "true" man. The novel's title, *The Ideal Attained*, referred to their achievement of the "perfect" marriage.[45]

Other activists viewed the war as a distraction from the fundamental clash between monogamous marriage and individual freedom. In 1861, the same year Chase published *The Fugitive Wife*, for example, Thomas and Mary Gove Nichols, unsympathetic to the Union effort, left for England.[46]

The Civil War did not end the debate over marriage, free love, or the meaning of adultery, but it temporarily scattered activists across the country and the globe.[47] After the war, national scandals capped decades of marriage debate. Not only would marriage radicals redefine adultery but they would turn the act of adultery into a form of civil disobedience to protest the deeper problems of marital hypocrisy and false morality.

CHAPTER 9

Adultery as Social Protest

In 1872, Victoria Woodhull's public accusation that the Reverend Henry Ward Beecher had committed adultery with his parishioner Elizabeth Tilton launched the biggest American sexual scandal of the nineteenth century. Beecher was an abolitionist, suffragist, and the married pastor of the popular Plymouth Church in Brooklyn. Elizabeth was the wife of his best friend and fellow reformer, the newspaper editor Theodore Tilton. After cooperating with Beecher to deny the charges, Tilton eventually sued him for criminal conversation in 1875. Historians have written many books about Woodhull and the Beecher-Tilton scandal, focusing on Woodhull's political agenda, her genius for publicity, or her anger at the famous Beecher family. This particular accusation of adultery, and its origin and aftermath—the focus of the next two chapters—was a key moment in a larger postwar campaign by free lovers against legal, monogamous marriage.[1]

Before the Civil War, both free lovers and moderate reformers had used adultery as a metaphor for loveless marriages and unwanted sexual relations. In the postwar period, marriage reformers became more aggressive. They politicized actual cases of marriage, divorce, and adultery to unmask the hypocrisies, lies, and pain caused by the legal bond, and to further their free-love cause, which they rebranded with the more expansive term *social freedom*. A few activists even used their own unconventional marriages as examples, turning the act of adultery into a form of civil disobedience by flouting laws that proscribed adultery. In this radical redefinition, the act of adultery became virtuous, and legal marriage became the site of hypocrisy and immorality.

* * *

After the Civil War, the writings of Marie Howland, among others, contributed to a renewed debate over the legal institution of marriage. Marie Case and Edward Howland had spent much of the Civil War in Europe. The couple detested slavery, but they viewed the war as barbaric. And, despite their socialist beliefs in the brotherhood of man, fighting racism was not their priority. Since Marie's divorce from her husband Lyman Case was not yet final, she and Edward also traveled abroad for greater social freedom as a couple. In Guise, France, they stayed in a new utopian community founded by businessman Jean-Baptiste André Godin. Disgusted with the living conditions of workers, and inspired by Charles Fourier, Godin created a cooperative society at his ironworks, replacing the phalanx with the Familistere, also known as the Social Palace. On their return to the United States, Marie and Edward Howland became the chief proponents of Godin's social theories.[2]

Marie Howland's reputation as a socialist and marriage reformer grew after their return. During Reconstruction, Marie published a novel that ended with the establishment of a Social Palace in a New England town. She translated Godin's *Social Solutions* for American audiences. As a radical, Marie Howland advocated women's sexual autonomy. Drawing on Fourier and Godin, she criticized both marriage and moralism, shaping the direction of postwar marriage critiques.

The Howlands were an unconventional couple. They had embraced sexual equality and bohemianism in the Unitary Home and Pfaff's Cellar, and they continued to do so after they married and settled in rural Hammonton, New Jersey. After New York courts granted Marie's divorce on the grounds of adultery in July 1865, she had married Edward on a trip to Scotland. True to their free-love beliefs, however, Marie maintained her friendship with Lyman Case for the rest of his life.[3] Though Marie denied being a bohemian—she thought of herself as "a simple, plain hard-working woman"—evidence suggests otherwise. She continued to dress as she had in the Unitary Home, in simple, unrestrictive, soft cotton gowns, "loose white or cream-colored mull with ribbons."[4] Marie's religious beliefs were similarly ethereal, and she identified primarily with spiritualists and later theosophists. She and Edward smoked cigars and cigarettes, and welcomed visitors from New York City, including Edward F. Underhill and Ada Clare, to their home near the New Jersey shore. After the 1874 death of Ada Clare, they buried her on their property.[5] Marie and Edward also became leaders in their local Grange, a social, intellectual and political hub for farmers founded in 1867, which functioned much as the League's Grand Order of Recreation had intended for New York City workers before garnering the scandalous nickname Free Love Club. Within their supportive, loving partnership, Edward tolerated and may have even approved Marie's close relationships with other women and men, including Ada Clare, Albert K. Owen, founder of the cooperative Topolobampo colony in Mexico, and Christian Hoffman, one of Owen's rich investors. When she and Edward eventually moved to Topolobampo, she scandalized some of their fellow colonists by swimming naked.[6]

Marie and Edward Howland promoted Godin's theories to Americans struggling with a turbulent postwar economy. During Reconstruction, the emancipation of slaves, the growing power of corporations and monopolies, especially the railroads, and the organization of farmers and workers into groups like the Grange and the Knights of Labor, augured a growing economic conflict. In 1872, the year before a global financial panic, Edward published an article reviewing the French edition of Godin's *Solutions Sociales* titled "The Social Palace at Guise." Edward wrote that Godin, and France more broadly, had inaugurated a "social system based upon liberty and human love." Like more moderate marriage reformers, the Howlands prioritized happiness, and they believed that the "love and sympathetic interest of members for each other" distinguished the Familistere.[7] As a manufacturer of cast-iron stoves, Godin had quickly recognized that neither higher wages nor shorter hours transformed the lives of his employees and their families. As Edward wrote approvingly, Godin believed that refinement and culture came from "social sympathy and friendly association."[8] Like the Unitary Home, the Familistere replaced the isolated household with opportunities for "social intercourse" in a setting that featured comfortable rooms and ample, nutritious meals. Godin went further by creating a "palace" that had the potential to house 1,500 people, with community spaces and private sleeping apartments as well as a nursery, school, theater, shops, and baths. Godin's goal was to enable workers to realize both their material and moral aspirations: "It is precisely because it affords him [the worker] the right conditions for the full development of his *physical* life, that it opens to the world a new horizon for our *moral* life."[9]

Edward constructed his portrait of the Familistere to be inoffensive. The focus of his article was its benefit for workingmen and their children. Throughout the article, the family, with a father at its head, remains intact, and the domestic circle is protected within the larger palace. Women might

Figure 11. Interior view of the grand communal Familistere
from Edward Howland, "The Social Palace at Guise,"
Harper's New Monthly Magazine, 44 (April 1872).

chose to care for their children but, as the article makes clear, the children
raised by the community grew up well-educated, well-behaved, and generous with their peers. The article's only indication that the Familistere
offered a more radical experiment was its system of governance. The community elected two councils, one composed of twelve men, and one composed of twelve women. Though the two councils sometimes worked
together, Edward Howland emphasized that the female council's responsibilities included "the domestic functions, the quality of the supplies, the
general neatness and healthfulness, the care taken with the children."[10]

Marie Howland's novel, *Papa's Own Girl*, published in 1874, portrayed
the Familistere as a potential site for women's liberation. Howland's novel
focuses on the intertwined lives of two women: Clara Forest, the daughter
of Dr. Forest, a radical New England town doctor, is the title character, and
Susie Dykes, her friend and future business partner, works in the Forest
household and falls in love with Clara's brother, Dan. Unlike his sister,
however, Dan does not inherit his father's ideals, and he seduces and
impregnates Susie. Both the doctor and Clara become Susie's champions
when she refuses to marry Dan. As Dr. Forest consoles Susie, "It is not you,

but conventional society that makes it wrong to have a child by one you love, and right by one you loathe, if you happen to be married to him."[11] Susie almost changes her mind in order to regain respectability and give her daughter legitimacy. When she declines Dan again, she voices the view of marriage reformers that marriage without love was a form of adultery: "I felt ashamed to marry Dan. It seemed to me so unholy a thing, when he does not love me."[12] Susie raises her child with the help of a lonely older woman, one of the doctor's friends.

Throughout the novel, Howland criticizes conventional models of marriage. Unlike her husband, Mrs. Forest is overly concerned with respectability and status. She blames Susie for Dan's actions, and worries about what the better families in town will think. As a result, she is overjoyed when Clara falls in love with Albert Delano, a wealthy, handsome Bostonian and an "excellent match." Dr. Forest horrifies his wife when he describes his daughter in her wedding gown as like a "victim tricked out for sacrifice."[13] After a short honeymoon period, their marriage falls apart when Albert neglects Clara to spend time with another, needier woman. In a chapter titled "The Sanctity of Marriage," Clara leaves Albert, giving him a cause (desertion) to legally divorce her. But, as she writes to him, "You have been really divorced from me since the time when you took another to your heart." With her friend Susie, Clara defines marriage as something greater than a legal bond. She tells her scandalized mother that "fidelity that came from love, would be a compliment to me; but ought I to be flattered by a chastity that was merely forced by a promise?" Here, Clara expands the adultery metaphor, arguing that not only was loveless marital sex a form of adultery but faithfulness to that legal bond had no significance. Postwar free lovers expanded upon this point, arguing that a violation of a false marriage could be redemptive. After all, as Clara concludes, "There is no marriage when love is dead."[14] With Dr. Forest's wholehearted approval, she moves in with Susie and her daughter, and this future divorcée helps the unwed mother run her thriving flower nursery.

In addition to delineating the virtues of two social outcasts, Howland's plot rewards Clara and Susie for their violations of sexual mores. Albert Delano eventually files for divorce, and he gloats to Clara that "I shall be free to marry, 'as though the defendant [Clara] were actually dead,'" but the law would not allow her to remarry while he lived. Even Albert's sister Charlotte struggles with the wisdom of the law, wondering "How can you remain bound to him, when he marries another wife. It is not common sense."[15] When Dr. Forest introduces Clara to the noble, high-minded Count von Frauenstein, a wealthy European who plans to emulate Godin by building a Social Palace in their town, she hides her love to protect him from the legal ban on her remarriage. Von Frauenstein does not press his attentions on Clara, but waits until she gives him a signal. As both the doctor and count believe, "it was woman's prerogative to call, the lover's to answer." When he learns of the divorce law, von Frauenstein dismisses the obstacle, noting that the penalty is a mere fine, and the law rarely enforced. In contrast to her earlier wedding, Dr. Forest endorses Clara's decision to marry the count, telling the couple "let us have a gloriously radical marriage ceremony, after our wicked latitudinarian hearts."[16] At the end of the novel, Clara von Frauenstein gives birth to their child in a private room in the Social Palace, which has as one of its principal industries her and Susie's flower business.

Though *Papa's Own Girl* was controversial, and even banned by the Boston Public Library, Howland's novel ended with marriage. This decision may have been a nod to the social conventions that she attacked in the book. But Howland, a divorcée like her character Clara Forest, had also married a broad-minded, loving partner in Edward Howland. She later described Edward as "a real husband—friend, comrade, mentor, brother, lover."[17] For Marie Howland, the problem was not a marriage based on love, but the false morality that forced couples to marry (in Susie's case) or stay married (in Clara's first marriage) without it. Despite her lived radicalism, Howland still believed in love. As she wrote in the novel, "To Clara, love was her religion—the one necessity of her higher life."[18] Howland wrote *Papa's Own Girl* as a political novel, advocating the reform of marriage and divorce laws, and prioritizing women's right to choose and consent to love.

More provocatively, Howland invoked Fourier's theories of attraction to justify women's autonomy. In *Papa's Own Girl*, residents of the Social Palace hung the flags of France and the United States, as well as a banner declaring, "*Attractions are proportional to destinies.*"[19] In 1886, when Howland published her English translation of Godin's *Social Solutions*, she hailed it as offering a "peaceable solution" to the "contest between labor and capital." Marie agreed with Godin that capitalists, who had gotten rich from the labor of others, must use their wealth to create institutions for the "Support, Progress, and Harmony of Human Life." As she knew, however, Godin's ideas extended beyond the relations between labor and capital. In

Social Solutions, Godin echoed Fourier, and the philosophy underpinning the Unitary Home, declaring that "Whatever conduces to our Happiness is *good*" and "Whatever conduces to our unhappiness is *evil*."[20] He viewed law and society as suppressing individual happiness. Among the "natural affections" that should be liberated, he included "love of sex," "procreation," and "paternity and maternity." In place of the law of man, he advocated "the law of nature" and the "free expression of the attractions of the heart." To address any potential consequences of this free expression, he stated that "All children are legitimate."[21] Similarly, in *Papa's Own Girl*, Howland acknowledged society's prejudices by having Count von Frauenstein legally adopt Susie's daughter, thus alleviating the mother's fears about her child's treatment.

By publishing her novel and translation, Marie Howland hoped to stimulate the implementation of Godin's theories in the United States. The Grange encouraged members to read her books. Albert K. Owen, a would-be western railroad magnate, made a pilgrimage to meet Howland after reading *Papa's Own Girl*. She advised him on his proposed communitarian settlement in Sinaloa, which she called a "Mexican Familistere," including a recommendation against a mixed-race commune. She and Edward also edited its newspaper, the *Credit Foncier of Sinaloa*, eventually moving to Topolobampo in 1888. Ultimately, Marie was disappointed. With no wealthy backer like Godin, the settlement struggled. She also disliked many of her fellow colonists, most of whom were half-hearted socialists, outraged by her penchant for skinny-dipping and her romance with Christian Hoffman. In 1892, after a long illness, Edward died at Topolobampo, a terrible loss for Marie.[22] After leaving the colony in 1893, she traveled around the country, finally settling in the progressive, single-tax community in Fairhope, Alabama, where she died in 1921.[23] Though Marie did not achieve her dream of Godin's Familistere, she remained an unrepentant communitarian and free lover, viewing women's sexual freedom as an essential precondition and result of socialism.

Throughout her career, Howland had rejected Americans' concern for women's sexual reputation. She viewed legal marriage as creating a false system of morals and rules that crushed women's autonomy. Within her fictional socialist Familistere, she presented her own partnership with Edward Howland as a model for loving, open, equal relationships.

After the Civil War, Marie Howland's *Papa's Own Girl* became one entry in a larger campaign by spiritualists, feminists, communitarians and

Figure 12. Marie Howland, with Edward Howland (in wheelchair), and an unknown man in Topolobampo, Mexico. Topolobampo Collection, Special Collections Research Center, Henry Madden Library, California State University-Fresno.

other reformers to expose the moral sham of the American marriage system. As the nation emerged from the violence of war and emancipation, activists reformulated their message for new audiences of political radicals, including workers, suffragists, and freed people. Few Americans, these critics observed, practiced chastity and self-control before or after marriage. They vowed to bring these adulteries into the open.

*   *   *

In 1869, a man named Daniel McFarland shot his ex-wife's fiancé. Living in New York City, Daniel and his wife, Abby Sage, an actress and writer, had associated with reformers and journalists attached to the *New York Tribune*. In 1867, Abby left her husband, claiming that Daniel was drunk and abusive. He accused her of an affair with the journalist Albert Richardson. Abby moved to Indiana to meet the state's one-year residency requirement, which had been increased several years earlier, securing her divorce in October 1869. The next month, Albert Richardson announced that he and Abby would marry. A furious Daniel McFarland responded by pulling a gun on Richardson in his *Tribune* offices. With Richardson on his deathbed, Henry Ward Beecher married Albert and Abby.

McFarland's public and legal defense rested on the "unwritten law" of adultery that entitled a husband to shoot his wife's lover. As Elizabeth Cady Stanton complained about the press coverage of the case, "One would really suppose that a man owned his wife as the master the slave, and that this was simply an affair between Richardson and McFarland, fighting like two dogs over one bone." As either a slave or a bone, the wife was mere property, without a will of her own. In contrast, Stanton presented the woman's view, that she "has a right to choose between a base, petty tyrant and a noble, magnanimous man."[24]

The McFarland-Richardson case added fire to the national debate over marriage and divorce, and exacerbated a recent schism among women's rights activists. In 1866, feminists formed the ill-fated American Equal Rights Association to advocate for universal suffrage rights. After an internal struggle over whether or not to support the Fifteenth Amendment, which did not enfranchise white or black women, activists formed two competing organizations: the National Woman Suffrage Association, founded by Stanton and Susan B. Anthony, and the American Woman Suffrage Association, founded by Lucy Stone and her husband, Henry

Blackwell. Though the organizations disagreed over strategy and personality, they also had profoundly different positions on the marriage question. As her comments on the McFarland-Richardson case made clear, Stanton continued her push for divorce reform, which had caused such consternation in 1860. In contrast, Stone, a marriage skeptic in the 1850s, now became the institution's vigilant defender, viewing scandal as dangerous to her cause. She also had personal reasons for her staunch moralism, since she believed her marriage to Henry Blackwell was threatened by his intimate friendship with "Mrs. P," probably their neighbor Abby Patton. After black men's voting rights, their contrasting attitudes toward marriage became the defining difference between the NWSA and the AWSA.[25]

Elizabeth Cady Stanton taunted her respectable rivals by suggesting that Stone and the American Woman Suffrage Association "call an indignation meeting and pass resolutions of censure" on Henry Ward Beecher, the president of the AWSA, for violating the "old order" by presiding over the wedding of a divorced woman.[26] Though her suggestion was sarcastic, Stanton was not the only one to point out the moral and legal inconsistences of Beecher's participation in the Richardson wedding. Some commentators viewed Abby's marriage to Albert Richardson as bigamous. Even though she had divorced, they viewed remarriage as immoral, and in some jurisdictions like New York, it was also illegal. In the view of these marriage advocates, she should not have remarried until after Daniel McFarland's death. Further, her claim of Daniel's drunken cruelty might have been grounds for divorce in Indiana, but it did not meet religious or New York State requirements for divorce.

Many New Yorkers questioned the validity of such divorces. Samuel Love, Mary Fenn Davis's first husband, had viewed his wife's Indiana divorce as invalid, and sued again in New York State. Catharine Beecher, Henry's sister as well as a national expert on homemaking, argued that religion and New York State law allowed "only one crime" to justify divorce: adultery. If Abby had divorced Daniel for adultery, Catharine argued, she was "morally free to marry again," but she had not. She believed that Abby's remarriage defied "the authority of the Lord Jesus Christ" and the *"law of marriage."* She did not mention her brother's role.[27]

Daniel McFarland's subsequent acquittal further outraged marriage reformers, narrowing the divide between moderates and radicals. Stanton proposed an "entire revision of the laws of New York on marriage and divorce" to an audience of furious women at New York City's Apollo Hall on May 17, 1870. At the beginning of her speech, she made sure to defend herself from the inevitable charges of free love, noting that she had been married to her husband for thirty years. Stanton also clarified that she had no personal stake in the case, and had never met Daniel McFarland or Abby Richardson. In what may have been an allusion to Warren Chase's pamphlet *The Fugitive Wife*, Stanton used the term to describe the plight of Abby Richardson. In relying on the unwritten law, the verdict had discounted her divorce and remarriage, and declared Abby "still the wife of the criminal whom for years she had loathed."[28]

Echoing her 1860 speech, Stanton asserted a marital standard of mutual happiness. "Divorce at the will of the parties is not only right," she argued, "it is a sin against nature, the family, and the State for a man or woman to live together in the marriage relation in continual antagonism, indifference, disgust." She assured her audience that "many pure minded, able men and women" agreed with her that, "a physical union should in all cases be the outgrowth of spiritual and intellectual sympathy." Some of her speech echoed the views of spiritualists like Mary Fenn Davis, as she referred to woman as "the mother of the race" who had been degraded by the "lust and selfishness of men." Yet Stanton almost invited accusations of free love when she compared Abby's first marriage to prostitution and adultery, and asserted that only love legitimized sexual relationships between men and women.[29] Feminists were quick to differentiate themselves from free lovers and other radicals, but at this moment and others, their criticisms converged.

In the wake of the McFarland-Richardson case, Theodore Tilton, the handsome, feminist, thirty-five-year-old editor of the *Independent*, joined in Stanton's call for more liberal divorce laws. A former member of the American Equal Rights Association, Tilton had tried, and failed, to reunite the opposing factions of the women's suffrage movement. In 1870, an article about his views on marriage and divorce had ended his career at the *Independent*, a liberal Christian newspaper, and estranged him from longtime friend Henry Ward Beecher, who had been a regular contributor. Like both moderate and radical marriage reformers, Tilton defined marriage by love alone; anything else was a "sin against God." "When love departs," he continued, "then marriage ceases, and divorce begins." He viewed the public commitment to lifelong, loveless marriages as a "sham morality" and a violation of any "just moral sense."[30]

These ideas firmly aligned Tilton with Stanton and the National Woman Suffrage Association, but they also revitalized an old friendship with the free lover Stephen Pearl Andrews, who had articulated similar views in the *New York Tribune* almost two decades earlier. Tilton had known Andrews since he was a thirteen-year-old aspiring phonographer.[31]

Since his disruptive appearance at the 1858 women's rights convention, Andrews had maintained his position as the nation's leading free lover. In the intervening years, he had expanded his radical social theories to include a universal language called Alwato; a new theory of everything, or "universology;" and a proposal for a worldwide system of government, under the leadership of the Pantarch (Andrews). He saw the McFarland-Richardson case as his own Bull Run, a temporary defeat from which victory, a "new civilization" based on individual sovereignty, emerged. In some ways, he was right to take the case personally, as McFarland's defense lawyers had blamed "fourierites" and "free-lovers" for Abby's divorce.[32]

Andrews also continued to torment the women's movement. Uninvited and unwelcome, he attended their conventions. At every opportunity, Andrews linked free love and women's rights, even publicly contradicting his friend Tilton's efforts to separate the two. Just as the abolition of slavery had caused a political and social revolution, Andrews argued that "Female Suffrage means, therefore, Radical Social Revolution, Constructive Socialism, and New Social Order, upon the basis of the dissolution of legal or force marriage." He also claimed, with some cause, that suffragists in the NWSA agreed with him, and had transformed their demand for suffrage into a call for the "complete social enfranchisement of the sexes." Andrews defined "social" enfranchisement as sexual equality and freedom.[33]

*　　*　　*

In May 1871, Andrews introduced Theodore Tilton to the suffrage movement's newest star, Victoria Woodhull. In early 1870, Woodhull, a little-known spiritualist medium, had caused a sensation when she and her sister Tennie Claflin opened a Wall Street brokerage with the financial support of Cornelius Vanderbilt. Andrews met her soon after the firm opened, and began writing for the sisters' radical newspaper *Woodhull and Claflin's Weekly*, also backed by Vanderbilt, which eventually reached 20,000 subscribers. By December, Woodhull had submitted a memorial to Congress arguing that women, as citizens of the United States, had won the right to vote under the Fourteenth and Fifteenth Amendments. Since the constitution did not explicitly exclude women from voting, she argued, they already had that right. Members of the National Woman Suffrage Association, impressed with her testimony before the House Judiciary Committee, transformed her argument into their "New Departure" strategy, and Woodhull and other activists registered to vote across the country.

The same month that he introduced Tilton to Woodhull, Andrews moved into her complicated household, which included her first husband, Dr. Canning Woodhull, whom she had married at the age of fifteen, her new husband, Colonel James Blood, and various members of her extended family. Andrews's second wife, Esther, had recently died, and the bustle of Woodhull's home, where he and Esther had stayed for several months the previous year, may have assuaged his grief. Andrews gloried in the vibrant intellectual community at 15 East Thirty-Eighth Street, whose visitors included socialists Albert Brisbane and Josiah Warren, and suffragists Elizabeth Cady Stanton, Susan B. Anthony, and Isabella Beecher Hooker (another of Henry's sisters), among many others. He later compared Woodhull's house to the revolutionary Parisian salon of Madame Marie-Jeanne Roland.[34]

While Andrews did not care about Woodhull's unusual marital history, some women's rights activists did. These putative allies viewed her friendship with Stephen Pearl Andrews as another reason to question her reputation. Prodded by her sister Catharine, Isabella Beecher Hooker launched an investigation of Woodhull's connections. Lyman Case, former resident of the Unitary Home and now a journalist, lawyer, and businessman living near Hooker in Hartford, Connecticut, apparently persuaded her that Andrews was a "hypocrite and a villain." The exact nature of Case's accusation is unclear, but it prompted Andrews's son William, a Union army veteran, to write in defense of his father's reputation as a husband. His father, William wrote, was "morally, intellectually, and physically the most perfect man and gentleman I have ever known." William Andrews also took the opportunity to attack Case for his behavior during his marriage to Marie Howland.[35]

To end the gossip, Susan B. Anthony invoked the sexual double standard and female inequality. As she wrote, "When we shall require of the *men*, who speak—vote, work for us—to *prove* that they have never been unduly familiar with any woman—never guilty of trifling with or desecrating womanhood—it will be time enough for us to demand of the *women* to *prove* that *no man has ever trifled with* or desecrated them." Echoing the arguments of moral reformers, Anthony's language made Woodhull, and all women, the potential victim of men's actions. Stanton went further. Enough women, in her view, had been "sacrificed to this sentimental, hypocritical, prating about purity." Rejecting the standard of respectability, Stanton argued that, "this is one of man's most effective engines, for our division & subjugation."[36]

Stanton's and Anthony's opponents in the American Woman Suffrage Association disagreed, and passed a resolution denouncing "recent attempts in this city [New York] and elsewhere to associate the Woman Suffrage cause with the doctrine of Free Love, and hold it responsible for the crimes and follies of individuals."[37] Though Victoria Woodhull's name was not mentioned, her reputation was the clear subtext. Once again, the issues of marriage, adultery, and free love deepened the divide created by the Fifteenth Amendment.

Responding to the rumors, Tilton wrote Woodhull's biography to establish the "whiteness of her life." In addition to defending her name, Woodhull wanted the biography to justify her campaign for the presidency in the 1872 election. Born in Homer, Ohio, in 1838—making her a bit young to be president—Woodhull grew up in "respectable poverty." Tilton's goal was to distinguish Woodhull from her abusive, dysfunctional family, but his description of her religious devotion, spending part of each day in the "spirit-realm," communing with the ancient Greek orator Demosthenes, who she said had written her suffrage memorial, probably hurt more than helped.[38]

The account of Victoria's marriage to Canning Woodhull, a drunken womanizer who spent their wedding night at a brothel, aimed to appeal to a broad swath of marriage reformers. Spiritualists and women's rights activists were primed to sympathize with her plight when they read that her son, the product of this wretched sexual union, was a "half idiot" and a "hopeless imbecile." After two children and eleven years of marriage, she divorced Woodhull. According to Tilton, Victoria's second marriage to Colonel Blood, a fellow spiritualist, communist, and internationalist, was a true marriage, and Blood was a "reverent husband to his spiritual wife." They welcomed her unfortunate, dissipated ex-husband into their home for "noble" humanitarian reasons. No woman, Tilton argued, was more "unsullied." He concluded by addressing Victoria Woodhull's views of marriage. Her position was no different from that of Elizabeth Cady Stanton or the British philosopher John Stuart Mill, he argued, with whom she believed that "marriage is of the heart and not of the law, that when love

ends, marriage should end with it." Many Americans, Tilton admitted, classified this definition with free love.[39]

*   *   *

Just two months after the biography's publication, Woodhull gave a speech
on the theme "And the Truth Shall Make You Free," destroying any hope
of reconciliation with her critics. She had invited Henry Ward Beecher to
introduce her, hoping to use his moral stature to prop up her own, but he
declined. Instead, on November 20, 1871, Tilton introduced her to a full
house of three thousand at Steinway Hall in New York City. Her friend and
mentor Stephen Pearl Andrews, who probably wrote most of the address
on the "Principles of Social Freedom," was in the audience.[40] Woodhull
began with a testament to Andrews's theory that the universe was composed of trinities, including the political trinity of freedom, justice, and
equality. She recounted the history of individual freedom, from the quest
for religious independence in the sixteenth century through the struggle for
political independence in the American and French Revolutions. Yet true
self-government, Woodhull continued, did not yet exist. In a reference to
the Seneca Falls Declaration of Sentiments, she described male domination
of women as a form of despotism worse than that of King George III. "If
self-government be the rule, every self must be its subject," she stated. Every
individual had an inherent, "inalienable," right of self-ownership, answer-
able only to herself and God. In this speech, as well as in the pages of her
newspaper, Woodhull had become the newest spokesperson for Andrews's
"individual sovereignty."[41]

Finally, Woodhull addressed the subject of her sexual reputation.
"What I believe to be the truth I endeavor to practice," she told the audience, "and, in advocating it, I shall *speak* so *plainly* that *none* may complain that I did not make myself understood." Woodhull condemned the
arbitrary laws and "sham respectability" of American society, which had
fostered the prostitution of "*scores of thousands of women*" and "*hundreds
of thousands of men.*" As she explained, she "denominated" men as prostitutes because the act that changes "a woman into a prostitute must also
necessarily change the man into the same," a critique of the sexual double
standard that moral reformers might have endorsed. But rather than
seeing marriage as the solution, she believed it was the problem. Woodhull viewed love as "superior" to all laws, and the only basis for sex or

Figure 13. Victoria Woodhull, feminist, free lover, and spokesperson
for Stephen Pearl Andrews's theory of individual sovereignty.
Billy Rose Theatre Division, The New York Public Library for the
Performing Arts; Astor, Lenox and Tilden Foundations.

marriage. She compared the current state of marriage to both legalized prostitution and legalized adultery, arguing that, "by this Higher Law . . . marriages of convenience, and, still more, marriages characterized by mutual or partial repugnance, are adulterous." Woodhull proclaimed a radical, individual "*right* to love," a right that she believed deserved government protection.[42]

Furthermore, Woodhull embraced the "epithet" of free lover. She told the scandalized audience, "I have an *inalienable, constitutional,* and *natural* right to love whom I may, to love as *long* or as *short* a period as I can; to *change* that love *every day* if I please, and with *that* right neither *you* nor any *law* you can frame have *any* right to interfere."[43]

Free love was not to blame for crime and licentiousness, she argued, but its antithesis: legal marriage. As an example, she used the McFarland-Richardson case: "McFarland murdered Richardson because he believed that the law had sold Abby Sage *soul* and *body* to him, and, consequently, that he *owned* her, and that no other person had *any* right to her favor, and that she had *no* right to bestow her love on any other person, unless *that ownership* was first satisfied." Freedom, Woodhull continued, was always better than slavery. She did not predict an amoral free love future because "the highest sexual unions" were "monogamic."[44] Rather, she envisioned a society in which women freely chose their sexual companions, unrestrained by law or public opinion, chose when and with whom to have children, and, as a result, created better families.

As Stephen Pearl Andrews probably intended, Woodhull's speech forced women's rights activists and other moderates to pick a side on the marriage question. Though she had not challenged feminists directly, Woodhull had invoked both suffrage factions in her speech. Much to their horror, she twice quoted the American Woman Suffrage Association's *Woman's Journal* in support of her arguments. Like Andrews, she also referred to the National's broad platform in support of women's "social" as well as political equality. The McFarland-Richardson case, which had inspired activists like Stanton and Tilton, who did not identify as free lovers, highlighted the similarities between their moderate arguments and those of Andrews and Woodhull. Any criticism of marriage underscored the truths of free love, Andrews and Woodhull believed, and women's rights could not be fully achieved without complete sexual freedom. Suffragists in the AWSA had never supported Woodhull. Over the next six months, members of the NWSA scorned her as well, refocusing their energies on the vote. Women's rights activists did their best to sideline the debate over marriage, and especially, free love.[45] Newer, more adamant and fierce defenders of marriage also emerged to condemn free lovers, contributing to the intensity of the Beecher-Tilton scandal, and culminating decades of debate over marriage.

CHAPTER 10

Adultery as Civil Disobedience

As Victoria Woodhull and her allies agitated the marriage question and challenged the institution's hallowed moral status, they confronted a growing number of voices defending the value and permanence of marriage. Since the Emancipation Proclamation of 1863, the Union army, abolitionists, missionaries, and the federal government had been encouraging legal marriage among former slaves, which confirmed the right to marry as a fundamental freedom. Many African Americans seized this opportunity to establish the permanence of their family relationships. Following the devastation of the war, northern and southern whites also reunited around the shared pleasures of the private domestic sphere. For proponents of marriage, any attack on the institution was a sign of moral decline and a threat to the future of the nation. Prominent voices emerged to attack free lovers, and call for stricter legal and religious supervision of marriage and divorce.[1]

Catharine and other members of the Beecher family were part of the chorus of marriage defenders. Isabella Beecher Hooker, who had investigated Victoria Woodhull, was an exception, remaining loyal to her fellow suffragists in the National Association. Though some marriage defenders attacked Woodhull and free lovers specifically, others expanded their critique to encompass broader American legal and religious practices. Divorce rates rose significantly in the postwar period—157 percent between 1867 and 1886, according to one government statistician. The feminist Elizabeth Cady Stanton, an advocate for more liberal divorce laws, pointed out the demand for divorce in the single state of Massachusetts, with an estimated 1,500 cases in one year.[2] Marriage defenders worried about the apparent demise of monogamous, lifelong unions, and blamed communitarians, spiritualists, women's rights activists, and free lovers.

The most prominent spokesperson for the pro-marriage forces was
Theodore Dwight Woolsey, president of Yale College, the alma mater of
the Seventh-Commandment sermonizer Timothy Dwight; Henry's father,
Lyman Beecher; and the defrocked John Humphrey Noyes. Woolsey
bemoaned the rising rates of divorce across the nation. He found inspira-
tion for his 1869 *Essay on Divorce and Divorce Legislation* in the "extremely
lax" divorce laws in his home state of Connecticut. Once a bastion of Puritan morality, the state had experienced a declension, in danger of "becoming a teacher and propagator of low views of the marriage relation." In
contrast, Woolsey praised New York State law, which limited divorces to
adultery, and prohibited "the defendant found guilty of adultery from marrying during the life-time of the innocent."[3]

In some ways, Woolsey's book resembled the New York State Senate's
1847 report on adultery, seduction, and abduction, though his goal was not
to pass new laws but to revoke current ones. In addition to surveying state
laws on divorce, he noted that most states criminalized adultery, with only
New York and South Carolina following England in viewing adultery as a
civil matter. Woolsey also detailed the various criminal penalties attending
adultery. He expressed some nostalgia for the colonial period, when Massachusetts had made it a capital crime, with lesser sentences such as whipping
and wearing the letter "A." Since then, Woolsey remarked, state govern-
ments had been "softening" their laws on adultery and expanding their
grounds for divorce.[4]

For Woolsey, religion was the solution. He observed that "the feeling of
the sanctity of marriage is passing away," with more Americans desiring "to
be free from the marriage bond on grounds of which were, of old, regarded
as insufficient" and politicians wanting to "gratify such a desire." In addition, divorcées moved freely in polite society, and no "moral indignation"
met the "adulterer or adulteress."[5] Woolsey viewed marriage as a "divine
institution" and the "starting point of the family and the state." As such,
marriage was "more than a contract," and "there are sacred obligations
which are violated by adultery and must be protected."[6] To avert a crisis,
Woolsey proposed that churches enforce their doctrines, with adultery
alone offering a cause for divorce. He advised ministers to refuse to marry
divorced individuals, and churches to censure members whose marriages
or divorces violated religious law. Woolsey also wanted churches to lobby
states to pass laws reinforcing these religious practices. Woolsey proposed
that these laws include a ban on adulterers marrying the person with whom

they committed the crime, a ban on the remarriage of the guilty party during the lifetime of the innocent spouse, and the criminalization of adultery, the sentence for which should immediately follow any divorce decree, without trial.[7]

Another writer, Dr. John B. Ellis, focused on the destructive effects of free lovers, whom he identified broadly as the "Oneida Communists, Individual Sovereigns . . . Spiritualists, Advocates of Woman Suffrage, or Friends of Free Divorce."[8] His *Free Love and Its Votaries*, published in 1870, relied heavily on British journalist William Hepworth Dixon's survey of polygamous practices among various European and American religious sects, *Spiritual Wives* (1868), which included excerpts from Oneida communist George Cragin's account of his courtship and tumultuous marriage to Mary Cragin. Where Dixon included some editorializing, Ellis added harsh criticisms, calling his book a catalog of "terrible facts," subjecting free lovers, women's rights activists and kindred groups to more vicious and sustained criticism than ever before. After giving Noyes's perspective on monogamous marriage as "selfish," "unholy," and fostering "secret adultery," for example, Ellis characterized complex marriage itself as adulterous and incestuous. He viewed Noyes and the male communists as acting on lust, so that both men and women wore the "signs of sexual excess . . . in their faces." While women had the right to say no to sex, he asserted, in practice they were forced to agree through the process of mutual criticism. Ellis bemoaned the plight of young people in the Oneida Community, sympathizing more with the young men, indoctrinated into complex marriage at the age of fourteen by "hideous and loathsome" older women, than with their female counterparts. He also invoked medical science to show the dangers of intercourse at such a young age. Ellis concluded that Noyes and his followers waged war on religion and purity, and he considered his book a weapon to be used against them.[9]

Dixon and Ellis found a common target in Andrew Jackson Davis and his spiritualist followers. In *Spiritual Wives*, Dixon accused Davis of being a "parody" of Swedenborg, the eighteenth-century Swedish visionary, and described Davis's readers as "ignorant dupes" of a man interested only in personal aggrandizement. Davis offered nothing new, he argued, but "the heat, the petulance, the ignorance, the irreverence of his books," especially the multivolume *Great Harmonia*. Dixon called the *Great Harmonia* "hostile to marriage," suggesting that it encouraged spiritualists to change partners in pursuit of love. He named Jackson Davis himself as a prime

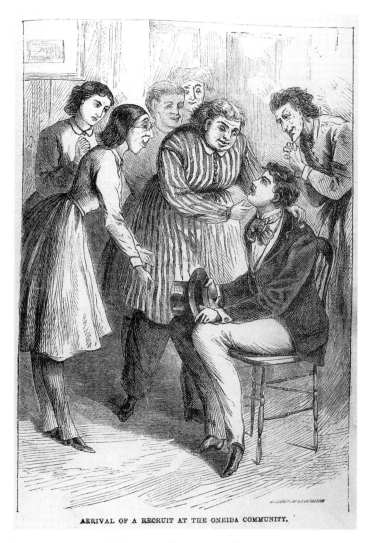

ARRIVAL OF A RECRUIT AT THE ONEIDA COMMUNITY.

Figure 14. Cartoon criticizing complex marriage, from John B. Ellis, *Free Love and Its Votaries*. Shows a handsome young man being scrutinized by older female free lovers. Courtesy of the Oneida Community Mansion House.

RECEPTION OF A FEMALE CONVERT AT THE ONEIDA COMMUNITY.

Figure 15. Cartoon criticizing complex marriage, from John
B. Ellis, *Free Love and Its Votaries*. Shows a beautiful young
woman surrounded by the eager men of the Oneida Community.
Courtesy of the Oneida Community Mansion House.

offender, repeating the rumor that Davis had seduced Mary Fenn Love away from her "surprised and outraged husband."[10] Ellis continued the attack, identifying Davis as a plagiarist and con man, who perverted the more respectable, Christian spiritualism of Swedenborg, and his American followers in the New Church. Even more than the Oneida Community or the Mormons, Ellis viewed free love's "alliance with Spiritualism" as its "most dangerous" manifestation.[11]

Ellis also warned his readers about secular free lovers. He devoted a chapter to Stephen Pearl Andrews's defunct Modern Times colony, which he called "the queerest company of men and women ever seen in America," and a "strange and abominable place." He accurately characterized Andrews as "opposed to the institution of Christian marriage," and described members living in "open adultery."[12] Like other defenders of marriage, Ellis revived the literal, familiar and legal meanings of adultery to combat the metaphoric and figurative ones. Undoubtedly inspired by Woolsey, Ellis also discussed divorce, and blamed free love for "stripping marriage of its religious character." Noting that most Americans ignored strictures against divorce and remarriage, he cited the wedding of Abby Sage and Albert Richardson, referring to Henry Ward Beecher as "by no means alone" in agreeing to officiate at such an event. Both free lovers and women's rights activists, Ellis believed, were complicit. He argued that "Free Love is gaining ground in society," and reminded women that their status had risen only with "Christian marriage." Even the strict laws of New York, he believed, "had little or no practical value" in defending the institution. Ellis saw New York City as the headquarters of "a villainous and powerful Divorce 'Ring,'" lawyers willing to procure divorces for their clients by any means, including manufacturing evidence of infidelity.[13]

Ellis's book was a delicate, perhaps deliberate balance of moralizing and titillating. His mysterious identity clouds insight into his motivations. The 1870 census lists a twenty-nine-year-old medical doctor named John B. Ellis in Oneida County, New York, making him a close, and possibly aggrieved, neighbor of the community. The same John B. Ellis who wrote Free Love and Its Votaries, however, also wrote an insider's guide to Washington, D.C., and claimed to be a longtime resident. Further, John Humphrey Noyes believed "John B. Ellis" to be a pseudonym manufactured by the publishing company, which had hired an established writer to plagiarize Dixon. A New York City homeopathic physician, author, inventor and Swedenborgian named John B. Ellis is another possible, though less likely, candidate.[14]

Whoever he was, the author of *Free Love and Its Votaries* worried about being prosecuted for obscene libel. This was an offense under English common law that had been enforced in the antebellum period unevenly and without clear definition. Then, in 1865, the federal government passed laws making it more difficult to send obscene materials through the U.S. mail. After the Civil War, more states began to criminalize obscenity, including New York State in 1868. Though Dixon had successfully battled accusations of obscenity in England, Ellis took pains to avoid arrest. Rather than using the mail, he printed an abbreviated prospectus for potential buyers, which included engraved caricatures of Oneida Community members and their practices, and advertised for agents to sell his book.[15]

Given her acquaintance with Tilton, Stanton, Anthony, and thus Woodhull, Harriet Beecher Stowe, sister of Henry and Catharine and author of *Uncle Tom's Cabin*, had personal, political, and religious motives for defending marriage. In her novel *My Wife and I* (1871), Stowe broke with convention and constructed her plot around a man's search for a wife, highlighting the importance of the decision for men as well as women. The main character, Harry Henderson, the son of a New England minister who moves to Manhattan to become a journalist, views marriage as "sacred as religion, indissoluble as the soul, endless as eternity." For Stowe, men like Harry must be worthy of their wives, "manly and true, and above all pure in thought and imagination and in word."[16] His choices, which unfold over the course of the novel, include his childhood sweetheart, Susie; his cousin Caroline; the beautiful gold-digger Miss Ellery; and Eva Van Arsdel, a wealthy socialite, who also happens to be lovely, educated, and devout. Eva knows that marriage is a serious decision, not to taken "lightly or unadvisedly," and she also believes in marrying for love.[17] As she had with *Uncle Tom's Cabin*, Stowe wrote *My Wife and I* as a protest novel, but with an opposing agenda to Howland's *Papa's Own Girl*. Stowe wanted to save marriage by demonstrating its transcendent moral value.

Though she believed the institution of marriage to be a sacred calling for most men and women, Stowe endorsed a limited definition of women's independence. She advocated for female education and, in some cases, she encouraged women to pursue careers. With her unmarried sister Catharine, Stowe defended women's right not to marry, as long as they devoted themselves to charitable or productive work. Two characters in the novel, cousin Caroline and Eva's older sister, Ida, decide to remain single in order to become medical doctors. Addressing criticism of marriage, Caroline reflects that "the rare, real marriage, that occurs one time in a hundred, is the true ideal state for man and woman, but it doesn't follow that all and everything that brings man and woman together in marriage is blessed."[18] Complaining of women's sheltered, indulged status, Ida Van Arsdel offers a more individualistic rationale: "*I* want to live while I live, and to keep myself in such trim that I can *do* something—and I won't pet myself or *be petted*." More so than Caroline, Ida has radical friends, and she brings Harry and Eva to a weekly salon hosted by Mrs. Stella Cerulean, a charming, brilliant, freethinking suffragist. Ida believes these conversations were essential to achieving women's rights, but Harry criticizes her friends for abandoning the common-sense virtues of the Bible. Confirming her demure femininity, Eva describes herself as too weak to pursue such a public life.[19]

Stowe's mild characterization of women's rights activists as misguided changed when she introduced Audacia Dangyereyes, a character based on Victoria Woodhull. This bold, jaunty, and curly-haired young woman enters Henderson's office uninvited, and, violating social convention, before they have been formally introduced. She proceeds to caress his arm and gaze into his eyes, and then informs Harry that he hasn't "the least idea" of the emancipation of women despite his public support of the cause. Repeating the "if I please" in Woodhull's speech on social freedom, Audacia states her right to behave like a man: "I claim my right to smoke, if I please, and to drink, if I please; and to come up into your room and make you a call, and have a good time with you, if I please."[20] Horrified at her willingness to adopt masculine behaviors, Henderson subscribes to her newspaper, *Emancipated Woman,* in order to get rid of her. Her paper, when he receives it, endorses the "wildest principles of French communism." Not unlike Andrews, Harry associates her with Madame Roland, but he refers to Roland at the guillotine, crying, "O Liberty, what things are done in thy name!"[21] When Audacia faces charges of blackmail and swindling, Ida becomes disillusioned with her friend Mrs. Cerulean, a lady of "family and position" as well as "dignity and delicacy," who continues to support the "persecuted" younger woman.[22] For Stowe, Mrs. Cerulean, possibly modeled on Elizabeth Cady Stanton, represents the National Woman Suffrage Association's dangerous alliance with Woodhull.

Harriet Beecher Stowe and other vocal defenders of marriage blamed easy divorce, non-conformist religious groups, free lovers, and, of course, women's rights for the current, threatened state of the institution. More than Woolsey or Ellis, however, Stowe condemned the women's movement for fostering activists like Woodhull and offering a respectable platform for their ideas. In her last appearance in the novel, Audacia is promoting her new book, "The Universal Empyreal Harmoniad, Being an Exposition of the Dual Triplicate Conglomeration of the Infinite," a clever mockery of Woodhull and her intellectual mentor Stephen Pearl Andrews.[23] The book ends with the happy marriage of Harry Henderson and Eva Van Arsdel. They wed in Eva's Episcopal church, and she willingly promises to obey him. Otherwise, Eva declares, "I shouldn't think myself really married."[24] Though her focused criticism of the women's movement differed from that of Woolsey and Ellis, Stowe also viewed established religion as the only sure protection against the threats of divorce and free love. More conservative than her brother Henry, Stowe nonetheless offered positive portrayals of a variety of American religions, from Jews, Catholics, and Quakers, to Congregationalists and Episcopalians, for sharing a devotion to marriage. She hoped for a similarly united religious front against the forces of free love.

*   *   *

The conflict between Woodhull and the Beecher family, orchestrated in part by Stephen Pearl Andrews, soon exploded. In October 1870, Andrews had written an article for *Woodhull and Claflin's Weekly* entitled, "Henry Ward Beecher Arraigned and Charged by Stephen Pearl Andrews With A Series of Falsehoods, Slander, Moral Cowardice, and Other Conduct Unbecoming a Minister." He vowed to hold the reverend to the "strict logic" of his "public and private deportment."[25] Two years later, he and Woodhull acted on his threat. Free lovers had long believed that legal marriage was another form of adultery and prostitution. It also provided respectable cover for illicit behavior. Once the public knew the truth about the "private deportment" of such eminent Americans, they believed, this flawed moral regime would collapse, and a new era of loving, mutual, and free relationships emerge.

A spiritualist named Moses Hull joined in the exposure campaign, becoming Victoria's ally in what both friends and enemies considered a "Wood-Hullian" vanguard of free-love spiritualists. As a young boy in Indiana, Hull had embraced the label of abolitionist, enduring bullying from his schoolmates. By the age of sixteen, he became a preacher, eventually dedicating his talents to Ellen Harmon White, the leader of the Seventh-Day Adventists. Ellen White pitted her followers, including Hull, against spiritualists, distinguishing her own visions from their trances. But Hull began to question White's doctrines and methods, and left the Adventists for spiritualism in 1865.[26] Three years later, he published his first tract on marriage, "That Terrible Question: A Few Thoughts on Love and Marriage." This former abolitionist had predicted that only war would bring an end to slavery, and he predicted another war over marriage. Hull saw signs of this growing rebellion in newspaper reports of adultery, prostitution, and licentiousness. He blamed these crimes on the "inharmonies" in most legal marriages. These bonds, Hull wrote, "often prove to be more galling than those which bind the slave to his master." The poor conditions of Civil War prisons provided an even better comparison than slavery: "When the key which should fasten two *souls* in wedlock only manacles human bodies, where the spirits are not united, the dark cell in which persons are held is so horrible that Libby Prison and Fort Anderson become palaces compared with it."[27] Like other spiritualists, he advocated "true marriage," a union of souls that transcended earthly relations. Rather than the law, Hull believed that love should guide human actions.[28]

True to his earlier promise in "That Terrible Question," Hull joined Woodhull's exposure campaign, and he was not alone. Hull's wife, Elvira, and his lover, Mattie, became outspoken advocates and practitioners of social freedom. The "Wood-Hullites" turned the pages of *Woodhull and Claflin's Weekly* into a vehicle to further redefine adultery, exposing the hidden wrongs of legal, respectable marriages. In many respects, their efforts were the result of decades of agitation, in which marriage reformers had used adultery as a term to characterize and condemn unhappy, loveless marriages as a violation of the self. Now, the act of adultery became a means of civil disobedience, a confrontation with the laws of marriage. They also defined the act of adultery as more honest and authentic than the public hypocrisy that surrounded the institution, which enabled Americans to say one thing and do another.

In the November 2, 1872, issue of *Woodhull and Claflin's Weekly*, Victoria began a "series of aggressive moral warfare" on the marriage question, with the goal of inciting a "social revolution." As a self-identified "agitator," Woodhull offered her own "Detailed Statement" of the "Beecher-Tilton Scandal Case," which she considered "one of the most stupendous scandals that has ever occurred in any community." The bulk of the article took the form of a Q and A with a reporter, an interview that she believed had been suppressed. Andrews helped her prepare the article for publication, adding his own ideological framework to the beginning and end of the interview. "The supercedure of marriage in the near future, by some kind of socialistic arrangement is as much a foregone conclusion with all the best thinkers of to-day," Andrews/Woodhull asserted, "as was the approaching dissolution of slavery no more than five or ten years before its actual dissolution." The majority of Americans, they believed, "act upon the new doctrines [of marriage] while they profess obedience to the old." They called this current system "organized hypocrisy." After she had challenged this false system, Woodhull condemned the subsequent attack by businessmen, clergymen, and social elites, all leading practitioners of moral duplicity. Their assault convinced her that she needed to use all the weapons at her disposal. Just as the abolitionist William Lloyd Garrison had denounced specific slave-holders, she too would name names. "Reputations had to suffer," she argued, "to create a new public opinion."[29]

Following Andrews's initial foray, Woodhull chose Henry Ward Beecher's reputation as her target. As she told the reporter, Woodhull believed that the married reverend was an "ultra-socialist reformer," and one who held "substantially the same views that I entertain on the social question." Further, he lived them. Nevertheless, she believed Beecher had succumbed to the opinion of the "religious and moralistic public" and refused to admit his true practices. In other words, he was "a hypocrite." Woodhull did not condemn him for his marital infidelity, then, but for his "unfaithfulness" to their shared belief in social freedom. The reporter asked, incredulously, "Do you mean to say that Mr. Beecher disapproves of the present marriage system?" Woodhull responded, "Mr. Beecher told me that marriage is the grave of love, and that he never married a couple that he did not feel condemned." She accused Beecher of moral cowardice for not admitting it publicly, as she had urged him to do when she invited him to introduce her at Steinway Hall.[30]

The swirling drama involved a number of women's rights activists as well as Beecher, his friend Tilton, and Tilton's wife, Elizabeth. Woodhull first learned of Beecher's extramarital affair from suffragist Paulina Wright Davis, whose friendship with Elizabeth Tilton prompted the confession of her "criminal relations" with Beecher while Theodore was on a lecture tour. Elizabeth Cady Stanton confirmed the facts, having learned of the affair from her friend and coworker Theodore Tilton. During his collaboration with Victoria, Theodore further revealed details of his wife's adultery. Though he was in anguish over his broken marriage and friendship,

Victoria apparently reassured him that "the fault and the wrong were neither in Mr. Beecher, nor in Mrs. Tilton, nor in himself; but in the false social institutions under which we still live." "True manliness," Victoria told him, glories "in protecting the absolute freedom of the woman who was loved." She encouraged Theodore to welcome Beecher back into his home, an action that also brought the doomed Beecher into conversation with Woodhull.[31]

While Woodhull condemned Beecher's hypocrisy, she praised his loving sexual relationship with Elizabeth Tilton. It was natural that his "great nature" led him to "the intimacy and embraces of the noble and cultured women about him." Woodhull called this "amative impulse" "one of the noblest and grandest of the endowments of this truly great and representative man." She described Mrs. Tilton as "tender, loving" and understandably susceptible to "the charms of the great preacher's magnetism." In contrast to society's condemnation of Elizabeth's adulterous relationship, her "love of loving and being loved," Woodhull argued, was "the best and most beautiful of things, the loveliest and most divine of things." She believed the only wrong was in trying to "prohibit," "prescribe and regulate" their right to love.[32]

Woodhull's article became the bombshell that she had intended, but she was one of its first casualties. Shortly after publication, Anthony Comstock, an anti-obscenity activist working with the Young Men's Christian Association, alerted the United States marshals, who arrested her for violating the federal law against sending obscene materials through the mail, which had been renewed in 1872. Comstock also pointed the marshals toward Stephen Pearl Andrews, but a sympathetic judge decided the sixty-year-old philosopher was too old for prison. Woodhull spent four weeks in Manhattan's Ludlow Street jail before she was exonerated.[33]

Comstock subsequently pursued a stronger and more expansive anti-obscenity law at the federal level. Passed in 1873 and nicknamed the Comstock law, the bill inaugurated a new era of prosecution of free lovers, birth control activists, and pornographers. State and federal obscenity laws tried to dictate what reformers wrote about love and sex. Free love radicals now faced greater consequences for their criticism of marriage. Moderate reformers, especially women's rights activists and spiritualists, found themselves tarred by association.

While Woodhull had lost the support of women's rights activists, she still had the endorsement of many spiritualists, who re-elected her president of the National Association of Spiritualists. For now, the subjects of Wood-hull's article, Beecher and Tilton, denied everything she had said.

The following summer, Moses Hull launched the next stage of the cam-paign in the pages of *Woodhull and Claflin's Weekly*. He expanded upon some of the key themes in Woodhull's "The Beecher-Tilton Scandal Case," i.e., that truth was essential to exposing hypocrisy and establishing freedom, and that individuals should understand their emotional, physiological incli-nations as right and natural, rather than wrong or sinful. Hull differed in that his article offered "A Personal Experience," as well as a testament to extramarital sex. He began by stating his view that the "entire confinement of one man to one woman," and vice versa, was "abominable." While admitting that promiscuity was not for everyone, Hull believed that "a change of sexual relations" offered physical and spiritual improvement for some people, just as fresh air or travel did for others. Hull also told readers than he practiced what he preached. Instead of destroying someone else's reputation, Hull jeopardized his own.[34]

Hull allowed readers a rare glimpse inside a marriage. For years, he was faithful to his marriage vows, and accepted the reformist principle of sexual self-control. In doing so, this man of "brain, heart and soul" wrote, "I died daily." Hull also had sex with his wife, but when he did, it made them both miserable. He confessed that, "like thousands of ignorant husbands who daily do the same thing, I had abused my wife until sexual pleasure between us was impossible." Finally, Hull accepted "the law of God" over the laws of marriage, and he had sex with women who offered "the love, the intellec-tual and spiritual food" he needed. Hull had never visited a prostitute because he defined God's law as love. As long as he did not gratify "animal feeling," or pay for sex, he did not define his behavior as licentious. Instead, his repeated offenses "against man-made institutions wherever God's law in me commanded," Hull revealed, had led him to "peace, happiness, and intellectual growth." His extramarital affairs also improved his legal mar-riage. He explained, "I find the theory and practice which came to me, brought my wife and myself the joys that had long departed from our household." Hull's wife had the "same privileges," and though he did not know whether she had acted upon them, their mutual home had since become "the model of domestic happiness."[35]

Like free lovers before him, Hull redefined adultery to imagine new forms of marriage. He offered more than a metaphorical alternative, however, when he shared his own lived experience. To those who defined adultery as a "violation of the marriage bed," he responded that those in false marriages "adulterate every time" they had sex. Unhappy marriages, involuntary marital sexual relations, in his view, allowed "a communion of the male and female organs without a corresponding communion of souls." In contrast, his extramarital affairs had brought him together with women who shared his higher commitment to love, free choice, and mutuality. A good spiritualist, Hull believed that only this "blending" of souls vindicated the sexual act. More often than not, this spiritual connection occurred outside of legal marriage.[36]

The more interesting party to Moses Hull's revelations was his wife, Elvira. After all, Moses benefited from the sexual double standard, and she did not. Her reputation, not his, would suffer the most. Even in their community of like-minded spiritualists and women's rights activists in Vineland, New Jersey, public morality favored legal, monogamous marriage. To these fellow reformers, the couple shared a respectable twenty-year bond, which had produced four daughters. When Moses told Elvira about his new theory of sexual and spiritual communion, she made "a scene," but, according to Moses, she soon realized the "latent powers" his extramarital activities provided to them both. It is possible that Elvira was happy to be relieved of the burden of her husband's sexual demands.[37]

Elvira Hull soon offered her own free-love perspective for curious readers of *Woodhull and Claflin's Weekly*. After Moses told her everything, Elvira confirmed that she had suffered for a "long, long time," but her suffering grew from her false sense of ownership over her spouse. The reality of their marriage meant periods of "sexual starvation" or sexual "abuse." As she wrote, "nature" had made Moses a traveling lecturer, just as "nature" required her to stay home and care for their daughters. As time passed, however, she realized that Moses's theories worked: "my health grew better; Moses grew more human . . . and more loveable." He had become a better husband, and Elvira Hull concluded, "Thank God for Social Freedom!" While she detested, "lust, license, libertinism, and lewdness," Elvira praised "free, untrammeled, spontaneous love." For those who worried about the impact of their unusual relationship on their children, Elvira reassured her audience that she planned to "educate my daughters entirely above danger of unhappy marriages and so-called unfortunate alliances." Her daughters would be better prepared for marriage and motherhood than she had been. Elvira did not, however, reveal if she had embarked on any extramarital dalliances of her own.[38]

Figure 16. Elvira Hull, spiritualist who wrote of her experiences
with open marriage in the pages of *Woodhull and Claflin's
Weekly*. Courtesy of the University of Michigan Library, Special
Collections Research Center, Joseph A. Labadie Collection.

Spiritualists had the most to lose by the Hulls' admissions. They already
had to defend the respectability of their religious movement from charges
of free love, and now the Hulls openly embraced it. As one spiritualist
complained, "Wood-Hullites would have it believed that all Spiritualists
are Free-lovers, which means free-lusters." Another described Moses as a
"contaminating influence."[39] One leading spiritualist accused Elvira of
"following in the Woodhull trail" and practicing "promiscuous sexual

indulgence," even though she had admitted no such thing. Moses viewed these criticisms as a sign that "the battle rages as never before." Elvira published another explanation of her views, denying any "promiscuous sexual indulgence." She suggested that their critics were unable to differentiate between "liberty and license."[40]

Though the Hulls continued to agitate for social freedom, their unorthodox relationship led to legal complications. Moses and Elvira remained good friends and coworkers, but they agreed that "in the highest and truest sense" they should not be husband and wife. In addition, Moses had met another spiritualist lecturer named Mattie Sawyer, who, despite being married, became his sexual soul mate. Mattie and her first husband, Christopher Sawyer, whom she married at age seventeen, had agreed that their marriage was over. In August 1874, the Sawyers announced the annulment of their marriage contract at a Silver Lake, Massachusetts gathering. They told fellow spiritualists that they "would be recognized no longer as husband and wife," declaring themselves "free from all obligations to each other." Then, as "independent sovereigns," Mattie and Moses Hull made their own "Declaration of Independence" from "man-made institutions." They argued that "every individual is endowed with instinct, telling when and with whom to form a companionship, and when to dissolve it." For now, they pledged to each other their "manhood and womanhood." These extra-legal actions showed their disdain for the laws of marriage. Though their relationship lasted for over thirty years, it is unclear if Moses ever legally married Mattie. After Elvira divorced him and remarried a Dr. D. W. Allen, Moses might have wed, and incurred some penalties as the guilty party, but Mattie's self-annulment meant she was still married to Sawyer. Suspicious New Jersey neighbors had Moses and Mattie arrested, probably on a charge of adultery, though the judge dismissed the case.[41]

Meanwhile, Mattie Sawyer joined Moses Hull on the free love battleground. In 1874, Moses seized the opportunity of his temporary notoriety to publish his own paper, *Hull's Crucible*, which printed letters of support for his "Personal Experience" revelation. Like Woodhull, he charged his most vociferous critics with engaging in behaviors that they condemned, such as keeping secret concubines and hiding illegitimate children. Henry Ward Beecher and other clergyman, Hull noted frequently, were the worst offenders. Mattie Sawyer wrote a poem for the newspaper entitled "Social Freedom," which declared her willingness to suffer for her beliefs:

Figure 17. Mattie Sawyer, spiritualist and free lover, who formed an extralegal union with Moses Hull. Courtesy of the University of Michigan Library, Special Collections Research Center, Joseph A. Labadie Collection.

Only a woman, I stand to-night
On a platform broad and free.
I take to my soul the sacred right
Of God-given liberty.
I know I will meet the skeptics' stare,
The censure of the critic ear;
But having the truth the world I dare;
I will strike and make them hear.

Sawyer's poem described many women's despair in legal marriages, forced to have sex with their husbands in exchange for financial support: "There are wives worse than widowed to-night/ Whose divinest loves are cold/ Their womanhood sank in blackest night/ They bartered their souls for gold." Joining her fellow female free lovers, Mattie wrote of the glorious inevitability of individual sovereignty: "Oh! Social Freedom! The ignorant world/ Defines thee in a vulgar way/ At thy teachers' calumnies are hurled/ But thy tide they cannot stay."[42]

The Wood-Hullites and other advocates of social freedom had changed adultery into a political act. They exposed its common practice among their enemies, including Henry Ward Beecher and other prominent religious figures, to show the hypocrisy of their public morality. In their own experimental alternatives, they modeled loving, free relationships. Their "marriages," they believed, were more moral and less licentious than the legal institution. As they had intended, free lovers' exposure of adultery caused chaos for their enemies in the Beecher family, as well as among their potential allies in the women's rights and spiritualist movements. The Wood-Hullites also paid a price, risking their reputations and their freedom. They waited to see if their actions might still destroy Henry Ward Beecher.

*　*　*

In January 1875, Beecher's civil trial for criminal conversation began. After Victoria Woodhull published her accusations, Henry Ward Beecher and the Tiltons had remained silent. But in 1874, Theodore Tilton decided to go public in order to vindicate himself. In the aftermath of the scandal, he had suffered more than Beecher. While Beecher still had his wife and position at Plymouth Church, Theodore's marriage had disintegrated, and his association with Woodhull had damaged his professional reputation. The first hearing, in Beecher's own parish, exonerated the pastor thanks in part to Elizabeth Tilton's testimony. Reversing her previous statements, Elizabeth admitted that she and Beecher had become close and loving friends, but denied that they had committed adultery.

Theodore followed this verdict with a civil suit against Beecher for $100,000. The defendant, Tilton asserted, had "debauched and carnally knew" his wife with the intention of depriving him "of the comfort, society, aid, and assistance of the said Elizabeth . . . and to alienate and destroy her affection for him." In addition to Beecher's alleged adultery, free love—as a theory, practice, and critique of marriage—was also on trial. Both plaintiff and defendant subpoenaed Stephen Pearl Andrews. Tilton's lawyers accused Beecher of engaging in free love, while Beecher's defense countered that it was Tilton who associated with free lovers.[43]

Victoria Woodhull was notably absent from a long roster of witnesses that included other women. Despite being the subject of much of the testimony, Woodhull likely presented too much risk for either the plaintiff or defendant. She made only one appearance in court. Beecher's attorney, William Evarts, had subpoenaed her letters from Tilton, and Woodhull came to protest. In a brief statement, she told the judge, "I have been imprisoned several times for the publication of this scandal," and that during her imprisonment, her office had been "ransacked."[44] Woodhull accused the Beecher and Tilton camps of the robbery, speculating that they already had most of her papers.

Neither Elizabeth Tilton nor Eunice Beecher, Henry's wife, could testify for or against their husbands, but they sat in the courtroom as other women offered indirect testimony of their spouses' misdeeds. For example, Emma Moulton, who was married to Tilton's ally Frank Moulton, claimed to have heard Beecher's confession of adultery. She testified that she had asked the Rev. Beecher how he could preach against adultery "when you are implicated in it yourself?" He apparently replied, "I feel more fit for it than ever before."[45] Another female witness connected Tilton to free-love radicalism. Hannah Augusta Moore, who had boarded with the Tiltons for a number of years, testified that Theodore often stayed out past midnight. She also told the court about one gathering at the Tiltons' home that had been dominated by Stephen Pearl Andrews. Andrews had talked "hour after hour," Moore remembered, "and I can't remember a solitary sentence the creature said, not one." The conversation, she testified, involved "spheres, spiritual influences, and things of that sort, but the talk I can't repeat, for it was beyond me altogether, or beneath me, somehow." Moore reported that Theodore seemed delighted to host these reformers, but Elizabeth acted stunned by their presence in her parlor.[46]

In addition to denying the adultery, Beecher's defense focused on tying Tilton to Andrews, Woodhull, and free love. Several times, William Evarts tried and failed to enter Theodore's biography of Woodhull into evidence as proof of their shared commitment to social freedom. Evarts argued that the book "was a most definite, authentic, deliberate form of allying himself in the view of a religious and general public with these doctrines of free love, and with this lady as one of its advocates and champions."[47] The defense also asserted that Tilton knew of Woodhull's intention to publish the exposé in advance. Theodore responded that his collaboration with Woodhull had been a deliberate attempt to bury the story. When the defense suggested that Tilton had a sexual relationship with Woodhull, he testified that her husband was always home when he visited, and they had taken him on a tour of the house to prove it was not a brothel. Yet if Theodore had an affair with Victoria, it would not have been his first, and everyone in the courtroom knew it. In her article on "The Beecher-Tilton Scandal Case," which was admitted into evidence, Woodhull revealed that when Tilton told her of his wife's adultery, he admitted he was no "vestal virgin." Her response had been to berate him for holding Elizabeth to moral standards that he had not met.[48]

On the seventy-eighth day of the trial, Tilton's lawyer called Stephen Pearl Andrews to the stand, hoping to prove that his client was not a free lover. As the ghostwriter of parts of "The Beecher-Tilton Scandal Case," and someone who had been aware of Woodhull's intentions for months, Andrews testified that Tilton had not known of their plans for publication. When asked about Hannah Moore's testimony regarding the "spheres" gathering at Tilton's house, Andrews explained that he attended with his late wife, a trance medium, who had sat with Theodore to study his character. He testified that there had been nothing improper about that night. Andrews also noted his long relationship with Tilton, and the fact that he had introduced his friend to Woodhull. While he was living at Woodhull's house, Andrews stated, Tilton had visited many times, and he was always "courtly" and "reserved." More damningly, he testified that Tilton had written the biography in the bedroom shared by Mrs. Woodhull and Colonel Blood, and that he had once spent the night in the house.[49]

Figure 18. Stephen Pearl Andrews, leader of the free-love movement
for twenty-five years. Courtesy of the University of Michigan Library,
Special Collections Research Center, Joseph A. Labadie Collection.

Andrews's testimony also revealed that Woodhull's house had replaced
the Unitary Home as the center of free love. To show that Tilton was one
of many guests, Andrews presented a long list of visitors, from socialists
and feminists to politicians and generals. Radicals of all sorts, their opponents, and the merely curious gathered at Woodhull's house for stimulating
conversation and conviviality. There, he and Woodhull had learned of the
Beecher-Tilton affair from Elizabeth Cady Stanton. They also discussed

their shared views on "the sovereignty of the individual." When Tilton's attorney asked him to explain the meaning of the phrase, Andrews replied that the theory covered "the whole ground" of marriage and divorce "as a branch of the larger doctrine." When asked if he meant promiscuous intercourse between the sexes, Andrews responded "yes and no," as only individuals could determine a natural inclination for promiscuity. Seeking more clarity, Tilton's lawyer asked if he believed couples should be able to separate at will. Yes, Andrews responded, the government should never intervene in the relationship between two individuals. Though Tilton had participated in these conversations on radical topics, Andrews excused his friend by noting that he had always offered "a vein of strong dissent."[50]

A more negative assessment of Tilton's presence in Woodhull's salon came from Charles Cowley, a Massachusetts lawyer and witness for Beecher. Cowley had served as Woodhull's attorney when she sued the proprietors of Boston's Tremont Temple for denying her the use of their venue. Since then, he had specialized in divorce cases, and had become an advocate for divorce and labor reform. In 1871, when he visited her home in Manhattan, the other guests included Andrews, Tilton, and Albert Brisbane, and they discussed marriage, spiritualism, and the illiberal New York divorce statute. However much they might have agreed about divorce reform, Cowley impugned Tilton's motives and character. When Woodhull described Beecher as a fellow advocate of free love, he testified, Tilton had offered the outlandish estimate that forty of Beecher's mistresses sat in the pews every Sunday. Contrary to Andrews's assessment of their relationship as chaste, Cowley described Theodore and Victoria as "enamored of each other." Woodhull allegedly told Cowley that Theodore Tilton was her "ideal of a man." Cowley thus confirmed the defense's argument that it was Tilton, not Beecher, who was the free lover and adulterer.[51]

The civil trial lasted for over one hundred days, and the jury, perhaps unsurprisingly, was unable to reach a decision. In adultery trials, hung juries occurred with some regularity.[52] Cases of sexual misconduct, like that of seducer Sherman Booth, often involved the malleable, subjective issue of the character of accuser and accused. Did Henry Ward Beecher and Elizabeth Tilton have a sexual relationship? Or had Tilton destroyed his own marriage by his involvement with Woodhull? Despite the lack of verdict, Beecher emerged victorious. He retained his position as a celebrated minister and pastor of Plymouth Church. With Tilton's character as much on trial as his own, Beecher and his lawyers had largely succeeded in labeling the moderate suffragist as a free lover. Tilton's career never recovered, and he eventually moved to France.

As a trial over free love, the verdict was clear. Both Beecher and Tilton had distanced themselves from social freedom, and portrayed free love as the enemy of marriage. Witnesses described Andrews and Woodhull as freaks or lunatics, with an overt hostility to marriage and morality. Though they might have bristled at the names, both Woodhull and Andrews had described marriage as an oppressive relic, and love and self-determination as the future. Deliberately, and with forethought, they publicized Henry Ward Beecher's adultery to expose the moral pretense of legal marriage. Instead, the civil trial upheld a hypocritical system, which defended marriage and, by extension, condoned adultery. Without legal marriage, as free love advocates knew, there would be no need for civil or criminal adultery.

The Beecher-Tilton scandal, trial, and verdict had a devastating impact on the broad movement for marriage reform. Suffragists, spiritualists, and other moderates distanced themselves from free lovers, and ultimately, the entire question of marriage. Free lovers experienced a defeat that would chasten their movement for several decades. Woodhull renounced free love, divorced Colonel Blood, and left the United States for England, blaming Stephen Pearl Andrews for her vilification.[53] Andrews tried to continue the fight, but he could no longer be considered the leader of a free-love movement, an informal position he had held for twenty-five years. Further, he never found a replacement for Julia Branch or Victoria Woodhull, who had served as compelling, newsworthy exemplars of his radical theories.

For over two decades, religious and secular free lovers, as well as moderate marriage reformers, had used the adultery metaphor to describe loveless marriages. For these gurus, activists, and writers, love alone justified sex and anything else was adulterous intercourse. Like defenders of the institution, its critics viewed adultery as the opposite of marriage. But their redefinition of adultery also necessitated a new type of marriage. Rather than an enduring legal and religious bond, these reformers envisioned the union as a voluntary arrangement between two individuals, who chose to be together out of love. In their lectures, newspapers, and books, they idealized this mutual love as pure and faithful, even if it existed outside of the law, and they urged couples to separate if love faded. The McFarland-Richardson case exemplified the shared critique of marriage among moderates and radicals. Suffragists, abolitionists, and free lovers agreed that Abby

Sage had a fundamental right to divorce a husband she did not love, for whatever reason, and marry one she did.

When the postwar campaign failed to damage Beecher or the legal institution, the metaphor and act of adultery lost power as a way for activists to resist or reimagine marriage. By the end of the 1870s, the marriage question had become a liability for reformers, and most American social movements dropped the controversial issues of marriage, divorce, and individual sexual rights. The institution's defenders had succeeded in associating free lovers with adultery, immorality, and obscenity, and portraying spiritualists and suffragists as their willing, dangerous dupes. Yet marriage reformers themselves also mobilized adultery in contradictory ways, rendering the concept almost meaningless. They used it as a negative to categorize loveless and involuntary marital sexual relations, while also conceptualizing legal adultery—extramarital sex—as a positive manifestation of mutual love. To a certain extent, the Beecher jury's indecision reflected this definitional uncertainty. With the difficulty of determining the nature or fact of any sexual relationship, the narrow, legalistic understanding of adultery as a violation of marital sexual fidelity triumphed.

But marriage reformers no longer needed the adultery metaphor. It disappeared not only because censors and moralists marginalized marriage reformers, but also because their ideas were absorbed, sometimes indirectly, into the mainstream. Activists had helped reinvent the legal institution around individual choice, mutual desire, and true love.

Epilogue

For over four decades, a loose coalition of women's rights activists, abolitionists, spiritualists, communitarians, free lovers, and bohemians challenged the legal institution of marriage. Marriage reformers used adultery as a metaphor for the personal violation of forced, lifelong monogamy. The concept of adultery was an adaptable, familiar, and useful conceptual link between radical, legal, and mainstream views of marriage. It also allowed these activists to bridge personal experiences and political meanings. The reformers described in these chapters defined any sex act that was not an expression of true, consensual love as adulterous. False, unhappy marriages were adulterous. They believed that women, as well as men, had the moral capability and individual right to determine when and with whom they would have sex. Adultery was a betrayal of the self or God, in other words, not a betrayal of man-made marriage laws. After the Civil War, free lovers also adopted adultery as a form of civil disobedience, a deliberate violation of these laws and a way to overthrow the social and cultural conventions of marriage.

During the nineteenth century, many Americans considered marriage reformers laughable or crazy. Scholars have largely accepted this portrayal, and marginalized these reformers in their histories of nineteenth-century social movements. Their bohemian rejection of middle-class values, their self-aggrandizement, and their often scandalous personal lives do not help their cause. Yet these reformers had a lasting and overlooked impact on how Americans think about marriage. Reformers articulated new ideals of love, choice, and consent. The marriage question became central to other reform movements, including at various times abolition, communitarianism, spiritualism, and women's rights. As participants in a national conversation about marriage, even moderate marriage reformers grappled with and absorbed the more radical critiques of the free lovers.

In their sexual relationships, marriage reformers made a genuine, if sometimes self-serving, effort to apply their principles. Their experiments in marriage created alternatives to monogamy, defying legal understandings of adultery. In communities such as Oneida, Modern Times, and the Unitary Home, open forms of marriage were essential to the larger goal of creating a cooperative, egalitarian society. Marriage reformers also negotiated new rules for intimacy, applying them to their own relationships. A true marriage was a loving, consensual partnership. Love was a spiritual as well as sexual connection, and it was imperative for individuals to find and marry their true love. They redefined adultery as sexual intercourse without love. They also acknowledged that love could be misguided, mercurial, or non-exclusive and non-monogamous. For these reasons, some marriage reformers advocated abolishing the institution or expanding the causes for divorce.

A few marriage reformers invited scandal, mockery, and outrage, which allowed their colleagues, subsequent generations, and historians to label them as the radical, quixotic fringe. After Comstock and the Wood-Hullite scandals, the climate for reform also shifted from debates about the true meaning of marriage and betrayal to sexual purity, especially in campaigns against obscenity, prostitution, and polygamy, which would dominate American social reform for the rest of the century.

But it was not simply that censorship, eccentric behavior, or resurgent sexual purity and pro-marriage campaigns diminished free love and the adultery metaphor. By the end of the nineteenth century, reformers no longer needed the metaphor because it had done its work: in American society, marriage and love were becoming ever more synonymous. Even opponents of marriage reform, defenders of the legal status quo such as Harriet Beecher Stowe, believed that the marital bond should be based on affection.[1] The sometimes shocking and provocative metaphor of adultery disappeared because its critique had been accepted. In this way, the ideas of marriage reformers were both exiled to the margins and embraced in the middle.

American law and policy gradually adjusted to the once-scandalous expectations that free lovers had used the vivid metaphor of adultery to convey. Jurists granted women more rights within marriage, and reinterpreted the law to establish marriage as an exchange of love rather than labor. In the early twentieth century, progressive reformers began policing the marriages of immigrants to make sure they reflected the American value of love.[2] Access to divorce for those who were unhappily married also continued to expand. Only New York State refused to change, leaving adultery as the only cause until 1966.

Criminal adultery statutes remained in place, however, and New York finally passed its own law in 1907 in an attempt to make it harder for couples, like Lyman Case and Marie Howland, to collude on the charge of adultery in order to divorce. Activists protested such laws as a violation of individual rights, and in the twentieth century they began to challenge them on the grounds of privacy.[3] Though the legal struggle continued, marriage would never be the same.

At the same time, a new generation of African Americans viewed marriage as an essential civil right. Like their predecessors in moral reform, upwardly mobile and middle-class African Americans saw their marital respectability as an argument for equal citizenship. Now that African Americans had access to the legal protections of marriage, states counteracted these benefits by using the law to police their sexual behavior. In 1880, for example, 161 Americans were in jail for adultery. The majority of those imprisoned for adultery were men, with a total of fifty-three white, native-born men and thirty-four African American men. Only forty-eight women, mostly white, native-born women, had been convicted of the charge.[4] Such numbers indicate that law enforcement might have been acting on behalf of American wives, but the disproportionate representation of black men suggests a goal of enforcing sexual (and probably racial) conformity within marriage. The punitive aspects of the law did not deter African Americans from love or marriage. As historian Tera Hunter points out, marriage was "one of the few civil rights that was safe from revocation at the century's end, which heightened its eminence all the more."[5]

*   *   *

In the 1870s and 1880s, marriage reformers continued their personal search for true love in a newly hostile political environment. Emancipation had confirmed the centrality of marriage to American society. Marriage conveyed rights, but it had lost none of its power to constrain. States continued to use the laws to proscribe individual behavior, and activists also faced the threat of censorship and prosecution. As a result, reformers focused anew on improving monogamous marriage through true love and mutual desire. And many reformers turned inward, struggling to reconcile their intimate relationships with their marital ideals.

In 1885, spiritualist Andrew Jackson Davis annulled his marriage of 29 years to his former soul mate, Mary Fenn Robinson Love Davis. The New

York courts had recently decided the case of the *People v. Faber*, affirming that "a person from whom a divorce has been obtained in this State commits bigamy in marrying and cohabiting with another during the lifetime of the person who obtained such judgment of divorce."[6] New York law not only limited divorce to cases of adultery, as we have seen, but also decreed the guilty party could not remarry while the former spouse was living. After *People v. Faber*, Davis apparently realized that his marriage was illegal. The newspapers rightly mocked his convoluted rationale for an annulment, which "concealed all the facts" about Mary's prior divorce in the state of Indiana. Contradicting the account in his autobiography *The Magic Staff*, Davis now claimed that ever since he learned of her first husband's subsequent suit in New York, "he ceased to cohabit with [Mary], but continued to maintain a brotherly and fraternal relation and to hold her out as his wife, because of their business relations." The census indicated that they had been living in the same household in 1860, 1870, and 1880, but Davis probably used the term "cohabitation" to refer to sexual intercourse.[7] He had long emphasized the importance of spiritual as well as physical communion, and the corresponding practices of self-control and mutual consent. It is certainly possible that the couple's sexual relations ceased soon after their marriage, which produced no children.

As one newspaper observed, Jackson Davis now had to rewrite his autobiography, which emphasized his attachment to Mary as a spiritual bond for all eternity, rather than "His Wife for Business Only."[8] Indeed, the same year as his annulment, Davis published a sequel to *The Magic Staff* called *Beyond the Valley*. He recounted that soon after their marriage in 1855, a spirit told him that Mary was a "*co-worker*" only, with a shared mission to teach the "basis of true marriage."[9] Jackson was devastated, but he endured the "temporary marriage" for the sake of their "public work" and out of consideration for her reputation and feelings. It was not until November 1884 that he told Mary their marriage was over. The new autobiography included his early realization that their relationship was not a true spiritual match.[10] He also reprinted a fourteen-page letter he had written to Mary, declaring their relationship, which he had publicly described as fraternal, as "*incestuous*," a different kind of sexual violation than adultery.[11]

While the Davises and other marriage reformers emphasized love over the law, most activists pursued conjugal love within the boundaries of the legal institution. With love as the only legitimating force in sexual relationships, reformers also advocated liberal divorce. Davis, as the newspapers noted, "invoked the machinery of the law" to end his marriage. To Mary, he argued that they must end their marriage for "true social order and progression—for the sake of purity of life and nobility of feeling," and most of all to "be true" to themselves.[12] These same ideals—purity, love, higher law, individual autonomy—had brought Mary and Jackson together. Twenty-nine years later, Jackson called upon these virtues to justify the dissolution of their partnership. They also led Mary to consent to the legal proceedings.

Mary's reaction combined acceptance with the knowledge that she bore the legal, social, and moral consequences. Jackson's 1885 autobiography also included Mary's short response to his letter, offering "*no opposition*" to his case. Writing that she appreciated his honesty and commitment to principle, Mary nonetheless expressed trepidation about her new status as a "divorced wife." In a letter to a friend, she emphasized her surprise and pain: "It seems a strange fate that I should again be bereft of that protecting love which cannot change, and banished from the heart of the domestic circle. Once I could not have believed such an ending of our happy life together would be possible."[13] Unlike Jackson, who remarried within the year, Mary was not free to marry again; she had lost forever the respectability and protection that married life provided. Instead, according to the laws of New York, she was an adulterer and would-be bigamist.[14] In the end, the Davis marriage was no different than any other legal bond.

The late annulment, as well as his quick remarriage, damaged Jackson Davis's reputation as an advocate for true love, but he continued to work as a clairvoyant physician. In 1883, he graduated from the homeopathic United States Medical College, an institution for which he had helped create a Chair of Psychological Science and Magnetic Therapeutics. For the rest of his life, Davis devoted himself to the practice of medicine, even though he and other spiritualist healers were on the defensive against allopathic physicians.[15]

After the Civil War, Paschal Beverly Randolph infused his marital advice with Rosicrucianism and magical mysticism. In *Eulis! The History of Love: Its Wondrous Magic, Chemistry, Rules, Laws, Modes, Moods, and Rationale* (1874), he described a sexual encounter with "a dusky maiden of Arabic blood" when he was traveling in Jerusalem. Randolph claimed this woman had taught him the "white magic" principle of love. This magic offered the key to sexual health and happiness, he wrote, "especially in our marriage matters in the false society of to-day; and furthermore, that by obedience to law, herein set forth, the ELIXIR of life may be found." Randolph explained that this elixir was the magnetic fluid exchanged between men and women in the sexual act. The danger, Randolph warned, was in the misuse of sexual intercourse, calling marriage without love a "desecration."[16] He and other marriage reformers had trouble following their own sexual and marital advice.

Randolph also repudiated accusations that he was a "Wood-Hullite." In September 1873, he attended a spiritualist convention, during which one faction rebelled against Victoria Woodhull's leadership. Though Randolph had defended her "right to a fair hearing in her bold, iconoclastic attack upon the wrongs of woman, and the injurious marriage system of to-day," he believed his speech had been misunderstood. Yes, he had declared that, "a female adulteress or harlot is no worse than a male libertine or voluptuary," but Randolph defended it as a "plea for the female outcast" rather than an "abrogation of marriage." He had gone to the convention, Randolph claimed, to debate Moses Hull, whom he described as "a boasting libertine." Moses Hull had not attended, but Randolph proceeded to castigate him as "lost and conscienceless" and a "human brute." In stressing his differences from the Wood-Hullites, Randolph again cast himself as a defender of marriage.[17]

Randolph knew that any association with the Wood-Hullites posed a threat to his career. In 1872, in the midst of a struggle with unsavory business partners in Boston, P. B. had been arrested for obscenity, or selling literature on "Free Lovism" and "reputable concubinage," and spent two days in jail. On his release, he wrote a fictional account of a trial to prove his innocence of the charge of free love. Calling it *The Great Free-Love Trial,*" Randolph composed the imaginary jury of men from all religions and races. The prosecutor charged him as "*the* most *dangerous* man and author on the soil of America, if not of the entire globe."[18]

Randolph's fictional defense criticized free lovers as well as their doctrines. He described advocates of social freedom as fanatics and rogues. A typical free-love woman, he asserted, was a "worn-out debauchee, a freedom-shrieking woman of faded charms, sharp voice, rapid tongue, overplus of brain, paucity of soul, little passion and less love." He described the men as "actually heartless, unemotive, spasmodically lecherous, bent on world-saving, themselves wholly lost." Randolph admitted that his knowledge came from firsthand experience among them, yet he assured readers that he had learned that free love led to unhappiness, disease, and death.

Rather than encouraging husbands and wives to leave their marriages, as free lovers did, Randolph showed them how to restore their relationships using magnetic principles. Without leaving their seats, his fictional jury declared Randolph "not guilty."[19]

Though Randolph did not mention Andrew Jackson Davis by name, the spiritualist certainly matched his description of a longhaired, world-saving fanatic, and one whom Randolph considered "spasmodically lecherous." Since their clash at the 1858 Utica convention, P. B. had new reasons to despise Davis. Before the Civil War, Jackson Davis had less interest in the problem of racial slavery than in the oppressive institution of marriage. Following emancipation, he and other white spiritualists imagined a segregated afterlife, with whites occupying a separate part of Summerland from people of African descent. Davis believed that racial differences were fixed, and could not be changed on earth or in heaven. Randolph's romantic theories of race, and celebration of his own blendedness, offered a direct challenge to Davis and other white spiritualists. He also continued to attack Jackson Davis as an amoral, marriage-destroying free lover.[20]

Randolph was a unique figure in nineteenth-century reform. His racial identification as an Indian, conglomerate, or black man changed depending on his situation, establishing his independent expertise on love, sex, and marriage. Randolph refused to be classed with abolitionists, spiritualists, or free lovers. Attuned to the changing political climate, Randolph's vehement arguments in favor of marriage undoubtedly helped persuade readers and censors alike. After his arrest, however, Randolph's business suffered, and he left Boston for Toledo, Ohio, where he met and married a nineteen-year-old white medium named Kate Corson. She helped Randolph market his books and elixirs, and they had a son named Osiris, but the relationship was tumultuous. In July 1875, fifty-year-old Randolph committed suicide, his personal quest for true love and spiritual enlightenment incomplete. As in life, Randolph's death showed his isolation.[21]

Moses Hull, one of Randolph's key nemeses, was undeterred by the backlash to his open marriage, divorce, and extralegal relationship with Mattie Sawyer. He also seems to have escaped the interest of Anthony Comstock. For a time, Hull turned to radical politics, using his newspaper *Hull's Crucible* to promote the Greenback Party. His daughter Mary Florence followed in her father's footsteps and formed a contractual union with a "vigorous young man" named Horace Johnson, a store clerk. Their 1877 agreement declared them "equal partners" and stated that "neither Church nor State have any business with our affairs." In conclusion, the couple vowed that, "when mutual love shall no longer justify our conjugal union, we shall part, giving the State as little trouble in our parting as we have coming together."[22] In the 1890s, Moses Hull began training younger spiritualist lecturers, and with the generous donation of a Wisconsin spiritualist, became the founding president of the Morris Pratt School, which educated spiritualists and mediums. When he died on a fundraising trip in 1907, aged seventy-two, Hull's partner, Mattie, and his daughter Alfaretta continued running the school. Mattie was now known by the last name Hull.[23]

The Hulls' experimentation with loving, contractual partnerships bolstered rather than damaged the legal institution. Observers saw little difference between Mattie and Moses's relationship and any other marriage. Those who wrote their own equal contracts, as well as those who married in a church, parlor, or office, wanted their intimate partnerships to be characterized by choice, love, and companionship. One critical newspaper observed that the union of Mary Florence and Horace Johnson had involved even more complicated paperwork and publicity than a legal marriage. They predicted that, after "a longer life experience," the couple will learn that "their greatest freedom [was] in and not outside the protection of the Christian religion and the State law." This newspaper viewed marriage as conveying rights as well as restrictions, a position that freed people and Mary Fenn Davis understood only too well.[24]

In the 1870s, Oneida Community members also began to view complex marriage as more coercive than conventional marriage. In part, the community was under attack from the same sexual-purity forces than targeted free lovers in the east and Mormons in the west. Further, as John Humphrey Noyes aged, younger men competed for his position and prerogatives, particularly the initiation of young women into complex marriage. With Noyes losing his spiritual authority, and no clear successor emerging, younger members began to find monogamy more appealing. After the community voted to dissolve complex marriage on August 28, 1879, younger members rushed to marry, with or without the approval of their elders. Harriet Skinner, one of the spiritual elders, called the movement toward marriage "a kind of baptism" brought on by an "irresistible power." She commented, "it looks as if marriage would eat up Communism."[25] Harriet Skinner was right. The Oneida Community turned its shared businesses into a joint stock company, and in order to avoid legal prosecution Noyes went to Canada, where he died in 1886.

MOSES HULL

Figure 19. Moses Hull, one of the eponyms of the free-love Wood-Hullite branch of spiritualism, who had violated the laws against adultery as an act of civil disobedience. Courtesy of the Special Collections Research Center, Syracuse University Libraries.

Figure 20. John Humphrey Noyes moved to Canada after the
dissolution of complex marriage and the Oneida Community.
Courtesy of the Oneida Community Mansion House.

Most marriage reformers had never abandoned monogamous marriage
in the first place. Even free-love radicals such as Edward Underhill, the
former manager of the Unitary Home, had been married. After his first
wife, Mary, died in 1874, Underhill wed Evelyn T. Stoddard, one of his
phonographers, now called stenographers. As the chief stenographer for the

Surrogate's Court, which handled all probate and estate cases in New York County, Underhill had become a respected, and apparently wealthy, professional. One reporter observed that Underhill "employs a number of female typewriters and stenographers, who are noted for their fair faces and figures." Women had started moving into the white-collar workforce, so it was their good looks, rather than the gendered structure of Underhill's office, that made these employees noteworthy. In 1888, Evelyn Underhill asked for a separation, also known as a limited divorce, from her husband, for "desertion and failure to support." A reporter discovered that the couple still lived in the same house, and questioned the likely success of her suit. As predicted, the judge denied her motion, and the couple was still married when Edward Underhill died in 1898, indicating the suit was a marital disagreement that had escalated.[26]

Reformers searched for love in and outside of legal marriage. As Mary Booth was on her deathbed in New York City, Sherman Booth had written that he was in love with a "young lady," but it would not be "*right*" to marry her as long as Mary Booth was "*in life*."[27] In 1867, two years after his wife's death, Sherman married Augusta Ann Smith, a woman thirty years his junior, with whom he had five children. Sherman and his new wife moved to Chicago, and he continued his career as a newspaper editor and Republican operative until his death in 1904.[28] In 1865, Mathilde Anneke, his former housemate, returned to the Wisconsin and soon became a leader in the state and National Woman Suffrage Association. With her in Milwaukee was a new female companion, a schoolteacher named Caecilie Kapp, who later taught German and French at Vassar. Anneke's husband, Fritz, died in 1872, and Anneke did not remarry before her death in 1884.

In her partnerships with Mary Booth and Caecilie Kapp, Mathilde Anneke participated in a larger pattern among feminists of rejecting heterosexual marriage in favor of loving relationships with other women. Susan B. Anthony recognized similar domestic partnerships in her 1877 speech on "Homes of Single Women." Anticipating Virginia Woolf, Anthony wrote, "A home of one's own is the want." She viewed women's domestic partnerships as "homes of exceeding joy and gladness, compared with the myriads of ill-assorted marriage homes, where existence, by night and by day, is but a living death!"[29] Anneke undoubtedly agreed. She had intimate knowledge of the Booth marriage, and she seemed content with long physical separations from Fritz, preferring loving relationships with women. Despite her criticism of marriage, Anthony offered no hint or possibility that these same-sex relationships might be as passionate as that of Mary and Mathilde, though a critical Henry James indicated their potential to warp women's true destiny—heterosexual marriage—in his 1886 novel *The Bostonians*.

*   *   *

The continued appeal of marriage and domesticity did not mean that free love disappeared. In the decades after the 1873 Comstock law, radical critics of marriage devoted much of their energy to evading and resisting its enforcer. In 1878, marriage reformers rallied to the defense of D. M. Bennett, arrested by Comstock for sending obscene material through the U.S. Post Office. Bennett had mailed *Cupid's Yokes*, a free-love pamphlet by Ezra H. Heywood, who had also been arrested by Comstock, and then pardoned at the highest level by President Rutherford B. Hayes. Heywood advocated the familiar ideals of true love, mutual consent, and physical health, believing that love should be "a free compact, dissolvable at will" rather than a "compulsive, hurtful, or irrevocable" bond. Acknowledging the new legal context, Heywood also called the Comstock law a "gag rule," an attack on free speech reminiscent of Congress's ban on antislavery petitions decades earlier, and referred to Comstock himself as a *"religious monomaniac."*[30] Bennett's lawyers made sure that no jurors were associates of Comstock or members of his New York Society for the Suppression of Vice. Both Andrew Jackson Davis and Theron T. Leland, phonographer and former resident of Modern Times, testified to the defendant's good character. His lawyers also compared the language of *Cupid's Yokes* favorably to passages in Shakespeare, Byron, Shelley, and Whitman. Nevertheless, Bennett was convicted and spent over a year in prison, highlighting the new risks of writing about love.[31]

In New York City and around the country, activists organized to fight the Comstock law. One of Bennett's lawyers, T. B. Wakeman, became president of the National Liberal League, which promoted the separation of church and state, and decried the Comstock law as a result of religious influence on the nation's laws. The league raised defense funds for Bennett and others arrested by Comstock. A new generation of female free lovers, including Lois Waisbrooker and Ida Craddock, also challenged Comstock's power.[32]

As with free love, this anti-Comstock coalition attracted those feminists still willing to question marriage, church, and state. Elizabeth Cady Stanton,

Elizabeth Smith Miller, Matilda Joslyn Gage, Amy Post, and Mathilde Anneke joined local liberal leagues, donated money, corresponded with freethinkers, and wrote for their newspapers. In return, liberals and free-thinkers endorsed women's suffrage, resolving "to do all they can by voice and vote to remove the subjection of woman, and to advance her social, material, and political emancipation." Now wholly focused on winning the vote, most suffragists rejected this support, or any alliance with free lovers and freethinkers. As a topic of debate and discussion, the marriage question had largely disappeared from their conventions.[33]

Within this liberal movement for free speech, Stephen Pearl Andrews continued to promote his universal system knows as the Pantarchy. At one convention of the Union Reform League, a relation of the liberal leagues, "the League became an Individual Sovereign Auxiliary of the Pantarchy." Such a relationship reflected his larger goal, for the Pantarchy was to be a beneficent collection of individuals and their associations into a larger "Temple of Humanity." He also offered a more pertinent resolution, "That since there is no obscenity in nature, no obscenity in Science, and no obscenity in Art . . . obscenity is mainly to be sought for and found in the minds of those very persons who complain of its existence."[34] Despite the humor in this motion, Andrews's proposals for a worldwide, individualistic socialism had become more abstract, appealing only to a small cohort of loyal followers. According to Andrews, the Pantarchy provided a self-fulfilling "School of Life" and "Science of Organization," and any ideal society that emerged would naturally be a Pantarchy. To teach the "Higher Life" of the Pantarchy, Andrews established a university. His university seems to have been one of the earliest for-profit educational scams, and Andrews received a number of letters withdrawing from any association with the school.[35]

By the time of his death in 1886, Andrews may have considered himself a Christ-like figure. Theodora Freeman Spencer, one of his devoted aco-lytes, wrote to Andrews's son William, a lawyer and Union army veteran, that "Mr. Andrews had thanked me in the last days of his life for preventing him from announcing himself as the Christ." Spencer, or Andrews himself, had also talked to a Unitarian minister named William R. Alger about this belief. In 1895, Alger wrote a poem that mocked Andrews for thinking he was the "foremost man on earth" and a "God in state." His "long haired, high cheeked, motley crew" viewed him as a "Yankee Christ." The poem also portrayed Andrews as "sunk in odium and shame," "his chance for social greatness vanished" after the Beecher-Tilton trial. Alger proclaimed him disappointed and repentant on his deathbed. William, an ardent defender of his father since Isabella Beecher Hooker had investigated Victoria Woodhull and her clique, once again came to his defense. In response, Alger protested that he viewed Andrews as a "great man."[36]

The eccentric life of Stephen Pearl Andrews illuminates the dilemma of marriage reform for modern audiences. Andrews was a colorful figure. Nineteenth-century Americans viewed him and his associates as fanatics and outsiders, and easily dismissed their criticism of loveless marriage as a form of adultery. In the nineteenth century, the powerful and flexible metaphor of adultery allowed these various reformers to discuss sex, individual freedom, and women's sexual equality, as well as to acknowledge the changeability of both love and marriage. Their ideas about love permeated American social movements, and shaped a national debate over marriage and the meaning of adultery. Now, their ideas about self-determination and mutual desire seem ordinary, and so familiar that they have passed almost unnoticed in American history.

NOTES

Introduction

1. Mary Gove Nichols, *Mary Lyndon or, Revelations of a Life* (New York: Stringer and Townsend, 1855), 135. On Nichols, see Jean L. Silver-Isenstadt, *Shameless: The Visionary Life of Mary Gove Nichols* (Baltimore: Johns Hopkins University Press, 2002); Patricia Cline Cohen, "The 'Anti-Marriage Theory' of Thomas and Mary Gove Nichols: A Radical Critique of Monogamy in the 1850s," *Journal of the Early Republic*, 34, no. 1 (Spring 2014): 1–20; and Helen Lefkowitz Horowitz, *Rereading Sex: Battles over Sexual Knowledge and Suppression in Nineteenth-Century America* (New York: Vintage, 2002), 288–298.

2. Most histories of nineteenth-century sexuality and marriage overlook this particular, conceptual critique of legal marriage. Horowitz mentions the adultery metaphor, but she does not analyze its use. See *Rereading Sex*, 348. On other marriage metaphors, see especially Amy Dru Stanley, *From Bondage to Contract: Wage Labor, Marriage, and the Market in the Age of Slave Emancipation* (New York: Cambridge University Press, 1998), 258; Nancy Cott, *Public Vows: A History of Marriage and the Nation* (Cambridge, MA: Harvard University Press, 2000), 63–67; Hélène Quanquin, "'There Are Two Great Oceans': The Slavery Metaphor in Antebellum Women's Rights Discourse as Redescription of Race and Gender," in Carol Faulkner and Alison M. Parker, eds., *Interconnections: Gender and Race in American History* (Rochester: University of Rochester Press, 2012), 75–104.

3. Horowitz, *Rereading Sex*, 251.

4. For example, Linda Gordon, "Voluntary Motherhood: The Beginnings of Feminist Birth Control Ideas in the United States," *Feminist Studies*, 1, nos. 3–4 (1973): 5–22; Ronald G. Walters, *American Reformers, 1815–1860* (New York: Hill and Wang, 1997, revised edition). Studies of free love tend to be focused on the movement itself, including Hal Sears, *The Sex Radicals: Free Love in High Victorian America* (Lawrence: University of Kansas Press, 1977), and Joanne Passet, *Sex Radicals and the Quest for Women's Equality* (Urbana: University of Illinois Press, 2003). Exceptions include Helen Lefkowitz Horowitz's *Rereading Sex*, which includes free lovers and other Americans in overlapping conversations about sex in nineteenth-century America, and John C. Spurlock, who identifies free love values as essentially middle class in *Free Love: Marriage and Middle-Class Radicalism in America, 1825–1860* (New York: New York University Press, 1988).

5. Stephanie Coontz, *Marriage, a History: How Love Conquered Marriage* (New York: Penguin, 2005); Debbie Cenziper and Jim Obergefell, *Love Wins: The Lovers and Lawyers Who Fought the Landmark Case for Marriage Equality* (New York: William Morrow, 2016).

6. Coontz, *Marriage, a History*, 5.

7. Clare A. Lyons, *Sex Among the Rabble: An Intimate History of Gender and Power in the Age of Revolution, Philadelphia, 1730–1830* (Chapel Hill: University of North Carolina Press, 2006), 1; Mary Beth Sievens, *Stray Wives: Marital Conflict in Early National New England* (New York: New York University Press, 2005). See also Andrew Cayton, *Love in the Time of Revolution: Transatlantic Literary Radicalism and Historical Change, 1793–1818* (Chapel Hill: University of North Carolina Press, 2013); Anya Jabour, *Marriage in the Early Republic: Elizabeth and William Wirt and the Companionate Ideal* (Baltimore: Johns Hopkins University Press, 2002).

8. Norma Basch, *Framing American Divorce: From the Revolutionary Generation to the Victorians* (Berkeley: University of California Press, 1999), 4, 8–10, chap. 1.

9. Cott, *Public Vows*, 18–21; Ruth Bloch, "The Gendered Meanings of Virtue in Revolutionary America," *Signs,* 13 (Autumn 1987): 37–58; Mary Kelley, *Learning to Stand and Speak: Women, Education, and Public Life in America's Republic* (Chapel Hill: University of North Carolina Press, 2008).

10. Lyons, *Sex Among the Rabble*, 310, 312; Anne M. Boylan, *The Origins of Women's Activism: New York and Boston, 1797–1840* (Chapel Hill: University of North Carolina Press, 2002).

11. Jacobs, *Incidents in the Life of a Slave Girl* (Boston: published for the author, 1861), 118. Tera W. Hunter, *Bound in Wedlock: Slave and Free Black Marriage in the Nineteenth Century* (Cambridge, MA: Belknap Press of Harvard University Press, 2017), 67. This book will not consider marriage, divorce, and adultery in slave states because of the absence of a movement for marriage reform, and because of the complicating context of slavery. See Loren Schweninger, *Families in Crisis in the Old South: Divorce, Slavery, and the Law* (Chapel Hill: University of North Carolina Press, 2012). For northern and southern differences on production and reproduction, see Susan E. Klepp, *Revolutionary Conceptions: Women, Fertility, and Family Limitation in America, 1760–1820* (Chapel Hill: University of North Carolina Press, 2009).

12. "Ohio Anti-Slavery Society," *The Philanthropist,* June 22, 1842.

13. Glenda Riley, *Divorce: An American Tradition* (New York: Oxford University Press, 1991), 62–66; Basch, *Framing American Divorce*, 58–59; Hendrik Hartog, *Man and Wife in America: A History* (Cambridge, MA: Harvard University Press, 2002), 264–265.

14. Theodore Dwight Woolsey, *Essay on Divorce and Divorce Legislation* (New York: Charles Scribner, 1869), 220; Cott, *Public Vows*, 51, 53.

15. Nathaniel Hawthorne, *The Scarlet Letter* (1850), 204, 268. See also "No. 68, in Senate, March 13, 1847," *Documents of the Senate of the State of New York, Seventieth Session,* 1847 (Albany: Charles Van Benthuysen, 1847); Mary Beth Norton, *Founding Mothers and Fathers: Gendered Power and the Forming of American Society* (New York: Knopf, 1996), 341–347.

16. James A. Clay, *A Voice from Prison* (Gardiner, ME: Bela Marsh, 1856), 25–26. See also Spurlock, *Free Love*, 167–168; David M. Turner, *Fashioning Adultery: Gender, Sex, and Civility in England, 1660–1740* (New York: Cambridge University Press, 2004), 4–5, 201.

17. Schweninger, *Families in Crisis in the Old South,* 70–71, Norton, *Founding Mothers and Fathers,* 346; Laura Hanft Korobkin, *Criminal Conversations: Sentimentality and Nineteenth-Century Legal Stories of Adultery* (New York: Columbia University Press, 1998), 20–24. By the 1880s, women began to sue other women for criminal conversation; see Korobkin, *Criminal Conversations,* 121–126.

18. Patricia Cline Cohen, Timothy J. Gilfoyle, and Helen Lefkowitz Horowitz, *The Flash Press: Sporting Male Weeklies in 1840s New York* (Chicago: University of Chicago Press, 2008), 18–20, 27.

19. Recent histories of the Oneida Community include Ellen Wayland-Smith, *Oneida: From Free Love Utopia to the Well-Set Table* (New York: Picador, 2016); Anthony Wonderley, *Oneida Utopia: A Community Searching for Human Happiness and Prosperity* (Ithaca: Cornell University Press, 2017).

20. Stephen Pearl Andrews, Horace Greeley, and Henry James, *Love, Marriage, and Divorce, and the Sovereignty of the Individual; a Discussion; and a Hitherto Unpublished Manuscript, Love, Marriage, and the Condition of Woman by Stephen Pearl Andrews* (Weston, MA: M & S, 1889, 1975); Carl J. Guarneri, *The Utopian Alternative: Fourierism in Nineteenth-Century America* (Ithaca: Cornell University Press, 1991).

21. Exceptions include Horowitz, *Rereading Sex*; Ann Braude, *Radical Spirits: Spiritualism and Women's Rights in Nineteenth-Century America* (Boston: Beacon Press, 1989); April Haynes, *Riotous Flesh: Women, Physiology, and the Solitary Vice in Nineteenth-Century America* (Chicago: University of Chicago Press, 2015).

22. See also William Leach, *True Love and Perfect Union: The Feminist Reform of Sex and Society* (New York: Basic Books, 1980); Chris Dixon, *Perfecting the Family: Antislavery Marriages in Nineteenth-Century America* (Amherst: University of Massachusetts Press, 1997).

23. Passet notes that historians of the women's rights movement have largely ignored free love, *Sex Radicals and the Quest for Women's Equality*, 4. See Spurlock, *Free Love*, 1–2; Stanley, *From Bondage to Contract*, 2–3; Pamela Haag, *Consent: Sexual Rights and the Transformation of American Liberalism* (Ithaca: Cornell University Press, 1999), chap. 2.

24. Carroll D. Wright, *Marriage and Divorce in the United States, 1867–1886* (New York: Arno Press, 1976) (Washington, DC: Government Printing Office, 1897), 9; Basch, *Framing American Divorce*, 80, 87; Cott, *Public Vows*, 106–107.

25. Cott, *Public Vows*, 72–73; Laurel Thatcher Ulrich, *A House Full of Females: Plural Marriage and Women's Rights in Early Mormonism, 1835–1870* (New York: Knopf, 2017); Sarah Barringer Gordon, *The Mormon Question: Polygamy and Constitutional Conflict in Nineteenth-Century America* (Chapel Hill: University of North Carolina Press, 2002). Marriage reformers shared more similarities with the Latter-day Saints than they acknowledged. Like Spiritualists, the Saints viewed marriage as an eternal connection. Saints also wanted marriages to be based on mutual love, and they allowed liberal access to divorce when unions proved uncongenial. The Saints viewed plural marriage as a private, spiritual matter, opposing government efforts to intervene. The Saints, the Oneida Community, and free lovers all agreed that their alternative marital forms curtailed sexual licentiousness rather than encouraging it. Despite these similarities, their efforts to reinvent marriage had different goals. Saints' vision of marriage was communal and familial; marriage reformers, even in the Oneida Community, emphasized the individual. On the larger historical conflict between monogamy and polygamy, see Sarah M. S. Pearsall, "'Having Many Wives' in Two American Rebellions: The Politics of Households and the Radically Conservative," *American Historical Review*, 118, no. 4 (October 2013), 1001–1028.

26. Victoria C. Woodhull, *A Speech on the Principles of Social Freedom, Delivered in Steinway Hall, Monday, Nov. 20, 1871, and Music Hall, Boston, Wednesday, Jan. 3, 1872* (New York: Woodhull, Claflin, 1872), 34. Historians have also compared the Oneida Community to the

Mormons. See Lawrence C. Foster, *Religion and Sexuality: The Shakers, the Mormons, and the Oneida Community* (Urbana: University of Illinois Press, 1981, 1984); Louis J. Kern, *An Ordered Love: Sex Roles and Sexualities in Victorian Utopias—The Shakers, the Mormons, and the Oneida Community* (Chapel Hill: University of North Carolina Press, 1981).

27. See especially Horowitz, *Rereading Sex*, 350–357; Korobkin, *Criminal Conversations*, 57–117; Richard Wightman Fox, *Trials of Intimacy: Love and Loss in the Beecher–Tilton Scandal* (Chicago: University of Chicago Press, 1999). Fox notes that Beecher and the Tiltons also prioritized love above the law. This book places their views in a larger reform context.

28. Martha S. Jones, *All Bound Up Together: The Woman Question in African American Public Culture, 1830–1900* (Chapel Hill: University of North Carolina Press, 2007), 28; James Oliver Horton, "Freedom's Yoke: Gender Conventions Among Antebellum Free Blacks," *Feminist Studies*, 12, no. 1 (Spring 1986): 51–76.

29. Andrew Jackson Davis, *The Magic Staff; An Autobiography of Andrew Jackson Davis* (New York: J. S. Brown, 1857), 480. Robert S. Cox overemphasizes Davis's abolitionism; see *Body and Soul: A Sympathetic History of American Spiritualism* (Charlottesville: University of Virginia Press, 2003).

30. See Cott, *Public Vows*, 63–67; Quanquin, "'There Are Two Great Oceans,'" 75–104. See also Gordon, "Voluntary Motherhood"; Lewis Perry, *Childhood, Marriage, and Reform: Henry Clarke Wright, 1797–1870* (Chicago: University of Chicago Press, 1980), 233–252; Sandra F. VanBurkleo, *Belonging to the World: Women's Rights and American Constitutional Culture* (New York: Oxford University Press, 2001).

Chapter 1

1. *McDowall's Journal*, 1, no. 4 (April 1833). On the moral reform movement, see Daniel S. Wright, *"The First Causes to Our Sex": The Female Moral Reform Movement in the Antebellum Northeast, 1834–1848* (New York: Routledge, 2006); Barbara J. Berg, *The Remembered Gate: Origins of American Feminism; The Woman and the City, 1800–1860* (New York: Oxford University Press, 1978); Carroll Smith-Rosenberg, "Beauty, the Beast, and the Militant Woman: A Case Study in Sex Roles and Social Stress in Jacksonian America," in *Disorderly Conduct: Visions of Gender in Victorian America* (New York: Knopf, 1985); Barbara Meil Hobson, *Uneasy Virtue: The Politics of Prostitution and the American Reform Tradition* (New York: Basic Books, 1987); Lori D. Ginzberg, *Women and the Work of Benevolence: Morality, Politics and Class in the 19th-Century U.S.* (New Haven: Yale University Press, 1990), 19–24, 77–78; Pamela Haag, *Consent: Sexual Rights and the Transformation of American Liberalism* (Ithaca: Cornell University Press, 1999), chap. 1.

2. *McDowall's Journal*, 1, no. 1 (January 1833).

3. American Society for Promoting the Observance of the Seventh Commandment, October 25, 1833; see also *Journal of Public Morals*, 1, no. 2 (June 1, 1836).

4. *McDowall's Journal*, 1, no. 10 (October 1833), and 1, no. 4 (April 1833).

5. *Journal of Public Morals*, 1, no. 1 (May 1, 1836).

6. Bertram Wyatt-Brown, *Lewis Tappan and the Evangelical War Against Slavery* (Baton Rouge: Louisiana State University Press, 1969, 1997), 70–71.

7. Timothy J. Gilfoyle, *City of Eros: New York City, Prostitution, and the Commercialization of Sex, 1790–1920* (New York: W. W. Norton, 1992); Clare A. Lyons, *Sex Among the Rabble: An Intimate History of Gender and Power in the Age of Revolution, Philadelphia, 1730–1830* (Chapel Hill: University of North Carolina Press, 2006).

8. *McDowall's Journal*, 1, no. 1 (January 1833).

9. *McDowall's Journal—Extra* (December 1833), and 1, no. 9 (Sept. 1833). Berg, *Remembered Gate*, 182.

10. John W. Kuykendall, "Martyr to the Seventh Commandment: John R. McDowall," *Journal of Presbyterian History*, 50, no. 4 (Winter 1972): 303.

11. *Advocate of Moral Reform*, June 1, 1837; *New York Evangelist*, May 29, 1841.

12. *Advocate of Moral Reform*, December 15, 1837. On moral reform strategies, see Berg, *Remembered Gate*; Smith-Rosenberg, "Beauty, the Beast, and the Militant Woman."

13. *Journal of Public Morals*,1, no. 2 (June 1, 1836); 1, no. 2 (May 1, 1836). Patricia Cline Cohen, *The Murder of Helen Jewett* (New York: Vintage Books, 1998), 313–315. The *Journal's* estimated population of prostitutes is probably based on John McDowall's estimate of 10,000 in New York City. Cline Cohen cites a report by officers of the City Watch that underestimated the number at 1,438. Historian Timothy Gilfoyle suggests between 5 and 10 percent of women aged fifteen to thirty-five had been prostitutes, or about 3,500. Cline Cohen, *Helen Jewett*, 71–72; Gilfoyle, *City of Eros*, 57–59.

14. *Journal of Public Morals* 1, no. 2 (June 1, 1836).

15. "Ohio Anti-Slavery Society," *The Philanthropist*, June 22, 1842.

16. *The Abrogation of the Seventh Commandment by the American Churches* (New York: David Ruggles, 1835), 3, 4. Graham Russell Gao Hodges, *David Ruggles: A Radical Black Abolitionist and the Underground Railroad in New York City* (Chapel Hill: University of North Carolina Press, 2010), 79–83; Carol Lasser, "Voyeuristic Abolitionism: Sex, Gender, and the Transformation of Anti-Slavery Rhetoric," *Journal of the Early Republic*, 28 (Spring 2008): 83–114; April Haynes, *Riotous Flesh: Gender, Race, and the Solitary Vice in Antebellum Physiology* (Chicago: University of Chicago Press, 2015).

17. *Abrogation of the Seventh Commandment*, 13, 6.

18. *Abrogation of the Seventh Commandment*, 9, 15–16.

19. *Abrogation of the Seventh Commandment*, 19.

20. *Advocate of Moral Reform*, May 1, 1837; Haynes, *Riotous Flesh*, 59–71; Margaret Washington, *Sojourner Truth's America* (Urbana: University of Illinois Press, 2009), 89–93. For stereotypes of African American women, see especially Deborah Gray White, *Ar'n't I a Woman? Female Slaves in the Plantation South* (New York: W. W. Norton, 1997); Martha S. Jones, *All Bound Up Together: The Woman Question in African American Public Culture* (Chapel Hill: University of North Carolina Press, 2007), 17–18.

21. *Advocate of Moral Reform*, June 1, 1838.

22. *Advocate of Moral Reform*, June 1, 1838. While historians of moral reform discuss the petition campaign against seduction, they neglect the simultaneous drive to criminalize adultery. Under common law, both seduction and adultery were also civil wrongs, and grounds for lawsuits seeking monetary damages. See Haag, *Consent*, 3–6; Jane E. Larson, "Women Understand So Little, They Call My Good Nature 'Deceit': A Feminist Rethinking of Seduction," *Columbia Law Review*, 93, no. 2 (March 1993): 374–472; Laura Hanft Korobkin, *Criminal Conversations: Sentimentality and Nineteenth-Century Legal Stories of Adultery* (New York: Columbia University Press, 1998), 20–26.

23. *Advocate of Moral Reform*, October 1, 1838. Susan Zaeske, *Signatures of Citizenship: Petitioning, Antislavery, and Women's Political Identity* (Chapel Hill: University of North Carolina Press, 2003).

24. "No. 68, in Senate, March 13, 1847," *Documents of the Senate of the State of New York, Seventieth Session, 1847* (Albany: Charles Van Benthuysen, 1847), 12–14.

25. *Advocate of Moral Reform*, January 15, 1839; "Importance of Petitions," *Advocate of Moral Reform*, November 15, 1838.

26. Wright, *Female Moral Reform Movement*, 150; Hobson, *Uneasy Virtue*, 67–69. On Wisconsin, see *The Trial of Sherman M. Booth for Seduction [. . .]* (Milwaukee: Wm. E. Tunis, 1859), 118.

27. On economic motivation see Gilfoyle, *City of Eros*, 59. On moral reformers' view of male sexuality see Ginzberg, *Women and the Work of Benevolence*, 20–21.

28. *Journal of Public Morals*, 1, no. 1 (May 1, 1836). Smith-Rosenberg, "Beauty, the Beast, and the Militant Woman," 113–116.

29. Patricia Cline Cohen, Timothy J. Gilfoyle, and Helen Lefkowitz Horowitz, *The Flash Press: Sporting Male Weeklies in 1840s New York* (Chicago: University of Chicago Press, 2008), 147–152.

30. For example, *Advocate of Moral Reform*, March 1, 1840. A petition from the Quaker antislavery stronghold of Farmington, New York, met with more success; see *Advocate*, July 15, 1839.

31. *Albany and New York Switch*, January 18, 1845; see also *The Flash*, October 30, 1841.

32. "Crimes About to Be Made Criminal," *New York Evangelist*, March 30, 1843; "American Female Moral Reform Society," *New York Evangelist*, May 29, 1841; Wright, *Female Moral Reform Movement*,151–154; Haag, *Consent*, 16.

33. "No. 68, in Senate, March 13, 1847," *Documents of the Senate*, 1, 4, 9, 11. David M. Turner, *Fashioning Adultery: Gender, Sex, and Civility in England, 1660–1740* (New York: Cambridge University Press, 2004), 4–5.

34. *Documents of the Senate*, 15, 16–17, 19.

35. *Documents of the Senate*, 24–25.

36. Wright, *Female Moral Reform Movement*, 164, chap. 6 passim; Berg, *Remembered Gate*, 211–212.

37. *Documents of the Senate*, 12. New York criminalized adultery in 1907. See Sewell Chan, "Is Adultery a Crime in New York?" *New York Times*, March 21, 2008.

Chapter 2

1. In 1865–66, George Cragin published his "Story of a Life" in a series in the *Circular*, the newspaper published by the Oneida Community. (See, for example, "Story of a Life, XLVI," *Circular*, March 19, 1866.) English journalist William Hepworth Dixon excerpted it extensively in his two-volume *Spiritual Wives* (London: Hurst and Blackett, 1868). John Humphrey Noyes describes Dixon's excerpts as "without much alteration" (Noyes, "Dixon and His Copyists," *Circular*, December 26, 1870). Dixon summarized and editorialized between passages, but his extensive excerpts are indeed unedited. Dixon, *Spiritual Wives*, 2: 90–95; George Cragin, "The Free Church of Old Time, No. 3," *Free Church Circular*, March 26, 1850; "The Last Voyage of the *Rebecca Ford*," *The Quadrangle*, April/May 1914 (typescript), George Cragin File, Box 44, Oneida Community Collection, Syracuse University [hereafter cited as Oneida Community Collection]. Though many historians of the Oneida Community mention George and Mary Cragin, none discuss their romance and marriage in detail, or recount the founding of the Oneida Community from their perspective. For example, Lawrence Foster,

Religion and Sexuality: The Shakers, the Mormons, and the Oneida Community (Urbana: University of Illinois Press, 1981, 1984), 93; Spencer Klaw, *Without Sin: The Life and Death of the Oneida Community* (New York: Penguin, 1993), 49; Ellen Wayland-Smith, *Oneida: From Free Love Utopia to the Well-Set Table* (New York: Picador, 2016), 32–33, 58–59; Anthony Wonderley, *Oneida Utopia: A Community Searching for Human Happiness and Prosperity* (Ithaca: Cornell University Press, 2017), 32–33, 46.

2. Dixon, *Spiritual Wives*, 2: 100; George Cragin, "Story of A Life," *Circular*, May 15, 1865.

3. George Cragin, "Story of a Life," *Circular*, May 15, 1865.

4. George Cragin, "Story of a Life, XVIII," *Circular*, June 19, 1865; Dixon, *Spiritual Wives*, 2: 89–90, 103–106.

5. George Cragin, "Story of a Life, XXVIII," *Circular*, Sept. 4, 1865.

6. *Advocate of Moral Reform*, January 1, 1837, and May 1, 1837; Dixon, *Spiritual Wives*, 2: 107–108.

7. George Cragin, "Story of a Life, XXIV," *Circular*, August 7, 1865; Cragin, "Story of a Life, XXXVII," *Circular*, December 4, 1865.

8. George Wallingford Noyes, ed., *Religious Experience of John Humphrey Noyes* (New York: Macmilllan, 1923), 127, 134–35; on Latourette and Truth see Margaret Washington, *Sojourner Truth's America* (Urbana: University of Illinois Press, 2009), 85–86; Nell Irvin Painter, *Sojourner Truth: A Life, a Symbol* (New York: W. W. Norton, 1996), 39–41.

9. Noyes, *Religious Experience of John Humphrey Noyes*, 137, 139. See also Foster, *Religion and Sexuality*, 78, chap. 3 passim.

10. Noyes, *Religious Experience of John Humphrey Noyes*, 140–143, 147.

11. A short but useful discussion of perfectionism is Neil Brody Miller, "Perfectionism," in Peter Hinks and John McKivigan, eds., *Encyclopedia of Antislavery and Abolition*, vol. 2 (Westport, CT: Greenwood Press, 2007), 527–529.

12. "Letter from Mrs. H. C. Green," *The Witness*, January 23, 1839; George Wallingford Noyes, ed., *John Humphrey Noyes, the Putney Community* (Oneida, NY: 1931), 35; George Cragin, "Story of a Life, XXXVII," *Circular*, December 4, 1865. Anne M. Boylan, *The Origins of Women's Activism: New York and Boston, 1797–1840* (Chapel Hill: University of North Carolina Press, 2002), 44–45.

13. "Letter from Wm. Green Jr.," *The Witness*, January 23, 1839. On William Green Jr. see Bertram Wyatt-Brown, *Lewis Tappan and the Evangelical War Against Slavery* (Baton Rouge: Louisiana State University Press, 1969, 1997), 112, 116, 118, 142.

14. *Advocate of Moral Reform*, December 15, 1837. See also George Cragin, "Story of a Life, XXXVII," *Circular*, December 4, 1865.

15. Noyes, *Putney Community*, 7–8; George Cragin, "Story of a Life, XXXVII," *Circular*, December 4, 1865.

16. Noyes, *Putney Community*, 17–18, 20.

17. George Cragin, "Story of a Life, XLII," *Circular*, January 8, 1866; Cragin, "Story of a Life, XLII," January 15, 1866; Dixon, 2: 116, 114–115, 118; Noyes, *Putney Community*, 36, 3; Foster, *Religion and Sexuality*, 81–82. The *Advocate of Moral Reform* removed George Cragin's name from its masthead as of December 1, 1839.

18. Cragin, "Story of a Life, XLIV," *Circular*, February 26, 1866; Dixon, *Spiritual Wives*, 2: 122.

19. Cragin, "Story of a Life, XLIV," *Circular*, February 26, 1866; Dixon, *Spiritual Wives*, 2: 124, 153, 144; Noyes, *Putney Community*, 38, 41.

20. Cragin, "Story of a Life, XLV," *Circular*, March 5, 1866.

21. Cragin, "Story of a Life, XLVI," *Circular*, March 19, 1866; Noyes, *Putney Community*, 44; Dixon, *Spiritual Wives*, 2: 146, 159, 172.

22. Cragin, "Story of a Life, XLVII," *Circular*, March 26, 1866; Dixon, *Spiritual Wives*, 2: 146; Noyes, *Putney Community*, 43.

23. Cragin, "Supplementary Chapter to the 'Story of a Life,' " *Circular*, July 30, 1866.

24. Noyes, *Putney Community*, 51, 53, 126, 194.

25. Noyes, *Putney Community*, 117, 120, 197–198, 201–202. See also Foster, *Religion and Sexuality*, 100–101; Klaw, *Without Sin*, 59–62.

26. Noyes, *Putney Community*, 209.

27. Noyes, *Putney Community*, 237.

28. Noyes, *Putney Community*, 317–318, 282–283, 301–302.

29. Noyes, *Putney Community*, 320, 342. Klaw, *Without Sin*, 68.

30. Mary Cragin to Brother Worden, March 2, 1850, Mary Cragin Folder, Box 44, Oneida Community Collection.

31. *First Annual Report of the Oneida Association; Exhibiting Its History, Principles, and Transactions to January 1, 1849* (Oneida Reserve: Leonard, 1849), 25.

32. *First Annual Report of the Oneida Association*, 19; Noyes, *Putney Community*, 386, 387, 393.

Chapter 3

1. George Wallingford Noyes, ed., *John Humphrey Noyes, the Putney Community* (Oneida, NY: 1931), 151.

2. For recent studies of the Oneida Community, see Spencer Klaw, *Without Sin: The Life and Death of the Oneida Community* (New York: Penguin, 1993); Ellen Wayland-Smith, *Oneida: From Free Love Utopia to the Well-Set Table* (New York: Picador, 2016); Anthony Wonderley, *Oneida Utopia: A Community Searching for Human Happiness and Prosperity* (Ithaca: Cornell University Press, 2017). On Noyes's views of birth control, see John Humphrey Noyes, *Male Continence* (Oneida, NY: Oneida Community, 1872).

3. The tumultuous relationship between Tryphena Hubbard and Henry Seymour is featured in an unofficial history of the Oneida Community based on original records, letters, and diaries. See Lawrence Foster and George Wallingford Noyes, eds., *Free Love in Utopia: John Humphrey Noyes and the Origin of the Oneida Community* (Urbana: University of Illinois Press, 2001), chaps. 16, 23, 27, 28. In his introduction to the volume, Foster notes the difficulty of implementing complex marriage and the significance of the Hubbard case to this process, x, xii, xxviii–xxx. See also Wonderley, *Oneida Utopia*, 72–74.

4. Biographical data for Henry Seymour and other early members is available in the Oneida Association Family Register, 1849, Box 7; for Henry Seymour's recollections, see Skaneateles Folder, Box 60, Oneida Community Collection.

5. Oneida Association Family Register, 1849, Box 7, Oneida Community Collection.

6. Foster and Noyes, *Free Love in Utopia*, 28–29, 94–97.

7. Foster and Noyes, 260–262.

8. Foster and Noyes, xxix. There are certainly other examples of members whose sexual desires could not be controlled by Noyes. For example, George Cragin to Brother Worden, March 8, 1851, George Cragin Letters, Box 44, Oneida Community Collection.

9. Foster and Noyes, *Free Love in Utopia*, 137, 139, 140–141, 142.

10. Foster and Noyes, 142. I have not been able to document the Seymours' divorce, but it did occur. See Foster and Noyes, 179.

11. Ellen Dwyer, *Homes for the Mad: Life Inside Two Nineteenth-Century Asylums* (New Brunswick, NJ: Rutgers University Press, 1987), 2, 11, 13, 15, 25, 59, 63, 86, 96, 102, 109–110. Dumping unwanted wives in insane asylums was the stuff of fiction, as, for example, the character Mary Leon in Fanny Fern's *Ruth Hall* (1854).

12. *New York Observer and Chronicle*, January 22, 1852; *First Annual Report of the Oneida Association* (Oneida: Leonard, 1849); see also Foster and Noyes, *Free Love in Utopia*, 146–147.

13. "The Past, Present, and Future," *Circular*, March 7, 1852.

14. "Two Kinds of Adultery," in Foster and Noyes, *Free Love in Utopia*, 156–157. Other marriage reformers also used this biblical example, including Thomas L. Nichols and Mary Gove Nichols. See T. L. Nichols and Mary S. Gove Nichols, *Marriage: Its History, Character, and Results; Its Sanctities, and Its Profanities; Its Science and Its Facts. Demonstrating Its Influence as a Civilized Institution, on the Happiness of the Individual and the Progress of the Race* (Cincinnati: Valentine Nicholson, 1854), 43.

15. Foster and Noyes, *Free Love in Utopia*, 187–191.

16. "Theocratic Platform," *Circular*, August 29, 1852.

17. Tryphena Seymour to Marcus L. Worden, December 1, 1861, and January 19, 1862, Tryphena Seymour Folder, Box 73, Oneida Community Collection.

18. Henry J. Seymour, "Letter to the *Outlook*," February 11, 1903, 10; Seymour, "Oneida Community: A Dialogue," 5–7, Special Collections, Syracuse University.

19. Foster and Noyes, *Free Love in Utopia*, 30, xxvii, xxxv.

20. Foster and Noyes, 115, 118.

21. Oneida Family Register, Box 7, Oneida Community Collection.

22. "The Last Voyage of the *Rebecca Ford*," typescript, *The Quadrangle*, April/May 1914, George Cragin File, Box 44, Oneida Community Collection. See also Foster and Noyes, *Free Love in Utopia*, chap. 18.

23. Foster and Noyes, 105, 113.

24. Foster and Noyes, 123–124, 128. On spiritualism, see especially Ann Braude, *Radical Spirits: Spiritualism and Women's Rights in Nineteenth-Century America* (Boston: Beacon Press, 1989).

25. *Circular*, January 18, 1852.

26. "Further Remarks on M.E.C.'s Experience," *Circular*, January 18, 1852.

27. Amy Dru Stanley, *From Bondage to Contract: Wage Labor, Marriage, and the Market in the Age of Slave Emancipation* (New York: Cambridge University Press, 1998), 24; On the marriages of enslaved men and women, see Tera Hunter, *Bound in Wedlock: Slave and Free Black Marriage in the Nineteenth Century* (Cambridge, MA; Belknap Press of Harvard University Press, 2017).

28. This pamphlet was also reprinted in *Bible Communism: A Compilation of the Annual Reports and Other Publications of the Oneida Association and Its Branches* (Brooklyn, NY: Office of the *Circular*, 1853), 5–18; Carl J. Guarneri, *The Utopian Alternative: Fourierism in Nineteenth-Century America* (Ithaca: Cornell University Press, 1991), chap. 9.

29. John Humphrey Noyes, *Slavery and Marriage: A Dialogue* (1850), 4, 6, 7.

30. Noyes, *Slavery and Marriage*, 7, 9, 10, 11.

31. Noyes, *Slavery and Marriage*, 12–13, 14.

32. Noyes, *Slavery and Marriage*, 8, 9; Noyes, *Putney Community*, 368.

Chapter 4

1. George Wallingford Noyes, ed., *John Humphrey Noyes, the Putney Community* (Oneida, NY: 1931), 168. See also John Humphrey Noyes, *History of American Socialisms* (Philadelphia: J. B. Lippincott, 1870) 27, 631; Carl J. Guarneri, *The Utopian Alternative: Fourierism in Nineteenth-Century America* (Ithaca: Cornell University Press, 1991); Sterling F. Delano, *Brook Farm: The Dark Side of Utopia* (Cambridge, MA: Belknap Press of Harvard University Press, 2004).

2. On the interconnection between religious and secular in early American history, see John Lardas Modern, *Secularism in Antebellum America With Reference to Ghosts, Protestant Subcultures, Machines, and their Metaphors* (Chicago: University of Chicago Press, 2011). John C. Spurlock notes the prevalence of marriage among free lovers in *Free Love: Marriage and Middle-Class Radicalism in America, 1825–1860* (New York: New York University Press, 1988). Helen Lefkowitz Horowitz identifies the radicals with an emerging belief that sex was "at the center of life" in *Rereading Sex: Battles over Sexual Knowledge and Suppression in Nineteenth-Century America* (New York: Vintage, 2002), 251, 252, 268–269.

3. Stephen Pearl Andrews published the exchange in book form in 1853, and an 1886 edition (with additional materials) is included in Stephen Pearl Andrews, *Love, Marriage, and Divorce, and the Sovereignty of the Individual: A Discussion Between Henry James, Horace Greeley, and Stephen Pearl Andrews, and a Hitherto Unpublished Manuscript, Love, Marriage, and the Condition of Women* (Weston, MA: M & S Press, 1975), 36; Lawrence Foster and George Wallingford Noyes, eds., *Free Love in Utopia: John Humphrey Noyes and the Origin of the Oneida Community* (Urbana: University of Illinois Press, 2001), 92, 71; Adam Tuchinsky, *Horace Greeley's* New-York Tribune*: Civil War-Era Socialism and the Crisis of Free Labor* (Ithaca: Cornell University Press, 2009), chap. 4.

4. Andrews, *Love, Marriage, and Divorce*, 31, 33, 43, 45, 49.

5. Guarneri, 2–3, 17–18, 33, 88–89, 94–96.

6. Andrews, *Love, Marriage, and Divorce, and the Sovereignty of the Individual*, 13.

7. Guarneri, *The Utopian Alternative*, 2–3, 17–18, 33, 88–89, 94–96; Marx Edgeworth Lazarus, *Love vs. Marriage* (New York: Fowler and Wells, 1852), 235, quoted in T. L. Nichols and Mary S. Gove Nichols, *Marriage: Its History, Character, and Results; Its Sanctities, and Its Profanities; Its Science and Its Facts. Demonstrating Its Influence as a Civilized Institution, on the Happiness of the Individual and the Progress of the Race* (Cincinnati: Valentine Nicholson, 1854), 172–173; Warren Chase, *The Life-Line of the Lone One; Or, Autobiography of the World's Child* (Boston: Bela Marsh, 1857), 123, 126.

8. Madeline B. Stern, *The Pantarch: A Biography of Stephen Pearl Andrews* (Austin: University of Texas Press, 1968), 152–153. Biographical information is available in Andrews's (partially destroyed) manuscript autobiography and a typed biography, Box 2, Stephen Pearl Andrews Papers, U.S. Mss. 19A, Wisconsin Historical Society [hereafter cited as Andrews Papers]. See also Spurlock, *Free Love*, chap. 6.

9. Andrews, manuscript autobiography, Andrews Papers.

10. Andrews, manuscript autobiography, Andrews Papers.

11. William S. Andrews, "Sketch of the Life of Stephen Pearl Andrews," *Woodhull and Claflin's Weekly*, December 9, 1871. Spurlock argues that the marriages of Stephen Pearl Andrews and other free lovers enabled them to assert "that they remained faithful out of love rather than coercion. For them, free love was an expression of the highest ideal of middle-class marriage." Spurlock, *Free Love*, 137.

12. Typed biography, Andrews Papers; Stern, The *Pantarch,* 38, 48–52, 55.

13. S. P. Andrews and August F. Boyle, *The Complete Phonographic Class-Book, Containing a Strictly Inductive Exposition of Pitman's Phonography,* eighth edition (New York: Andrews and Boyle, 1847), 6. Stern, *The Pantarch,* 58–64.

14. Typed biography, Andrews Papers.

15. Foster and Noyes, *Free Love in Utopia,* 24, 74; Guarneri, *The Utopian Alternative,* 286–287; J. A. Parkhurst, "Henry M. Parkhurst," *Popular Astronomy,* 16 (1908): 231–232. On Marie Stevens Howland see Robert S. Fogarty, "The Familistere: Radical Reform through Cooperative Enterprise," an introduction to Marie Howland, *The Familistere: A Novel* (Philadelphia: Porcupine Press, 1874, 1975), 1; Holly Blake. "Howland, Marie"; http://www.anb.org .libezproxy2.syr.edu/articles/15/15–00351.html; *American National Biography Online* February 2000. (Access Date: January 26, 2015).

16. "Obituary Notes," *New York Sun,* June 19, 1898; "Edward F. Underhill Dead," *New York Times,* June 19, 1898; "Autobiography of Theron C. Leland," *Browne's Phonographic Monthly* (December 1877): 202, 203–204. Judith Wellman, *The Road to Seneca Falls: Elizabeth Cady Stanton and the First Woman's Rights Convention* (Urbana: University of Illinois Press, 2004), 74.

17. "Declaration of Sentiments" is available at https://www.nps.gov/wori/learn/history culture/declaration-of-sentiments.htm. For more on Underhill see, Margaret Moore Booker, *Edward Fitch Underhill: Renaissance Man of Siasconset* (Nantucket: Nantucket Historical Association, 2014). I shared with Booker some of my early research, presented as "Curious Connections: Free Love, Feminism and Phonography" (Society for Historians of the Early American Republic conference, 2012). Some of this research is also found in chap. 7. See email correspondence between Carol Faulkner and Margaret Moore Booker, November 27–28, 2012, in possession of the author.

18. Josiah Warren, *Practical Details in Equitable Commerce, With a Preface by Stephen Pearl Andrews* (New York: Fowler and Wells, 1854), vi–viii; Roger Wunderlich, *Low Living and High Thinking at Modern Times, New York* (Syracuse: Syracuse University Press, 1992), 2, 3, 10, 15, 27, 69, 78, 101 and entire. See also Spurlock, *Free Love,* chap. 4.

19. Moncure Conway, "Modern Times, New York," in Taylor Stoehr, *Free Love in America: A Documentary History* (New York: AMS Press, 1979), 435; Wunderlich, *Low Living and High Thinking,* 60, 64, 73, 75–76, 86.

20. Wunderlich, *Low Living and High Thinking,* 53, 82.

21. Lazarus, *Love vs. Marriage,* 27, 180; Andrews, *Love, Marriage, and Divorce,* 14, 30, 40. Tuchinsky, *Horace Greeley's* New-York Tribune, 114–119.

22. Andrews, *Love, Marriage, and Divorce,* 43, 44, 47, 49. In 1851, Andrews had published similar arguments in *The Science of Society: The Constitution of Government in the Sovereignty of the Individual* (New York: Fowler and Wells, 1852).

23. Andrews, *Love, Marriage, and Divorce,* 55.

24. Andrews, *Love, Marriage, and Divorce,* 4, 6.

25. Though the adultery metaphor had appeared occasionally before 1850, its use grew among marriage reformers in the decade of the 1850s. Andrew Jackson Davis, who will be discussed in the next chapter, used the metaphor of "legalized adultery" three years before Andrews in "What Is the Philosophy of True Marriage?" *Spirit Messenger,* December 21, 1850.

26. Andrews, *Love, Marriage and Divorce,* 69, 71, 72. See also Nichols and Nichols, *Marriage,* 196–198, 205, chap. 17. On Mary Gove Nichols see Jean L. Silver-Isenstadt, *Shameless:*

The Visionary Life of Mary Gove Nichols (Baltimore: Johns Hopkins University Press, 2002); Patricia Cline Cohen, "The 'Anti-Marriage Theory' of Thomas and Mary Gove Nichols: A Radical Critique of Monogamy in the 1850s," *Journal of the Early Republic*, 34, no. 1 (Spring 2014): 1–20.

27. "S. P. Andrews and the Tribune," *Circular*, January 29, 1853; "Matter for Discussion," *Circular*, May 14, 1853.

28. Noyes, *History of American Socialisms*, 93; Stern, 84–85.

29. Stephen Pearl Andrews, "Love, Marriage, and the Condition of Women," manuscript, Andrews Papers. The scholar Charles Shively published this manuscript, which he believes was written in the early 1850s, in its entirety at the end of his 1975 reprint of Andrews, *Love, Marriage, and Divorce*. See especially 12, 38–40, 47.

30. Andrews, "Love, Marriage, and the Condition of Women," in *Love, Marriage, and Divorce*, 11, 54.

31. Andrews, "Love, Marriage, and the Condition of Women," in *Love, Marriage, and Divorce*, 3, 8, 9.

32. William S. Andrews, "Sketch of the Life of Stephen Pearl Andrews," *Woodhull and Claflin's Weekly*, Dec. 9, 1871; Frances Rose MacKinley, "In Memoriam," *Woodhull and Claflin's Weekly*, May 20, 1871.

33. Letter fragment, Williams S. Andrews to Isabella Beecher Hooker, December 1871, Andrews Papers; Andrews, "Love, Marriage, and the Condition of Women," in *Love, Marriage, and Divorce*, 8; Stern, *The Pantarch*, 92–93, 118–119.

Chapter 5

1. *New York Tribune*, November 26, 1856. Mary Fenn Davis bridges the suffrage-free love divide described by Linda Gordon, "Voluntary Motherhood: The Beginnings of Feminist Birth Control in the United States," *Feminist Studies*, 1, nos. 3–4 (Spring 1973): 5–22. See also Joanne Passet, *Sex Radicals and the Quest for Women's Equality* (Urbana: University of Illinois Press, 2003), 1.

2. On the legal and cultural standard of marital unity, see Nancy F. Cott, *Public Vows: A History of Marriage and the Nation* (Cambridge, MA: Harvard University Press, 2000), 3, 5, 10–11; Hendrik Hartog, *Man and Wife in America: A History* (Cambridge, MA: Harvard University Press, 2000), 105–108. On the centrality of love to nineteenth-century marriage, see Karen Lystra, *Searching the Heart: Women, Men, and Romantic Love in Nineteenth-Century America* (New York: Oxford University Press, 1989), 28, 9, 60, chap. 7.

3. Andrew Jackson Davis, "What Is the Philosophy of True Marriage?" *Spirit Messenger*, December 21, 1850.

4. Anne Braude, *Radical Spirits: Spiritualism and Women's Rights in Nineteenth-Century America* (Boston: Beacon Press, 1989), 3, 117–119, 135–136.

5. Lucretia Mott, *Discourse on Woman* (Philadelphia: T. B. Peterson, 1850); Mary Fenn's first appearance at a women's rights meeting was in 1853; see Elizabeth Cady Stanton, Susan B. Anthony, and Matilda Joslyn Gage, eds., *History of Woman Suffrage*, vol. 1, *1848–1861* (New York: Fowler and Wells, 1881), 587.

6. T .L. Nichols and Mary S. Gove Nichols, *Marriage: Its History, Character, and Results; Its Sanctities, and Its Profanities; Its Science and Its Facts. Demonstrating Its Influence as a Civilized Institution, on the Happiness of the Individual and the Progress of the Race* (Cincinnati: Valentine Nicholson, 1854), 117.

7. Elizabeth Cady Stanton to Susan B. Anthony, March 1, 1852, and Lucy Stone to Elizabeth Cady Stanton, August 14, 1853, in Ann Gordon, ed., *The Selected Papers of Elizabeth Cady Stanton and Susan B. Anthony*, vol. 1 (New Brunswick: Rutgers University Press, 1998), 195, 224. See also Cott, *Public Vows*, 66–67; Norma Basch, *Framing American Divorce: From the Revolutionary Generation to the Victorians* (Berkeley: University of California Press, 1999), chap. 3; Amy Dru Stanley, *From Bondage to Contract: Wage Labor, Marriage, and the Market in the Age of Slave Emancipation* (New York: Cambridge University Press, 1998); Ellen Carol Dubois, " 'The Pivot of the Marriage Relation': Stanton's Analysis of Women's Subordination in Marriage," in Dubois and Richard Candida Smith, eds., *Elizabeth Cady Stanton: Feminist as Thinker* (New York: New York University Press, 2007), chap. 5.

8. Andrew Jackson Davis, *The Magic Staff; An Autobiography of Andrew Jackson Davis* (New York: J. S. Brown, 1857), 494.

9. Davis, *The Magic Staff*, 491, 481. Warren Chase also claimed to have counseled the Loves, and encouraged Mary to take up a career as a lecturer. See Chase, *The Life-Line of the Lone One; Or, Autobiography of the World's Child* (Boston: Bela Marsh, 1857), 205–6.

10. Davis, *The Magic Staff*, 494, 518. Glenda Riley, *Divorce: An American Tradition* (New York: Oxford University Press, 1991), 62–66; Norma Basch, *Framing American Divorce*, 58; Hartog, *Man and Wife in America*, 265; Carroll D. Wright, *Marriage and Divorce in the United States, 1867–1886* (New York: Arno Press, 1976) (Washington: Government Printing Office, 1897), 81, 95.

11. Davis, *The Magic Staff*, 494.

12. Davis, *The Magic Staff*, 434, 498, 502. On his marriage to Catherine DeWolf, see also Davis to William Green Jr., July 10, 1848, Andrew Jackson Davis Papers, Yale Manuscripts and Archives, MS 677 (hereafter cited as Davis Papers).

13. Davis, *The Magic Staff*, 539, 540, 542.

14. Davis, *The Magic Staff*, 498–499. On Swedenborg's influence, see also Marx Edgeworth Lazarus, *Love vs. Marriage* (New York: Fowler and Wells, 1852), 210, 212.

15. Davis to William Green Jr., December 18, 1854, Davis Papers. For this criticism of Davis, see William Hepworth Dixon, *Spiritual Wives* (London: Hurst and Blackett, 1868), 2: 239–240; John B. Ellis, *Free Love and Its Votaries; Or, American Socialism Unmasked* (New York: United States Publishing, 1870), 406. For another accusation of plagiarism, see Davis, *The Magic Staff*, 453.

16. Davis to William Green Jr., February 17, 1855, Davis Papers.

17. Davis, *The Magic Staff*, 546–547.

18. Davis, *The Magic Staff*, 550–551.

19. Davis, *The Magic Staff*, 552. The Erie County, New York, Clerk's Office does not seem to have a copy of this decree. Email to the author from Patricia L. Fulwiller, Erie County Clerk's Office, January 1, 2014.

20. Andrew Jackson Davis, *The Great Harmonia*, vol. 4 (Boston: Colby & Rich, 1884, eighth edition), 306, 421.

21. Davis, *The Great Harmonia*, 4: 422; Andrew Jackson Davis, *The Genesis and Ethics of Conjugal Love* (New York: A. J. Davis Progressive Publishing House, 1874), 3, 52–53; Hartog, *Man and Wife*, 64.

22. Davis to William Green Jr., February 17, 1855, Davis Papers.

23. Mary Fenn Davis to William Green Jr., March 25, 1855, Davis Papers.

24. Andrew Jackson Davis to William Green Jr., October 27, 1857, see also letters dated September 25, 1855; August 26, 1856; September 19, 1857, Davis Papers.

25. Davis, *The Magic Staff*, 529; Davis to William Green Jr., February 17, 1855, Davis Papers.

26. "The 'Friends of Human Progress,'" *Liberator*, June 19, 1857.

27. Susan B. Anthony to Elizabeth Cady Stanton, September 29, 1857, in Gordon, 1: 354.

28. For discussion of other sex and marriage advice books, see Ronald G. Walters, *Primers for Prudery: Sexual Advice to Victorian America* (Englewood Cliffs, NJ: Prentice-Hall, 1974); Lystra, *Searching the Heart*, 101–117.

29. Robert Dale Owen, *The Moral Physiology; A Treatise on Popular Questions, or Means Devised to Check Pregnancy* (New York: 1836), v, 24, 40–1, 74. Noyes discussed Owen in his "Bible Argument," see *First Annual Report of the Oneida Association* (Oneida Reserve: Leonard, 1849), 17, 31–33.

30. Richard William Leopold, *Robert Dale Owen: A Biography* (Cambridge, MA: Harvard University Press, 1940), 155; Hartog, *Man and Wife*, 111. For states as primary regulators of marriage, see Cott, *Public Vows*, chap. 2.

31. S. J. [Sarah Jackson], *Letters to a Young Christian* (New York: American Female Guardian Society, 1852), 54, 56, 57; Bertram Wyatt-Brown, *Lewis Tappan and the Evangelical War Against Slavery* (Baton Rouge: Louisiana State University Press, 1969, 1997), 303.

32. For example, O. S. Fowler, *Fowler on Matrimony: Or the Principles of Phrenology and Physiology Applied to the Selection of Suitable Companions for Life* (Philadelphia: 1841).

33. O. S. Fowler, *Fowler on Matrimony*, 29, 38, 40.

34. Lorenzo N. Fowler, *Marriage: Its History and Philosophy, Founded on Phrenology and Physiology* (New York: Fowler and Wells, 1848), 86, 126, 136, 137.

35. O. S. Fowler, *Sexual Science; Including Manhood, Womanhood, and Their Mutual Interrelations; Love Its Laws, Power, Etc.* (Philadelphia: National Publishing, 1870), 636, 664, 665. See also O. S. Fowler, *Fowler on Matrimony*, 39–40.

36. O.S. Fowler, *Sexual Science*, 631, 632; see also Lorenzo Fowler, *Marriage*, 80, 140.

37. Lewis Perry, *Childhood, Marriage, and Reform: Henry Clarke Wright, 1797–1870* (Chicago: University of Chicago Press, 1980), 233, 181–182, 186, 194–195, 242–244. Mary Fenn Davis describes reading *The Unwelcome Child* in 1858; see *Proceedings of the Free Convention held at Rutland, VT, June 25th, 26th, 27th, 1858, Phonographic Report by J. M. W. Yerrinton* (New York: S. T. Munson, 1858) (Boston: J. B. Yerrinton and Son, 1858), 123.

38. Henry Clarke Wright, "Lectures of Andrew Jackson Davis," *Liberator*, March 3, 1854.

39. Davis, "Thoughts on H. C. Wright's Last Book," *Liberator*, June 2, 1854; Perry, *Childhood, Marriage, and Reform*, 252.

40. Lorenzo Fowler, *Marriage*, 197, 192.

41. O. S. Fowler, *Love and Parentage, Applied to the Improvement of Offspring Including Important Directions and Suggestions to Lovers and the Married Concerning the Strongest Ties and the Most Momentous Relations of Life* (New York: Fowler and Wells, 1844), v, 68, 71, 73–74, 134, 136.

42. Dr. P. Beverly Randolph and Mrs. M.J. Randolph, *Human Love, in Health and in Disease, Or, The Grand Secret* (Boston: P. B. Randolph, 1860), 10, 11–12. These marriage writers also criticized abortion; see, for example, O. S. Fowler, *Love and Parentage*, 68–69; Randolph and Randolph, *Human Love*, 9–10.

43. P. B. Randolph, the "Learned Pundit," and "Man with Two Souls." His Curious Life, Works, and Career. The Great Free-Love Trial. Randolph's Grand Defense. His Address to the Jury, and Mankind. The Verdict (Boston: Randolph Publishing House, 1872), 4, 50; "The Converted Medium," New-York Daily Tribune, November 25, 1858.

44. Randolph and Randolph, Human Love, 7. "Paschal Beverly Randolph," Year: 1850; Census Place: Albion, Calhoun, Michigan; Roll: M432_348; Page: 18B; Image: 41, Ancestry.com. 1850 United States Federal Census [database online]; and Year: 1860; Census Place: Boston Ward 6, Suffolk, Massachusetts; Roll: M653_521; Page: 876; Family History Library Film: 803521, Ancestry.com. 1860 United States Federal Census [database online].

45. P. B. Randolph, 3, 4, 18. Biographer John Patrick Deveney points out Randolph's equivocation on his racial background. See Deveney, Paschal Beverly Randolph: A Nineteenth-Century Black American Spiritualist, Rosicrucian, and Sex Magician (Albany: State University of New York Press, 1997), 5–6.

46. Randolph and Randolph, Human Love, 3, 4. Though ostensibly writing with his wife, Randolph employs the first person throughout the text.

47. Randolph and Randolph, Human Love, 6–8, 10.

48. Count de St. Leon [P. B. Randolph], Love and Its Hidden History. A Book for Man, Woman, Wives, and Husbands, and for the Loving and the Unloved: The Heart-Reft, Pining Ones (Boston: William White, 1869), 24, 25, 37, 38.

49. Count de St. Leon, Love and Its Hidden History, 69.

50. Count de St. Leon, Love and Its Hidden History, 6, 22, 49.

51. "The Converted Medium," New-York Daily Tribune, November 25, 1858. On Randolph's soured relationships with free lovers, spiritualists, and abolitionists, and his marriages, see Deveney, Paschal Beverly Randolph, 7, 9, 12, 93, 102, 205–206. Elizabeth Stordeur Pyror argues that "the word nigger became a slur in conversation with black social aspiration," in "The Etymology of Nigger: Resistance, Language, and the Politics of Freedom in the Antebellum North," Journal of the Early Republic, 36, no. 2 (Summer 2016): 205. In his exposé of spiritualism, B. F. Hatch called Randolph "true and honorable" for returning to his wife; see Spiritualists' Iniquities Unmasked (New York: 1859), 14.

52. Paschal Beverly Randolph, Eulis! The History of Love: Its Wondrous Magic, Chemistry, Rules, Laws, Modes, Moods, and Rationale; Being the Third Revelation of Soul and Sex. Also, Reply to "Why Is Man Immortal?" The Solution of the Darwin Problem. An Entirely New Theory (Toledo, OH: Randolph Publishing, 1874), 123. George Frederickson, The Black Image in the White Mind: The Debate on Afro-American Character and Destiny, 1817–1914 (Middletown, CT: Wesleyan University Press, 1987), chap. 4. For other African Americans who also celebrated distinct differences to challenge the racism of American society, see Mia Bay, The White Image in the Black Mind: African-American Ideas About White People, 1830–1925 (New York: Oxford University Press, 2000), 71–72, 195.

53. Nichols and Nichols, Marriage, iii, 16, 22.

54. Nichols and Nichols, Marriage, 197, 300, 399. Adin Ballou, the founder of the Hopedale Community in Massachusetts, published a rebuttal of the Nicholses' book; see Adin Ballou, True Love vs. Free Love: Testimony of a True Hearted Woman (Hopedale Press, 1855), 7–8. Patricia Cline Cohen, "The 'Anti-Marriage Theory' of Thomas and Mary Gove Nichols: A Radical Critique of Monogamy in the 1850s," Journal of the Early Republic, 34, no. 1 (Spring 2014): 1–20.

55. Thomas L. Nichols, *Esoteric Anthropology, A Comprehensive and Confidential Treatise on the Structure, Functions, Passional Attractions and Perversions, True and False Physical and Social Conditions, and the Most Intimate Relations of Men and Women* (New York: 1854), 171–174, 191–193, 200. Nichols was not alone in his misinterpretation of women's fertility, see Gordon, "Voluntary Motherhood," 9; Andrea Tone, *Devices and Desires: A History of Contraception in America* (New York: Hill and Wang, 2001), 43.

Chapter 6

1. Scholars have tended to emphasize successful reform unions over more troubled ones. For example, Chris Dixon, *Perfecting the Family: Antislavery Marriages in Nineteenth-Century America* (Amherst: University of Massachusetts Press, 1997). Some marriages began with high ideals, like those of Angelina Grimké and Theodore Dwight Weld, and Lucy Stone and Henry Blackwell, but even these couples struggled at times. See Gerda Lerner, *The Grimké Sisters from South Carolina* (Chapel Hill: University of North Carolina Press, 1967, 2004); Robert H. Abzug, *Cosmos Crumbling: American Reform and the Religious Imagination* (New York: Oxford University Press, 1994); Leslie Wheeler, ed., *Loving Warriors: Selected Letters of Lucy Stone and Henry B. Blackwell, 1853–1893* (New York: Dial, 1981); Andrea Moore Kerr, *Lucy Stone: Speaking Out for Equality* (New Brunswick: Rutgers University Press, 1992); Joelle Million, *Woman's Voice, Woman's Place: Lucy Stone and the Birth of the Woman's Rights Movement* (Westport, CT: Praeger, 2003); Sally G. McMillen, *Lucy Stone: An Unapologetic Life* (New York: Oxford University Press, 2015). Karen Lystra examines unhappy marriages among ordinary Americans in *Searching the Heart: Women, Men, and Romantic Love in Nineteenth-Century America* (New York: Oxford University Press, 1989), 206–19.

2. "A Stray Husband," *New York Daily Tribune*, March 12, 1850; William Wells Brown, "To the Public," *Liberator*, July 12, 1850; Ezra Greenspan, *William Wells Brown: An African American Life* (New York: W. W. Norton, 2014), 99, 128–129, 135–137, 176–177, 180–181, 212–214, 232–236. Charles S. S. Griffing to Friend [Samuel J.] May, March 1, 1863, Anti-Slavery Collection, Boston Public Library; Carol Faulkner, *Women's Radical Reconstruction; The Freedmen's Aid Movement* (Philadelphia: University of Pennsylvania Press, 2004), 174 n.5, 185 n. 57; Stacey M. Robertson, *Hearts Beating for Liberty: Women Abolitionists in the Old Northwest* (Chapel Hill: University of North Carolina Press, 2010), 153.

3. See letters from Mary to her mother Adaline and sister, Jane Corss, July 29, August 8, September 8, 1849, and September 28, 1849, Sherman M. Booth Family Papers, Milwaukee Manuscript Collection, Wisconsin Historical Society (hereafter cited as Booth Papers).

4. Mary Corss to Adaline Corss, September 30, 1849, Booth Papers. Diane S. Butler, "The Public Life and Private Affairs of Sherman M. Booth," *Wisconsin Magazine of History*, 82, no. 3 (Spring 1999): 166–197.

5. Byron (this could be either Byron Paine, a friend of the family, or Byron Corss, a relative) to Adaline Corss, November 13, 1849, Booth Papers.

6. Mary and Sherman Booth to Adaline Corrs, December 3, 1849, Sherman Booth to Adaline Corss, November 17, 1849, Booth Papers.

7. Mary to Adaline Corss, and Sherman to Adaline Corss, November 21, 1849, Booth Papers.

8. Sherman Booth to Adaline Corss, November 17, 1849; Mary Booth to Adaline Corss, November 27, 1849; Mary and Sherman Booth to Adaline Corss, December 3, 1849; Mary Booth to Adaline Corss, December 1849, Booth Papers; Lystra, *Searching the Heart*, 85. On

feminists' struggle to be classed as adults, see Corinne T. Field, *The Struggle for Equal Adulthood: Gender, Race, Age, and the Fight for Citizenship in Antebellum America* (Chapel Hill: University of North Carolina Press, 2014).

9. Mary Booth to Adaline Corss, November 27, 1849, Booth Papers.

10. Sherman Booth to Adaline Corss, November 17, 1849, Booth Papers.

11. On the Glover case, including Booth's involvement, see H. Robert Baker, *The Rescue of Joshua Glover: A Fugitive Slave, The Constitution, and the Coming of the Civil War* (Athens: Ohio University Press, 2006).

12. Sherman Booth to Adaline and Jane Corss, March 1, 1850, Booth Papers.

13. Mary Booth to Adaline Corss, March 4, 1859, Booth Papers.

14. Mary Booth to Adaline Corss, c. January 14, 1858, Mary Booth to Jane Corss, February 15, 1858, Booth Papers. Mischa Honeck, *We Are the Revolutionists: German-Speaking Immigrants and American Abolitionists After 1848* (Athens: University of Georgia Press, 2011), chap. 4; Bonnie S. Anderson, *Joyous Greetings: The First International Woman's Movement, 1830–1860* (New York: Oxford University Press, 2000), 26, 180–181, passim.

15. *The Trial of Sherman M. Booth for Seduction [. . .]* (Milwaukee: Wm. E. Tunis, 1859), 5, 7, 12.

16. *Trial of Sherman M. Booth*, 118, 77, 257. For an analysis of the public value of female chastity in the Booth case see Pamela Haag, *Consent: Sexual Rights and the Transformation of American Liberalism* (Ithaca: Cornell University Press, 1999), 14–18. Sharon Block, *Rape and Sexual Power in Early America* (Chapel Hill: University of North Carolina Press, 2006).

17. *Trial of Sherman M. Booth*, 127, 122, 130, 134.

18. Mary Booth to Adaline Corss, August 4 and August 8, 1859, Booth Papers.

19. Mary Booth to Adaline Corss, July 17 and August 8, 1859, Booth Papers; Mary Booth to Mathilde Anneke, January 3, 1865, Fritz and Mathilde Anneke Papers, Wisconsin Historical Society (hereafter cited as Anneke Papers).

20. Mathilde Anneke to Fritz Anneke, July 15, 1859, Anneke Papers, translated from German by Marjorie Galelli.

21. Mary Booth to Mathilde Anneke, January 3, 1865, Anneke Papers.

22. Sherman M. Booth to Jane Corss, November 18, 1849; [Lorenzo Crouse?] to Byron Corss, April 21, 1859, Booth Papers.

23. Ancestry.com. *U.S. Naturalization Record Indexes, 1791–1992 (Indexed in World Archives Project)* [database online]. Provo, UT: Ancestry.com Operations, 2010; "Home Again" advertisement, Milwaukee *Daily News*, April 8, 1856; Mathilde Anneke to Fritz Anneke, July [date unknown] and 10, 1859, Anneke Papers, translated from German by Marjorie Galelli.

24. Mathilde Anneke to Fritz Anneke, July [date unknown] 1859 and January 28, 1860, Anneke Papers, translated from German by Marjorie Galelli. Philip J. Deloria, *Playing Indian* (New Haven: Yale University Press, 1998), 34, 113. I have not been able to identify an American Indian ancestor.

25. *Trial of Sherman M. Booth*, 274, 283, 293. See also Mathilde Anneke to Fritz Anneke, January 28, 1860, Anneke Papers, translated from German by Marjorie Galelli.

26. Baker, *The Rescue of Joshua Glover*, chap. 7; see also Mathilde Anneke to Fritz Anneke, January 28, 1860, Anneke Papers, translated from the German by Marjorie Galelli.

27. Mary Booth to Mathilde Anneke, October 30, 1863, Anneke Papers. Bonnie S. Anderson notes the passionate relationship between Booth and Anneke in *Joyous Greetings*, 60;

Mischa Honeck sees their relationship as an experiment in women's independence and a "productive literary collaboration," but not necessarily sexual. See *We Are the Revolutionists*, 120, 133. Women had lived as married couples before, but the phenomenon of Boston marriages did not become well known until after the Civil War. See Rachel Hope Cleves, *Charity and Sylvia: A Same-Sex Marriage in Early America* (New York: Oxford University Press, 2014).

28. On the use of landscape in lesbian love poetry, see Lisa L. Moore, "The Swan of Litchfield: Sarah Pierce and the Lesbian Landscape Poem," in Thomas A. Foster, ed., *Long Before Stonewall: Histories of Same-Sex Sexuality in Early America* (New York: New York University Press, 2007), 253–276. On their antislavery writings, see Honeck, *We Are the Revolutionists*, 121–133.

29. Mary Booth to Mary Corss, November 8, 1861, January 14, 1864, Booth Papers.

30. Mary Booth to Mary Corss, March 18, 1864, Booth Papers; Mary Booth to Mathilde Anneke, January 3, 1865, Anneke Papers.

31. Mary Booth to Mary Corss, November 8, 1861, January 14, 1864, Booth Papers.

32. Letter from Mary, undated, and Mary Booth to Mathilde Anneke, July 28, 1863, Anneke Papers.

33. Box 5, Anneke Papers, and Mary H. C. Booth, *Wayside Blossoms* (Philadelphia: J. B. Lippincott, 1865), 17, 57.

34. "Alpine Lovers," *Wayside Blossoms*, 72.

35. Mary Booth to Mathilde Anneke, October 30, 1863, November 4, 1863, October 26, 1864, December 1, 1864, January 3, 1865, Anneke Papers.

36. Mary Booth to Mathilde Anneke, January 3, 1865, Anneke Papers; Booth, *Wayside Blossoms*, 22. On Louis Wust, see especially Mary Booth to Mathilde Anneke, October 26, 1864, December 1, 1864, January 3, 1865, January 28, 1865, March 7, 1865, Anneke Papers.

37. Mary Booth to Mathilde Anneke, July 23, 1863, Anneke Papers.

38. Mary Booth to Mathilde Anneke, July 30, 1864, January 28, 1865, March 3, 1865, March 7, 1865, Anneke Papers; Mary Booth to Mary Corss, March 27, 1865, Booth Papers.

39. Mary Booth to Mathilde Anneke, September 20, 1864. The *Daily Wisconsin* published her obituary, likely written by Sherman Booth, on April 12, 1865.

40. Mary Booth to Mathilde Anneke, January 3, 1865, October 30, 1863, Anneke Papers.

Chapter 7

1. *Theodore Tilton Against Henry Ward Beecher, Action for Crim. Con. Tried in the City Court of Brooklyn, Chief Justice Joseph Nielson, Presiding . . .* , 3 vols. (New York: McDivitt, Campbell, 1875), 3: 387.

2. "Cost the Limit of Price," *Liberator*, October 14, 1853.

3. See especially Mark A. Lause, *The Antebellum Crisis and America's First Bohemians* (Kent, OH: Kent State University Press, 2009); "The Vault at Pfaff's: An Archive of Art and Literature by the Bohemians of Antebellum New York" at http://pfaffs.web.lehigh.edu/.

4. Marie Howland to Edmund Clarence Stedman, April 21, 1907, Edmund Clarence Stedman Papers, Rare Books and Manuscripts, Butler Library, Columbia University (hereafter cited as Stedman Papers).

5. "Free-Love by a Female Visitor," *New York Tribune*, October 15, 1855.

6. Laura Stedman and George M. Gould, *Life and Letters of Edmund Clarence Stedman*, vol. 1 (New York: Moffat, Yard, 1910), 175.

7. Article clipping, "Marie Howland and Topolobampo: Her Life and Experiences in the Mexican Socialist Colony, Where Her Husband Died," in Box 18, Folder 3, Topolobampo Collection, Special Collections Library, Henry Madden Library, California State University, Fresno (hereafter cited as Topolobamo Collection). On Case's interest in Catholicism, see Lyman Case to Edmund Clarence Stedman, August 4, 1854, and September 8, 1854, and Marie Howland to Edmund Clarence Stedman, September 27, 1907, Stedman Papers.

8. "The Execution of Orsini and Pierri," *New York Herald*, April 5, 1858; "The Sympathizers With Orsini and Pierri," *New York Herald*, April 11, 1858; "Manifesto of the Admirers of Orsini—Defence of the Murder Demonstration," *New York Herald*, April 19, 1858; "Socialist Demonstration," *New York Herald*, June 24, 1858. Case was also opposed Sabbath laws; see "The Anti-Sabbatarian Movement," *New York Herald*, September 14, 1859.

9. "A Rich Development, Free Love Nowhere," *New York Times*, October 19, 1855; "The Free-Lovers' Troubles," *New York Times*, October 20, 1855. Lause, *America's First Bohemians*, 30–41; John C. Spurlock, *Free Love: Marriage and Middle-Class Radicalism in America, 1825–1860* (New York: New York University Press, 1988), 153.

10. "The Unitary Household," *New York Times*, June 25, 1858; "Practical Socialism in New-York: Revival of the 'Free-Love' Meetings—The 'Unitary Household,'" *New York Times*, June 22, 1858. On the Unitary Home, see Lause, *America's First Bohemians*, 64–73; Carl J. Guarneri, *The Utopian Alternative: Fourierism in Nineteenth-Century America* (Ithaca: Cornell University Press, 1991), 396–397; Dolores Hayden, *The Grand Domestic Revolution: A History of Feminist Designs for American Homes, Neighborhoods, and Cities* (Cambridge, MA: MIT Press, 1981), 33–35, 94–95.

11. "The Unitary Household," *New York Times*, June 25, 1858. Underhill's scandalous remarks on free love were reprinted in "Free Love in City and Country," *New York Herald*, June 26, 1858, and "The Unitary Household," *Circular*, July 1, 1858.

12. *Life and Letters of Edmund Clarence Stedman*, 165, 167–168; Marie Howland to Edmund Clarence Stedman, April 21, 1907, Stedman Papers; Lause, *America's First Bohemians*, chap. 1. On Anna Ballard see "The Vault at Pfaff's," https://pfaffs.web.lehigh.edu/node/54241.

13. *Life and Letters of Edmund Clarence Stedman*, 172–174; Marx Edgeworth Lazarus, *Love vs. Marriage* (New York: Fowler and Wells, 1852), 180–181.

14. Giancinto Achilli, *Dealings with the Inquisition: Or, Papal Rome, Her Priests, and Her Jesuits* (London: Arthur Hall, Virtue, 1851); *Achilli vs. Newman. A Full Report of This Most Extraordinary Trial for Seduction and Adultery Charged Against Dr. Achilli, the Apostate Catholic Priest, by the Celebrated Dr. Newman* (New York: Dewitt and Davenport, [1852]).

15. Marie E. Primo, typed history of "The Achille Family," and notes by Mary Leonard Beagle, Box 38, Oneida Community Collection; "Narrative of Facts; Concerning Giovanni Giancinto Achilli," *Circular*, December 27, 1860.

16. "The Unitary Home," *New York Tribune*, November 27, 1858.

17. "The Unitary Household," *Circular*, October 13, 1859.

18. Marie Howland to Edmund Clarence Stedman, April 21, 1907, Stedman Papers.

19. *Life and Letters of Edmund Clarence Stedman,* 159, 160, 166.

20. Marie Howland to Edmund Clarence Stedman, November 30, 1885, Stedman Papers.

21. Theresa Strouth Gaul, ed., *To Marry an Indian: The Marriage of Harriet Gold and Elias Boudinot in Letters, 1823–1839* (Chapel Hill: University of North Carolina Press, 2005), 76 n. 44; *Alumni Record of Wesleyan University* (Hartford, CT: Case, Lockwood, and Brainard, 1883), 399.

22. Marie Howland to Edmund Clarence Stedman, April 21, 1907 and September 27, 1907, Stedman Papers; Marie Howland to Albert K. Owen, July 9, 1885, Box 18, Folder 4, Topolobampo Collection. Case continued to have such relationships with younger, working-class women, leaving him vulnerable to blackmail. See Lyman Case to Edmund Clarence Stedman, February 7 [no year], June 19, 1891, March 7, 1892, Stedman Papers. On the marriage of Marie and Lyman Case, see also Holly Jacklyn Blake, "'Dependency Is Not Charming': Marie Howland on Women, Class and Community, 1836–1921" (PhD diss., State University of New York at Binghamton, 2002), 115, 120–124.

23. William S. Andrews to Isabella Beecher Hooker, December 1871, Andrews Papers.

24. Marie Howland to Edmund Clarence Stedman, April 21, 1907, Stedman Papers; "Edward Howland" obituary, New York Times, January 21, 1891.

25. William S. Andrews to Isabella Beecher Hooker, December 1871, Andrews Papers.

26. Marie S. Case v. Lyman W. Case, July 11, 1865, Record of the Supreme Court of New York, New York County Clerk Archives, New York, NY.

27. Marie Howland to Edmund Clarence Stedman, April 21, 1907, Stedman Papers; A .L. Rawson, "A Bygone Bohemia," Frank Leslie's Popular Monthly (January 1896): 99, 101–102.

28. Life and Letters of Edmund Clarence Stedman, 169. See also Mary Loeffelholz, "Stedman, Whitman, and the Transatlantic Canonization of American Poetry," in Joanne Levin and Edward Whitley, eds., Whitman Among the Bohemians (Iowa City: Iowa University Press, 2014).

29. Life and Letters of Edmund Clarence Stedman, 185–186. For the Unitary Home's new location see "The Unitary Home," Circular, April 14, 1859; "Unitary Household," New York Tribune, June 29, 1859.

30. Saturday Press, October 22, 1859, available on "The Vault at Pfaff's," http://digital.lib .lehigh.edu/pfaffs/spr/336/271/25/40/40/, accessed June 2, 2015.

31. Life and Letters of Edmund Clarence Stedman, 190–192.

32. Mary Gove Nichols, Mary Lyndon; Or, Revelations of a Life (New York: Stringer and Townsend, 1855), 135.

33. The Times reporter experienced "an odd sensation to see a good-looking woman rise to avow herself a Free-Lover." "Radicals in Council: The Rutland Convention—A Curious Gathering," New York Times, June 29, 1858. For her alleged "two husbands" see Benjamin F. Hatch, Spiritualists' Iniquities Unmasked, and the Hatch Divorce Case (New York: published for the author, 1859), 15; see also Ann Braude, Radical Spirits: Spiritualism and Women's Rights in Nineteenth-Century America (Boston: Beacon Press, 1989), 227 n. 50. On the unhappiness of her marriage, see Henry Clapp's remarks in the Proceedings of the Free Convention held at Rutland, VT, June 25th, 26th, 27th, 1858, Phonographic Report by J. M. W. Yerrinton (New York: S. T. Munson, 1858) (Boston: J. B. Yerrinton and Son, 1858), 56. In 1850, Julia was listed in the census under her father's name, Peckham, and in 1856, she applied for a passport under the name of Julia Branch. I have not been able to find records of her marriage or divorce, or examples of her poetry or other writings.

34. Leslie Wheeler, ed., Loving Warriors: Selected Letters of Lucy Stone and Henry B. Blackwell 1853–1893 (New York: Dial, 1981), 146–147.

Chapter 8

1. "The Woman's Rights Convention," New York Times, May 15, 1858. See also "Woman's Rights Convention," New York Tribune, May 14, 1858, available on Women and Social Movements in the United States, 1600–2000, http://asp6new.alexanderstreet.com.libezproxy2.syr

.edu/was2/was2.object.details.aspx?dorpid = 1000636081, accessed June 2, 2015; Martha Coffin Wright to Susan B. Anthony, June 8, 1858, in Ann Gordon, ed., *Selected Papers of Elizabeth Cady Stanton and Susan B. Anthony, vol.1: In the School of Anti-Slavery, 1840–1866* (New Brunswick: Rutgers University Press, 1998), 372–374.

2. "Radicals in Council," *New York Times*, June 29, 1858.

3. Leslie Wheeler, ed., *Loving Warriors: Selected Letters of Lucy Stone and Henry B. Blackwell 1853–1893* (New York: Dial, 1981), 135–136; see also Andrea Moore Kerr, *Lucy Stone: Speaking Out for Equality* (New Brunswick: Rutgers University Press, 1995), 78, 80–92; Joelle Million, *Woman's Voice, Woman's Place: Lucy Stone and the Birth of the Woman's Rights Movement* (Westport, CT: Praeger, 2003), 192–193, 197. These historians base their conclusions on the letters and travel schedules of Stone and Blackwell. Sally G. McMillen disagrees, interpreting their letters differently. See *Lucy Stone: An Unapologetic Life* (New York: Oxford University Press, 2015), 127, 131–133, 138.

4. Lori D. Ginzberg, *Elizabeth Cady Stanton: An American Life* (New York: Hill and Wang, 2009), 99. Historians have examined feminists' critique of marriage as legalized prostitution. For example, Amy Dru Stanley, *From Bondage to Contract: Wage Labor, Marriage and the Market in the Age of Slave Emancipation* (New York: Cambridge University Press, 1998), chap. 6; Ellen Carol DuBois, " 'The Pivot of the Marriage Relation': Stanton's Analysis of Women's Subordination in Marriage," in DuBois and Richard Candida Smith, *Elizabeth Cady Stanton: Feminist as Thinker* (New York: New York University Press, 2007). On Victoria Woodhull's view of marriage as legal prostitution, see Amanda Frisken, *Victoria Woodhull's Sexual Revolution: Political Theater and the Popular Press in Nineteenth-Century America* (Philadelphia: University of Pennsylvania Press, 2004), 38.

5. Sarah Grimké, "Marriage," in Gerda Lerner, *The Feminist Thought of Sarah Grimké* (New York: Oxford University Press, 1998), 108, 110–111; "The Free Love System," *New York Times*, September 8, 1855.

6. Martha Coffin Wright to Susan B. Anthony, June 8, 1858, in Gordon, *Selected Papers of Stanton and Anthony*, 372–374.

7. "Radicals in Council," *New York Times*, June 29, 1858; *Proceedings of the Free Convention held at Rutland, VT, June 25th, 26th, 27th, 1858, Phonographic Report by J. M. W. Yerrinton* (New York: S. T. Munson, 1858) (Boston: J. B. Yerrinton and Son, 1858), 5, 9.

8. "Depravity of the American Press," *Liberator*, Sept. 17, 1858. A number of historians mention Branch's speech, but they do not consider her career beyond the Rutland convention. John C. Spurlock, *Free Love: Marriage and Middle-Class Radicalism in America, 1825–1860* (New York: New York University Press, 1988), 145–146; Anne Braude, *Radical Spirits: Spiritualism and Women's Rights in Nineteenth-Century America* (Boston: Beacon Press, 1989), 71, 133; 227 fn50; Mark A. Lause, *The Antebellum Crisis and America's First Bohemians* (Kent, OH: Kent State University Press, 2009), 74–75; Taylor Stoehr, *Free Love in America: A Documentary History* (New York: AMS Press, 1979), 24–26, 263–264; William Leach, *True Love and Perfect Union: The Feminist Reform of Sex and Society* (New York: Basic Books, 1980), 82; Joanne E. Passet, *Sex Radicals and the Quest for Women's Equality* (Urbana: University of Illinois Press, 2003), 74, 114.

9. "Radicals in Council," *New York Times*. Lewis Perry speculates that this resolution may have been written by Henry C. Wright, but, given the similarity of their views, it is just as likely to have been written by Andrew Jackson Davis, who also addressed the gathering.

See Lewis Perry, *Childhood, Marriage, and Reform: Henry Clarke Wright, 1797–1870* (Chicago: University of Chicago Press, 1980), 252.

10. "Radicals in Council," *New York Times*. See also *Proceedings of the Free Convention*, 52–55.

11. "Radicals in Council," *New York Times*, June 29, 1858.

12. *Proceedings*, 82.

13. *Proceedings*, 71.

14. "Radicals in Council," *New York Times*. The convention's official *Proceedings* indicate that Henry Clapp Jr. spoke before Foster and Tiffany, defending Branch's right to criticize marriage. *Proceedings*, 56.

15. *Proceedings*, 60–61; see also "Radicals in Council," *New York Times*.

16. *Proceedings*, 122–123.

17. *Proceedings*, 67–68.

18. *Proceedings*, 67, 69.

19. *Proceedings*, 69, 70, 72.

20. "The Free Love Question-Letter from Mrs. Rose," *Liberator*, August 27, 1858. Bonnie S. Anderson, *The Rabbi's Atheist Daughter: Ernestine Rose, International Feminist Pioneer* (New York: Oxford University Press, 2017), 109–113.

21. Lucretia Mott to Martha Coffin Wright, July 6, 1858, in Beverly Wilson Palmer, ed., *Selected Letters of Lucretia Coffin Mott* (Urbana: University of Illinois Press, 2002), 274–275.

22. "Philanthropic Harmonial Convention," *Troy Daily Times*, September 11, 1858; "The 'Cause and Cure of Evil' Convention," *Utica Daily Observer*, September 13, 1858.

23. "Cause and Cure of Evil," *Utica Daily Observer*, September 13, 1858; "The Free Lovers Again," *New York Herald*, September 12, 1858.

24. H. W. B., "The Philanthropic Convention at Utica," *Circular*, September 16, 1858; "Speech of Mrs. Julia Branch," *Liberator*, October 1, 1858.

25. "The Free Lovers Again," *New York Herald*, Sept. 12, 1858.

26. "The Free-Lovers at Utica," *New York Times*, September 15, 1858; "The Men and Women at the 'Overcoming Convention,'" *New York Post*, September 16, 1858. George W. Noyes of the Oneida Community defended Branch against charges of encouraging prostitution: "Now we know but little of the person under discussion, but it strikes us there is some difference between a woman adopting Free Love as a principle, soberly subjecting it as a right to philosophical discussion and those who sell their persons in shame and secrecy for money." "A Would-be Wit," *Circular*, September 2, 1858.

27. "Cause and Cure of Evil," *Utica Daily Observer*.

28. "Cause and Cure of Evil," *Utica Daily Observer*.

29. "The Converted Medium," *New-York Daily Tribune*, November 25, 1858.

30. P. B. Randolph, *The Unveiling, Or What I Think of Spiritualism* (Newburyport: William H. Huse, 1860), 5, 6, 14, 15, 30.

31. "Cause and Cure of Evil," *Utica Daily Observer*; "Harmonial Pow-Wow," *Troy Daily Times*, September 14, 1858.

32. Andrew Jackson Davis to William Green Jr., August 15, 1859, and September 1859, MS 677, Davis Papers.

33. "City Items," *New York Tribune*, November 17, 1858. On bohemians decrying Mrs. Grundy see Lause, *America's First Bohemians*, 10; Joanna Levin, "'Freedom for Women From

Conventional Lies,': The 'Queen of Bohemia' and the Feminist Feuilleton," in Joanne Levin and Edward Whitley, eds., *Whitman Among the Bohemians* (Iowa City: Iowa University Press, 2014).

34. *New York Clipper*, May 7, 1859. Julia Branch Crosby died in 1867, and her husband died in 1878. "Died," *New York Tribune*, November 20, 1867; *New York World*, December 17, 1878.

35. "Tenth National Woman's Rights Convention," in Gordon, *Selected Papers of Stanton and Anthony*, 418, 419, 428–429, 431; *National Woman's Rights Convention, 10th: 1860 May 10–11: New York, NY* (Boston: Yerrinton and Garrison, 1860), 81, 83–84. See also Ginzberg, *Elizabeth Cady Stanton*, 97–101.

36. "Demise of the Unitary Home," *New York Tribune*, June 5, 1860.

37. Warren Chase, *The Fugitive Wife: A Criticism on Marriage, Adultery, and Divorce* (Boston: Bela Marsh, 1861), 7, 8, 9, 13, 14.

38. Chase, *The Fugitive Wife*, 16, 28, 39, 41, 80, 94.

39. Warren Chase, *The Life-Line of the Lone One; Or, Autobiography of the World's Child* (Boston: Bela Marsh, 1857), 147, 35, 73, 96.

40. Chase, *The Life-line of the Lone One*, 92, 148–149, 161. One of his opponents was B. F. Hatch, who described Chase's "character" as "too well known to need comment," but nevertheless compared him to a sailor who "finds a temporary wife in every Spiritual port." See *Spiritualists' Iniquities Unmasked* (New York: 1859), 14.

41. Chase carefully recorded his earnings for each year: in 1862, $449; in 1863, $582; and in 1864, $643. See Warren Chase, *Forty Years on the Spiritual Rostrum* (Boston: Colby and Rich, 1888), 11–12, 87, 91, 95.

42. "Edward F. Underhill Dead," *New York Times*, June 19, 1898.

43. John Patrick Deveney, *Paschal Beverly Randolph: A Nineteenth-Century Black American Spiritualist, Rosicrucian, and Sex Magician* (Albany: State University of New York Press, 1997), 168–170, 173–174, 176, p. 462–463, n. 1; *P. B. Randolph, the 'Learned Pundit,' and 'Man with Two Souls.' His Curious Life, Works, and Career. The Great Free-Love Trial. Randolph's Grand Defense. His Address to the Jury, and Mankind. The Verdict.* (Boston: Randolph Publishing House, 1872), 32, 38, 48; Martha Randolph, *Year: 1870*; *Census Place: Thibodaux, Lafourche, Louisiana*; Roll: *M593_516*; Page: *533A*; Image: *286952*; Family History Library Film: *552015*; Ancestry.com. *1870 United States Federal Census* [database on-line].

44. Wendy Hamand Venet, *Neither Ballots or Bullets: Women Abolitionists and the Civil War* (Charlottesville: University of Virginia Press, 1991), chap 5.

45. Eliza W. Farnham, *Woman and Her Era, in Two Volumes*, vol. 1 (New York: C. M. Plumb, 1865, second edition), and Eliza Farnham, *The Ideal Attained: Two Steadfast Souls, and How They Won Their Happiness* (New York: C. M. Plumb, 1865). On Farnham, see especially JoAnn Levy, *Unsettling the West: Eliza Farnham and Georgiana Bruce Kirby in Frontier California* (Berkeley, CA: Heyday Books, 2004), 215, 218–219; Ellen Carol DuBois, "Seneca Falls in Santa Cruz: Eliza Farnham and the Varieties of Women's Emancipation in Nineteenth-Century California," *Common-Place*, 9, no. 2 (January 2009), http://www.common-place-archives.org/vol-09/no-02/dubois/.

46. Jean Silver-Isenstadt, *Shameless: The Visionary Life of Mary Gove Nichols* (Baltimore: Johns Hopkins University Press, 2002), 231–233.

47. Most studies of free love and marriage neglect the Civil War years. Spurlock, *Free Love*; Passet, *Sex Radicals and the Quest for Women's Equality*, 42; Nancy E. Cott, *Public Vows:*

A History of Marriage and the Nation (Cambridge, MA: Harvard University Press, 2000), 75–79. Helen Lefkowitz Horowitz sees Comstock's Civil War experience as central to his postwar policing of sex, see *Rereading Sex: Battles over Sexual Knowledge and Suppression in Nineteenth-Century* (New York: Vintage, 2002), 305–318.

Chapter 9

1. In *Trials of Intimacy: Love and Loss in the Beecher-Tilton Scandal* (Chicago: University of Chicago Press, 1999), Richard Wightman Fox illuminates the history of the complicated, emotionally intimate friendship of Theodore Tilton, Elizabeth Tilton, and Henry Ward Beecher. Helen Lefkowitz Horowitz examines the clash between the sexual worldviews of Victoria Woodhull and Anthony Comstock in *Rereading Sex: Battles Over Sexual Knowledge and Suppression in Nineteenth-Century America* (New York: Vintage, 2002). Amanda Frisken shows how Victoria Woodhull turned the scandal into a vehicle for her celebrity as well as her political message of sexual equality, in *Victoria Woodhull's Sexual Revolution: Political Theater and the Popular Press in Nineteenth-Century America* (Philadelphia: University of Pennsylvania Press, 2004). On Woodhull, see Lois Beachy Underhill, *The Woman Who Ran for President: The Many Lives of Victoria Woodhull* (New York: Bridgeworks, 1995); Mary Gabriel, *Notorious Victoria: The Life of Victoria Woodhull, Uncensored* (New York: Algonquin, 1998), and Myra MacPherson, *The Scarlet Sisters: Sex, Suffrage, and Scandal in the Gilded Age* (New York: Twelve Books, 2014). On Beecher, see Debby Applegate, *The Most Famous Man in America: The Biography of Henry Ward Beecher* (New York: Doubleday, 2006).

2. "Foreward" to Marie Howland, *The Familistere: A Novel* (Philadelphia: Porcupine Press, 1975, based on the third edition from 1918), originally published as *Papa's Own Girl* in 1874. Howland touched on the Civil War only to condemn it. See Howland, *The Familistere: A Novel*, 155–164. For a detailed account of her European travels, see Holly Jacklyn Blake, "'Dependency Is Not Charming': Marie Howland on Women, Class and Community, 1836–1921" (PhD diss., State University of New York at Binghamton, 2002), 152–153, 159.

3. Marie Howland to Edward Clarence Stedman, December 16, 1893, Stedman Papers.

4. Marie Howland to Edmund Clarence Stedman, April 21, 1907, Stedman Papers; Marie Howland to Edmund Clarence Stedman, no date, Box 62, Stedman Papers.

5. Marie Howland, "Biographical Sketch of Edward Howland," *Credit Foncier of Sinaloa*, June 1 and June 15, 1891. On her religious beliefs, see especially Marie Howland to Albert K. Owen, July 25, 1889, Topolobampo Collection.

6. Blake, "Dependency Is Not Charming," 196–199, 316–325. For Marie Howland's experiences at Topolobampo, see especially Ray Reynolds, "Cat's Paw Utopia" (self-pub., 1972), 77–78, 81–83.

7. Edward Howland, "The Social Palace at Guise," *Harper's Monthly*, 44 (April 1872): 701. Marie Howland likely helped write and edit this article. See Folder 14, Box 18, Topolobampo Collection.

8. Edward Howland, "The Social Palace at Guise," 702.

9. Edward Howland, "The Social Palace at Guise," 703, 706.

10. Edward Howland, "The Social Palace at Guise," 715.

11. Marie Howland, *The Familistere*, 96. For more extensive treatments of *Papa's Own Girl* (in later editions retitled *The Familistere*), see Susan Lynch Foster, "Romancing the Cause: Fourierism, Feminism, and Free Love in *Papa's Own Girl*," *Utopian Studies*, 8, no. 1 (1997): 31–54; Blake, "Dependency Is Not Charming," chap. 5.

12. Howland, *The Familistere*, 188.

13. Howland, *The Familistere*, 209, 199.

14. Howland, *The Familistere*, 280, 289–290.

15. Howland, *The Familistere*, 396.

16. Howland, *The Familistere*, 460, 488–489.

17. Marie Howland to Edmund Clarence Stedman, December 25, 1896, Stedman Papers.

18. Howland, *The Familistere*, 393.

19. Howland, *The Familistere*, 532.

20. M. Godin, *Social Solutions*, translated from the French by Marie Howland (New York: John W. Lovell, 1886), iv, 74.

21. Godin, *Social Solutions*, 134–135.

22. Marie Howland to Albert K. Owen, October 8, 1880, September 18, 1885; "Marie Howland and Topolobampo: Her Life and Experiences in the Socialist Colony. Where Her Husband Died" (1894), Folder 3, Box 18, Topolobampo Collection.

23. Paul M. Gaston, *Women of Fairhope* (Athens: University of Georgia Press, 1984), 48–65.

24. "Editorial Correspondence by E. C. S. [Elizabeth Cady Stanton]," in Ann D. Gordon, ed., *The Selected Papers of Elizabeth Cady Stanton and Susan B. Anthony, vol. 2: Against an Aristocracy of Sex, 1866–1873* (New Brunswick: Rutgers University Press, 2000), 285, originally published in *Revolution*, December 23, 1869. Hendrik Hartog, *Man and Wife in America* (Cambridge, MA: Harvard University Press, 2000), 221–223. See also Hartog, "Lawyering, Husbands' Rights, and 'the Unwritten Law' in Nineteenth-Century America," *Journal of American History* (June 1997): 67–96; Nancy Cott, *Public Vows: A History of Marriage and the Nation* (Cambridge, MA: Harvard University Press, 2000), 107–109; Fox, *Trials of Intimacy*, 233–234.

25. Andrea Moore Kerr, *Lucy Stone: Speaking Out for Equality* (New Brunswick: Rutgers University Press, 1995), 105–106, 144, 143–157; Sally G. McMillen offers a more cautious interpretation of the affair in *Lucy Stone: An Unapologetic Life* (New York: Oxford University Press, 2015), 179–181. Faye Dudden, *Fighting Chance: The Struggle Over Woman Suffrage and Black Suffrage in Reconstruction America* (New York: Oxford University Press, 2011); Lisa Tetrault, *The Myth of Seneca Falls: Memory and the Woman Suffrage Movement, 1848–1898* (Chapel Hill: University of North Carolina Press, 2014).

26. Editorial Correspondence by ECS [Elizabeth Cady Stanton], in Gordon, ed. *Against an Aristocracy of Sex*, 286.

27. Catharine E. Beecher to ECS, May 16, 1870, in Gordon, ed. *Against an Aristocracy of Sex*, 335; Hartog, *Man and Wife in America*, 242–249.

28. "Speech by ECS to a Mass Meeting of Women in New York," in Gordon, ed. *Against an Aristocracy of Sex*, 337, 338.

29. "Speech by ECS to a Mass Meeting of Women in New York," in Gordon, ed. *Against an Aristocracy of Sex*, 342, 343, 347, 352.

30. Quoted in Fox, *Trials of Intimacy*, 235.

31. *Theodore Tilton Against Henry Ward Beecher, Action for Crim. Con. Tried in the City Court of Brooklyn, Chief Justice Joseph Nielson, Presiding [. . .]*, 3 vols. (New York: McDivitt, Campbell, 1875), 3: 389.

32. Stephen Pearl Andrews, "The Lesson of the McFarland Trial," *Woodhull and Claflin's Weekly*, May 20, 1871; "fourierites" and "free-lovers" quoted in Hartog, *Man and Wife in*

America, 227; Madeline B. Stern, *The Pantarch: A Biography of Stephen Pearl Andrews* (Austin: University of Texas Press, 1968), 95–100.

33. Stephen Pearl Andrews, "The Greeley-Tilton Free Love Controversy Again," *Woodhull and Claflin's Weekly*, September 23, 1871; Andrews, "Meaning of the Recent Woman's Rights Conventions," *Woodhull and Claflin's Weekly*, May 27, 1871; "Stephen Pearl Andrews," *Woodhull and Claflin's Weekly*, Jan. 27, 1872; Gabriel, *Notorious Victoria*, 94–95.

34. Andrews's testimony describes his residence in Woodhull's house, in *Theodore Tilton Against Henry Ward Beecher* 3: 388, 390, 392, 399; Gabriel, *Notorious Victoria*, 62–63, 65, 69, 73–77, 114; MacPherson, *Scarlet Sisters*, 9, 54–55, 63–67.

35. "SBA to Martha Coffin Wright," March 21, 1871, in Gordon, ed. *Against an Aristocracy of Sex*, 425, 426 n. 2; William Andrews to Isabella Beecher Hooker, December 1871, U.S. Mss 19A, Andrews Papers.

36. SBA to Martha Coffin Wright, March 21, 1871, and ECS to Lucretia Coffin Mott, April 1, 1871, in Gordon, ed. *Against an Aristocracy of Sex*, 425, 428.

37. *New York Tribune*, May 11, 1871, quoted in Beverly Wilson Palmer, ed., *The Selected Letters of Lucretia Coffin Mott* (Urbana: University of Illinois Press, 2002), 460 n. 3; Carol Faulkner, *Lucretia Mott's Heresy: Abolition and Women's Rights in Nineteenth-Century America* (Philadelphia: University of Pennsylvania Press, 2011), 207.

38. Theodore Tilton, *Biography of Victoria C. Woodhull* (New York: Golden Age, 1871), 3, 8, 11–12.

39. Tilton, *Biography of Victoria C. Woodhull*, 13–14, 16, 21, 23, 25, 26, 32; Gabriel, *Notorious Victoria*, 120.

40. On Andrews as her amanuensis, see Frisken, *Victoria Woodhull's Sexual Revolution*, 10; Gabriel, *Notorious Victoria*, 138–140, 143–150; MacPherson, *The Scarlet Sisters*, 52, 129–130.

41. Victoria C. Woodhull, *A Speech on the Principles of Social Freedom, Delivered in Steinway Hall, Monday, Nov. 20, 1871, and Music Hall, Boston, Wednesday, Jan. 3, 1872* (New York: Woodhull, Claflin, 1872), 4, 6, 8, 10.

42. Woodhull, *A Speech on the Principles of Social Freedom*, 11, 12, 14, 16, 17, 19.

43. Woodhull, *A Speech on the Principles of Social Freedom*, 23, 25.

44. Woodhull, *A Speech on the Principles of Social Freedom*, 27, 39.

45. Tetrault, *The Myth of Seneca Falls*, chap. 3.

Chapter 10

1. On marriage and Reconstruction policy, see Herbert Gutman, *The Black Family in Slavery and Freedom, 1750–1925* (New York: Pantheon, 1976); Laura Edwards, *Gendered Strife and Confusion: The Political Culture of Reconstruction* (Urbana: University of Illinois Press, 1997); Noralee Frankel, *Freedom's Women: Black Women and Families in Civil War Era Mississippi* (Bloomington: Indiana University Press, 1999). On the place of marriage in reuniting the states, see Nina Silber, *Romance of Reunion: Northerners and the South, 1865–1900* (Chapel Hill: University of North Carolina Press, 1997). On national interest in marriage and increased sexual moralism, see Gaines M. Foster, *Moral Reconstruction: Christian Lobbyists and the Federal Legislation of Morality, 1865–1920* (Chapel Hill: University of North Carolina Press, 2002); Norma Basch, *Framing American Divorce: From the Revolutionary Generation to the Victorians* (Berkeley: University of California Press, 1999); Nancy Cott, *Public Vows: A History of Marriage and the Nation* (Cambridge, MA: Harvard University Press, 2000), chaps. 4 and 5.

2. "Speech by ECS to a Mass Meeting of Women in New York," in Ann Gordon, ed., *The Selected Papers of Elizabeth Cady Stanton and Susan B. Anthony, vol. 2: Against an Aristocracy of Sex, 1866–1873* (New Brunswick, NJ: Rutgers University Press, 2000), 342. Gordon notes that Stanton's numbers were wrong, p. 354. On rising divorce rates, see Carroll D. Wright, *Marriage and Divorce in the United States, 1867–1886* (Washington, DC: Government Printing Office, 1897, (New York: Arno Press, 1976), 140. Norma Basch, *Framing American Divorce*; Glenda Riley, *Divorce: An American Tradition* (New York: Oxford University Press, 1991).

3. Theodore Dwight Woolsey, *Essay on Divorce and Divorce Legislation* (New York: Charles Scribner, 1869), preface, 182, 191.

4. Woolsey, *Essay on Divorce and Divorce Legislation*, 209, 211–212.

5. Woolsey, *Essay on Divorce and Divorce Legislation*, 217.

6. Woolsey, *Essay on Divorce and Divorce Legislation*, 234, 235.

7. Woolsey, *Essay on Divorce and Divorce Legislation*, 279, 242, 252, 258, 260.

8. John B. Ellis, *Free Love and Its Votaries; Or, American Socialism Unmasked: Being an Historical and Descriptive Account of the Rise and Progress of the Various Free Love Associations in the United States, and of the Effects of Their Vicious Teachings Upon American Society* (New York: United States Publishing, 1870), 10.

9. Ellis, *Free Love and Its Votaries*, 13, 165, 211, 180, 188, 218, 332. See also Michael Doyle, *The Ministers' War: John W. Mears, the Oneida Community, and the Crusade for Public Morality* (Syracuse: Syracuse University Press, 2018), 39–40.

10. William Hepworth Dixon, *Spiritual Wives*, 2 vols. (London: Hurst and Blackett, 1868), 2: 239, 249, 250, 251, 252.

11. Ellis, *Free Love and Its Votaries*, 405–406.

12. Ellis, *Free Love and Its Votaries*, 384, 389, 392.

13. Ellis, *Free Love and Its Votaries*, 450, 453, 467, 477, 484, 492.

14. On Ellis's identity, see John B. Ellis, *The Sights and Secrets of the National Capital: A Work Descriptive of Washington City in All Its Various Phases* (Chicago: Jones, Junkin, 1869); John Humphrey Noyes, *Dixon and His Copyists, a Criticism* (Oneida: Oneida Community, 1871), 37. On the Swedenborgian author and inventor, see "Obituary," *New York Sun*, December 6, 1896; "Dr. John Ellis's Will," *New York Tribune*, December 18, 1896.

15. "Agents Wanted for Free Love, and Its Votaries," *Progressive Batavian*, Batavia, New York, December 23, 1870; Ellis, *Free Love and Its Votaries*; Helen Lefkowitz Horowitz, *Rereading Sex: Battles over Sexual Knowledge and Suppression in Nineteenth-Century America* (New York: Vintage, 2002), 37, 361–362; Donna Dennis, *Licentious Gotham: Erotic Publishing and its Prosecution in Nineteenth-Century New York* (Cambridge, MA: Harvard University Press, 2009), 94–95, 254–258; P. B. Randolph, the *"Learned Pundit," and "Man With Two Souls": His Curious Life, Works, and Career. The Great Free-Love Trial. Randolph's Grand Defense. His Address to the Jury, and Mankind. The Verdict* (Boston: Randolph Publishing House, 1872), 67.

16. Harriet Beecher Stowe, *My Wife and I, or Harry Henderson's History* (New York: Fords, Howard, and Hulbert, 1871), 4, 40. Carol Faulkner, "Harriet Beecher Stowe on the Marriage Question," *Religion in American History* (blog), December 22, 2014, http://usreligion.blogspot.com/2014/12/harriet-beecher-stowe-on-marriage.html. For a more extended discussion of the novel and its relation to women's rights, see Amy Easton-Flake, "Harriet Beecher Stowe's Multifaceted Response to the Nineteenth-Century Woman Question," *New England Quarterly*, 86, no. 1 (March 2013), 29–59.

17. Stowe, *My Wife and I*, 173.

18. Stowe, *My Wife and I*, 107.

19. Stowe, *My Wife and I*, 194, 235–239.

20. Stowe, *My Wife and I*, 240–241. Myra MacPherson thinks there is more of Tennie in the portrait of Audacia Dangyereyes; see *The Scarlet Sisters: Sex, Suffrage, and Scandal in the Gilded Age* (New York: Twelve Books, 2014), 118.

21. Stowe, *My Wife and I*, 257.

22. Stowe, *My Wife and I*, 267.

23. Stowe, *My Wife and I*, 485.

24. Stowe, *My Wife and I*, 411.

25. Quoted in Mary Gabriel, *Notorious Victoria: The Life of Victoria Woodhull, Uncensored* (New York: Algonquin, 1998), 66.

26. Daniel Hull and others, *Moses Hull* (Wellesley, MA: Maugus Printing, 1907), 15, 20, 22–23, 29, 31. Ann Taves, "Visions," in Terrie Dopp Aamodt, Gary Land, and Ronald L. Numbers, eds., *Ellen Harmon White: American Prophet* (New York: Oxford University Press, 2014), 30–51.

27. Moses Hull, *That Terrible Question: Or, A Few Thoughts on Love and Marriage* (Chicago: Hazlitt & Reed, 1868), 3–4, 5.

28. Hull, *That Terrible Question*, 7, 9, 15, 24.

29. "The Beecher-Tilton Scandal Case," *Woodhull and Claflin's Weekly*, November 2, 1872, 9, 10. For similar spiritualist attacks on ministers, see Horowitz, *Rereading Sex*, 356; Amanda Frisken, *Victoria Woodhull's Sexual Revolution: Political Theater and the Popular Press in Nineteenth-Century America* (Philadelphia: University of Pennsylvania Press, 2004), 88. On Andrews's contributions to the article see his testimony in the later civil trial, *Theodore Tilton Against Henry Ward Beecher, Action for Crim. Con. Tried in the City Court of Brooklyn, Chief Justice Joseph Nielson, Presiding[. . .]*, 3 vols. (New York: McDivitt, Campbell, 1875), 3: 395.

30. "The Beecher-Tilton Scandal Case," 11, 12; Horowitz, *Rereading Sex*, 352; Frisken, *Victoria Woodhull's Sexual Revolution*, 93.

31. "The Beecher-Tilton Scandal Case," 12. Stanton initially denied her role, but later admitted that what Woodhull stated was true. Gordon, ed. *Against an Aristocracy of Sex*, 533–536; "Elizabeth Cady Stanton," *Woodhull and Claflin's Weekly*, August 15, 1874.

32. "The Beecher-Tilton Scandal Case," 9, 13.

33. Gabriel, *Notorious Victoria*, 184–197, 215; Horowitz, *Rereading Sex*, 358, 376–379; Frisken, *Victoria Woodhull's Sexual Revolution*, 95–102.

34. Moses Hull, "A Personal Experience," *Woodhull and Claflin's Weekly*, August 22, 1873, 3. Scholars mention Hull, but they do not offer an extensive analysis of his marriages or participation in the free-love movement. John C. Spurlock, *Free Love: Marriage and Middle-Class Radicalism in America, 1825–1860* (New York: New York University Press, 1988), 220–222, 225–226; Anne Braude, *Radical Spirits: Spiritualism and Women's Rights in Nineteenth-Century America* (Boston: Beacon, 1989), 123, 134; Joanne E. Passet, *Sex Radicals and the Quest for Women's Equality* (Urbana: University of Illinois Press, 2003), 45–46; Frisken, *Victoria Woodhull's Sexual Revolution*, 118, 182 notes 4 and 5.

35. Hull, "A Personal Experience," 4.

36. Hull, "A Personal Experience," 4.

37. Elvira Hull, "Socialistic; 'Facts are Stubborn Things,'" *Woodhull and Claflin's Weekly*, September 6, 1873. On Vineland, see William Leach, *True Love and Perfect Union: The Feminist Reform of Sex and Society* (New York: Basic Books, 1980), 87, 139.

38. Elvira Hull, "Socialistic."

39. "Woodhullism Gone to Seed and Burnt Its Shell in Moses Hull," *Religio-Philosophical Journal*, October 25, 1873; "Contaminating Influence of Moses Hull in New Hampshire," *Religio-Philosophical Journal*, September 20, 1873.

40. "Mrs. Elvira Hull," *Woodhull and Claflin's Weekly*, October 25, 1873; "In the Battle," *Woodhull and Claflin's Weekly*, October 4, 1873.

41. "The Spiritualists' Camp," *New York Sun*, August 12, 1874; Elvira Hull to Victoria Woodhull, *Woodhull and Claflin's Weekly*, December 16, 1873; Daniel Hull and others, *Moses Hull*, 39–42. On the friendship between Elvira and Mattie, see "The Real Brotherhood," *Hull's Crucible*, June 1, 1875, for a positive portrayal, and "Moses Hull and the Fruits of Free Love," *Religio-Philosophical Journal*, May 22, 1875 for a negative one.

42. Moses Hull, "The General Judgment" and "That Experience," *Hull's Crucible*, January 1, 1874, 1–2, 3; Mattie E. B. Sawyer, "Social Freedom," *Hull's Crucible*, January 8, 1874.

43. *Tilton Against Beecher*, 3:821; Richard Wightman Fox, *Trials of Intimacy: Love and Loss in the Beecher-Tilton Scandal* (Chicago: University of Chicago Press, 1999), 73–76, 405–406, chaps. 3 and 4 passim.

44. *Tilton Against Beecher*, 3: 507, 508–510.

45. *Tilton Against Beecher*, 1: 719; Fox, *Trials of Intimacy*, 94–95; Laura Hanft Korobkin, *Criminal Conversations: Sentimentality and Nineteenth-Century Legal Stories of Adultery* (New York: Columbia University Press, 1998), 92–93.

46. *Tilton Against Beecher*, 2: 185–186.

47. *Tilton Against Beecher*, 1: 239, 230. Fox, *Trials of Intimacy*, 122–124.

48. "The Beecher-Tilton Scandal Case," *Woodhull and Claflin's Weekly*, November 2, 1872, 12; *Tilton Against Beecher*, 1: 89, 233, 673.

49. *Tilton Against Beecher*, 3: 388, 390, 392, 395, 396, 401, 403.

50. *Tilton Against Beecher*, 3: 392, 404–405.

51. *Tilton Against Beecher*, 2: 258, 271, 280, 289; D. A. Sullivan, *A Sketch of Charles Cowley* (Lowell, MA.: 1882), 52–53, 44; Charles Cowley, *The Mistake of a Life! Or the Other Side of the Holbrook Divorce Case* (Boston: 1874); Charles Cowley, *Famous Divorces of All Ages* (Lowell, MA: Penhallow Printing, 1878).

52. For other examples, see *Boston Daily Bee Extra: Judge Merrick's Charge to the Jury, in the Dalton Divorce Case, The Phonographic Report of the Daily Bee, By Messrs. J. M. W. Yerrinton, and Rufus Leighton of Boston; and Messrs. Henry M. Parkhurst and William H. Burr, of New York* (Boston Daily Bee, 1857); *Boston Daily Bee Extra. Opening Address and Closing Argument of Richard H. Dana Jr., Esq., Counsel for Libellant, (Benj. F. Dalton,) in the Dalton Divorce Case, Phonographic Report of the Daily Bee* (Office of the Boston Daily Bee, May 1857); *Boston Daily Bee Extra. The Arguments of Counsel for Libellee, Helen Maria Dalton, in the Dalton Divorce Case, Consisting of the Opening Address of H. F. Durant, Esq., and the Closing Plea of Hon. Rufus Choate. The Phonographic Report of the Daily Bee* (Boston Daily Bee, May 1857); *Only Full Report of the Trial of Rev. I. S. Kalloch, on Charge of Adultery. Complete History of the Affair; Doings of the Church; Kalloch's Pulpit Defence; Arrest, Arraignment, Trial, and Result. With Accurate Portraits of Kalloch, and the Beautiful Lady in Black, and the Lecture Room of the Lechmerr* (Boston: Federhen and Co., 1857). For a guilty verdict, see Edward L. Pierce, *The Wareham Adultery Case* (Plymouth, MA.: 1867).

53. Gabriel, *Notorious Victoria*, 245; J. H. Blood, "What Broke Down the Woodhull Paper?" *American Socialist*, April 18, 1878.

Epilogue

1. Stephanie Coontz, *Marriage, a History: How Love Conquered Marriage* (New York: Penguin, 2005). For the further evolution of marriage, and marriage reform, in the twentieth century, see Kristin Celello, *Making Marriage Work: A History of Marriage and Divorce in the Twentieth-Century United States* (Chapel Hill: University of North Carolina Press, 2009); Rebecca L. Davis, *More Perfect Unions: The American Search for Marital Bliss* (Cambridge, MA: Harvard University Press, 2010); Leigh Ann Wheeler, *How Sex Became a Civil Liberty* (New York: Oxford University Press, 2013); Clare Virginia Eby, *Until Choice Do Us Part: Marriage Reform in the Progressive Era* (Chicago: University of Chicago Press, 2014).

2. Kimberley A. Reilly, "Labor as Love: Housework, Emotional Labor, and the Market, 1870–1920" (paper presented at the Berkshire Conference on the History of Women, Genders, and Sexualities, Hofstra University, June 1, 2017); Pamela Haag, *Consent: Sexual Rights and the Transformation of American Liberalism* (Ithaca: Cornell University Press, 1999), 98–110; Michael Grossberg, *Governing the Hearth: Law and the Family in Nineteenth-Century America* (Chapel Hill: University of North Carolina Press, 1985).

3. Sewell Chan, "Is Adultery a Crime in New York?" *New York Times*, March 21, 2008; S. N. Tuckman, "Unfaithfulness a Crime: Effects of the Laws of 1907 Upon Divorce Procedure," *New York Times*, August 23, 1907; Leigh Ann Wheeler, *How Sex Became a Civil Liberty*, ch. 4. This law passed in the midst of another, more successful campaign to abolish prostitution; see Timothy Gilfoyle, *City of Eros: New York City, Prostitution, and the Commercialization of Sex, 1790–1920* (New York: W. W. Norton, 1992), ch. 14.

4. Frederick Howard Wines, *Report on the Defective, Dependent, and Delinquent Classes of the Population of the United States as Returned at the Tenth Census (June 1, 1880)* (Washington: Government Printing Office, 1888), 504–519.

5. See Tera Hunter, *Bound in Wedlock: Slave and Free Black Marriage in the Nineteenth Century* (Cambridge, MA: Belknap Press of Harvard University Press, 2017), 15–16; Katherine Franke, *Wedlocked: The Perils of Marriage Equality* (New York: New York University Press, 2015). See also Ann duCille, *The Coupling Convention: Sex, Text, and Tradition in Black Women's Fiction* (New York: Oxford University Press, 1993); Michele Mitchell, *Righteous Propagation: African Americans and the Politics of Racial Destiny After Reconstruction* (Chapel Hill: University of North Carolina Press, 2004); Victoria Wolcott, *Remaking Respectability: African American Women in Interwar Detroit* (Chapel Hill: University of North Carolina Press, 2001); Anastasia Curwood, *Stormy Weather: Middle-Class African American Marriages Between the Two World Wars* (Chapel Hill: University of North Carolina Press, 2010).

6. "Love and Divorce," *New York Sun*, January 7, 1885; *People v. Faber*, in George Bliss, *The New York Code of Civil Procedure* (Albany: Matthew Bender, 1912), 3302.

7. *New York Sun*, February 1, 1885. "Andrew Jackson Davis," Year: *1860*; Census Place: *Orange Ward 2, Essex, New Jersey*; Roll: *M653_690*; Page: *402*; Family History Library Film: *803690*. Ancestry.com. *1860 United States Federal Census* [database online]. Year: *1870*; Census Place: *Orange Ward 2, Essex, New Jersey*; Roll: *M593_861*; Page: *345B*; Family History Library Film: *552360*, Ancestry.com. *1870 United States Federal Census* [database online]. Year: *1880*; Census Place: *Orange Ward 2, Essex, New Jersey*; Roll: *780*; Page: *94C*; Enumeration District: *107*, Ancestry.com. *1880 United States Federal Census* [database online].

8. *New York Sun*, February 1, 1885; "Divorce Suit of A. J. Davis," *Rochester Democrat and Chronicle*, February 3, 1885.

9. Andrew Jackson Davis, *Beyond the Valley: A Sequel to* The Magic Staff, *An Autobiography of Andrew Jackson Davis* (Boston: Colby and Rich, 1885), 17.

10. Davis, *Beyond the Valley*, 95, 96, 98.

11. Davis did not totally abandon the adultery metaphor, writing, "I denounce all such non-conjugal intercourse as *rape*, as *adultery*, as *fornication*, as a *prostitution* of the holiest, most tender, and most immortal tie that binds together one man to one woman." *Beyond the Valley*, 110–111.

12. *Weekly Auburnian*, January 23, 1885; Davis, *Beyond the Valley*, 113.

13. Davis, *Beyond the Valley*, 114; *Albany Evening Journal*, August 23, 1887.

14. *Weekly Auburnian*, January 23, 1885; *Syracuse Standard*, February 1, 1885.

15. Davis, *Beyond the Valley*, 226–227, 229–230, 235.

16. Paschal Beverly Randolph, *Eulis! The History of Love: Its Wondrous Magic, Chemistry, Rules, Laws, Modes, Moods, and Rationale; Being the Third Revelation of Soul and Sex. Also, Reply to "Why is Man Immortal?" The Solution of the Darwin Problem. An Entirely New Theory* (Toledo, OH: Randolph Publishing, 1874), 27, 30, 48, 88; Count de St. Leon [P. B. Randolph], *Love and Its Hidden History. A Book for Man, Woman, Wives, and Husbands, and for the Loving and the Unloved: The Heart-Reft, Pining Ones* (Boston: William White, 1869), 34.

17. Randolph, *Eulis!*, 134–137.

18. *P. B. Randolph, The "Learned Pundit," and "Man with Two Souls." His Curious Life, Works, and Career. The Great Free-Love Trial. Randolph's Grand Defense. His Address to the Jury, and Mankind. The Verdict* (Boston: Randolph Publishing, 1872), 64, 65, 66, 70, 77. John Patrick Deveney, *Paschal Beverly Randolph: A Nineteenth-Century Black American Spiritualist, Rosicrucian, and Sex Magician* (Albany: State University of New York Press, 1997), 195–204.

19. *P. B. Randolph, The "Learned Pundit,"* 88, 89, 91, 92, 96.

20. Randolph, *Eulis!*, 185; Robert S. Cox, *Body and Soul: A Sympathetic History of American Spiritualism* (Charlottesville: University of Virginia Press, 2003), 165, 195–197. Andrew Jackson Davis responded to Randolph, and associated his own views with those of Henry Ward Beecher; see Davis, *The Genesis and Ethics of Conjugal Love* (New York: A. J. Davis & Co. Progressive Publishing House, 1874), 3, 26–27, 44, 51, 52, 80, 97, 107.

21. Deveney, *Paschal Beverly Randolph*, 205, 239, 242–243.

22. "A Conjugal Contract," *New York Times*, January 4, 1877; "Free Love Doctrines as Exemplified in One Instance," *Brooklyn Eagle*, January 14, 1877.

23. Daniel Hull and others, *Moses Hull* (Wellesley, MA: Maugus Printing, 1907), 65, 74.

24. "Free Love Doctrines as Exemplified in One Instance," *Brooklyn Eagle*, January 14, 1877.

25. Quoted in Ellen Wayland-Smith, *Oneida: From Free Love Utopia to the Well-Set Table* (New York: Picador, 2016), 165. See also Michael Doyle, *The Ministers' War: John W. Mears, the Oneida Community, and the Crusade for Public Morality* (Syracuse, NY: Syracuse University Press, 2018).

26. "A Sad Court Stenographer," *New York World*, December 12, 1888; "Mrs. Underhill's Motion Denied," *New York World*, January 1, 1889; "Obituary Notes," *New York Sun*, June 19, 1898. The connection between free love and phonography remained. The free lover Ida Craddock trained in phonography. See Leigh Eric Schmidt, *Heaven's Bride: The Unprintable Life of Ida C. Craddock, American Mystic, Scholar, Sexologist, Martyr, and Madwoman* (New York: Basic Books, 2010), 46.

27. Mary Booth to Mathilde Anneke, January 3, 1865, Anneke Papers.

28. "Meeting of the Illinois Woman Suffrage Association in Chicago," February 12, 1869, in Ann D. Gordon, ed., *The Selected Papers of Elizabeth Cady Stanton and Susan B. Anthony, vol. 2: Against an Aristocracy of Sex, 1866–1873* (New Brunswick: Rutgers University Press, 2000), 218.

29. Susan B. Anthony, "Homes of Single Women," in Ellen Carol DuBois, ed., *The Elizabeth Cady Stanton and Susan B. Anthony Reader* (Boston: Northeastern University Press, 1981, 1994), 146–147. On Kapp, see Mary Booth to Mathilde Anneke, December 6, 1864, and February 9, 1865, Anneke Papers.

30. E. H. Heywood, *Cupid's Yokes: Or, The Binding Forces of Conjugal Life* (Princeton, MA: Co-operative Publishing, 1878); "Cupid's Yokes," *New York Herald*, March, 19, 1879; Helen Lefkowitz Horowitz, *Rereading Sex: Battles over Sexual Knowledge and Suppression in Nineteenth-Century America* (New York: Vintage , 2002), 410–424.

31. "Cupid's Yokes," *New York Herald*, March, 19, 1879; Horowitz, *Rereading Sex*, 424–433; Joanne E. Passet, *Sex Radicals and the Quest for Women's Equality* (Urbana: University of Illinois Press, 2003), 14.

32. Horowitz, *Rereading Sex*, 421–422; On Waisbrooker, see especially Passet, *Sex Radicals*, 113–122. On Craddock, see Leigh Eric Schmidt, *Heaven's Bride*.

33. *The Proceedings and Addresses of the Freethinkers' Convention* (New York: D. M. Bennett, 1878), 24; E.C.S. to the Editor, *Index*, in Gordon, ed., *The Selected Papers of Elizabeth Cady Stanton and Susan B. Anthony, vol. 3: National Protection for National Citizens* (New Brunswick: Rutgers University Press, 2003), 69–70, 399–400; Nancy A. Hewitt, *Radical Friends: The Activist Worlds of Amy Kirby Post, 1802–1889* (Chapel Hill: University of North Carolina Press, 2018), 275–276. On the suffrage movement's rejection of the marriage question, see Lisa Tetrault, *The Myth of Seneca Falls: Memory and the Women's Suffrage Movement, 1848–1898* (Chapel Hill: University of North Carolina Press, 2014), chap. 3.

34. *The Evolutionists: Being a Condensed Report of the Principles, Purposes, and Methods of the Union Reform League* (Princeton, MA: Co-operative Publishing, 1882), 6–7.

35. Letter from A. Boyle, March 8, 1872, and "First Sequential Exposition of the Constitution of the Pantarchy, 1876," Andrews Papers.

36. Letters from William S. Andrews, June 10, 1895, William R. Alger, June 21, 1895, and T. F. Spencer, June 24, 1985; William R. Alger, "Stephen Pearl Andrews as a Protagonist of Humanity," Andrews Papers; Madeleine Stern, *The Pantarch: a Biography of Stephen Pearl Andrews* (Austin: University of Texas Press, 1968), 148, 149, 151.

INDEX

abortion, 76
Achilli, Giancinto, 97
adultery, 2, 5, 10–11, 14, 23, 55–56, 157, 158–159; in American utopian movements, 49; among marriage reformers, 78, 82–85; Andrews' views of, 55–56; Beecher-Tilton affair, 116, 144, 151–157; as civil disobedience, 10, 115, 143, 151, 157; complex marriage (*see* complex marriage); Cragin/Smith adultery affair, 30–32; criminalization of, 14, 19–22, 34, 135, 160, 177n22; divorce and, 5, 23, 66–67, 99, 125, 135, 159–160; false marriage as adultery, 62, 68, 120, 147, 158; free love and, 62, 75–76, 120, 146, 158–159; Hull family and, 146–147, 166; Lazarus on, 54–55; legal punishments for, 5–6, 20, 22; as metaphor for loveless marriage, 1–2, 7–10, 13, 49–50, 55–56, 58, 62, 67, 70, 73–74, 77, 92, 101–102, 107, 112–113, 116, 120, 147, 156–159, 171, 173n2, 183n25, 203n11; "mutual love" and, 55–56, 62, 67; Noyes on, 32, 41; Oneida Community and, 40; perfectionism and, 27; as political act, 6, 151; as private dispute, 23; race and, 160; religious objections to, 14–15; same-sex relationships and, 88, 91; Seventh Commandment and, 5, 14–15, 17–18, 41; sexual double standard and, 56; slavery and, 17–18, 106; trials for, 155–156; "unwritten law" of, 124; virtuousness of, 6, 116, 143; women's campaigns against, 16–17
Advocate of Moral Reform, 16, 19, 25
Alger, William R., 170–171
Allen, Eliza, 44–45
Alwato, 127
American Equal Rights Association, 124
American Society for Promoting the Observance of the Seventh Commandment, 14
American Woman Suffrage Association, 124–125, 129, 132
Andrews, Esther B. Hussey, 57
Andrews, Jane, 51
Andrews, Mary Ann Gordon, 52, 54
Andrews, Stephen Pearl, 11, 49–59, 127, 170–171; antislavery views of, 51–52; Beecher-Tilton affair and, 10, 152–154, 156; criticism of, 139; free love and, 7, 10, 57–58, 67, 77, 101, 127, 152, 154; Free Love Club and, 93; individual sovereignty and, 7, 53–55, 58, 63; McFarland-Richardson case and, 127; Modern Times community and, 53–54; Pantarch and, 170; personal life of, 57–59; phonography and, 52–53, 93; Unitary Home and, 101; views of adultery, 55–56; views of marriage, 50–51, 54–58, 127; women's rights and, 57–58, 63; women's rights movement and, 103–104, 127; Woodhull and, 128, 130, 156; Woodhull-Beecher conflict and, 142, 156
Andrews, Thomas, 51
Andrews, William S., 58, 99, 128, 171
Anneke, Mathilde, 11, 81, 84–91, 168, 170
Anthony, Susan B., 68, 104–105, 124–125; same-sex relationships and, 168; sexual double standard and, 128; Woodhull and, 128
anti-obscenity laws, 140, 145, 163, 169; challenges to, 169–170; Comstock law, 9, 145, 159, 169
antislavery movement, 17–19, 106, 110; Andrews family and, 51–52; Booth family and, 79, 81, 86–87; marriage and, 106, 108; Noyes and, 46–47; sexual moral reform and, 17–18, 23, 46. *See also* slavery

Ballard, Anna, 95
Battle-Axe, 29

Beecher, Catharine, 125
Beecher, Eunice, 152
Beecher, Henry Ward: accused of free love
     philosophy, 152, 155; Beecher-Tilton affair
     and, 10, 116, 143–146, 151–157; McFarland-
     Richardson case and, 124–125, 139; Wood-
     hull and, 142–145
Beecher, Lyman, 135
Beecher-Tilton affair, 10–11, 116, 143–146,
     151–157
Bennett, D. M., 169
Beyond the Valley (Davis, 1885), 161–162
Biedermann, Julius, 85, 90
birth control, 69, 72; at Oneida Community,
     37, 43; sexual frequency and, 76
Blackstone, William, 63
Blackwell, Henry, 102, 104, 124–125
Blood, James, 128–129, 156
Bloomer, Amelia, 56
Bogue, Josephine, 97
Booth, Mary, 11, 78–92, 168; Cook seduction
     case and, 82–86; Indian identity of, 85, 90;
     marriage to Sherman Booth, 78–81; poetry
     of, 88–90; relationship with Anneke, 81,
     86–91, 189n27; relationship with Bieder-
     mann, 85, 90; sickness and death of, 90–91
Booth, Sherman, 78–86, 88, 155, 168; Cook
     seduction case, 82–86; Glover fugitive
     slave case and, 81, 86; marriage to Mary
     Booth, 78–81; relationship to Jane Corss,
     85
Boudinot, Mary Harriett, 98
Branch, Julia, 11, 101, 105–106, 108–111,
     194n26; free love philosophy and, 7, 9, 94,
     101, 105–109; women's rights movement
     and, 103–104, 111–112
Braude, Ann, 62
Brisbane, Albert, 50, 94, 128
Brook Farm, 36, 52
Brown, William Wells, 78

Case, Lyman, 94, 98–100, 117, 128, 160
Case, Marie Stevens. *See* Howland, Marie
Ceresco community, 36, 50, 113
Chase, Warren, 50, 113–114, 126, 195n40
Chatham Street Chapel, 15, 17, 27
Civil War, 113–115
Claflin, Tennie, 127
Clapp, Henry, Jr., 96, 99
Clare, Ada, 90, 100, 117–118

Clay, James A., 5–6, 54
Collins, John A., 37
Combe, George, 70
companionate marriage, 3
complex marriage, 7, 34–37, 58; abandoned
     by Oneida Community, 40–41, 165; birth
     control and, 37, 43; criticism of, 136–138;
     Noyes' beliefs on, 35–37, 39, 41, 47; patriar-
     chy and, 39–40; practiced at Oneida Com-
     munity, 35–39, 42–44, 136
Compromise of 1850, 46
Comstock, Anthony, 145
Comstock law, 9, 145, 159, 169; challenges to,
     169–170
Congdon, Charles Tabor, 95
Cook, Caroline, 82–86
Corson, Kate, 164
Corss, Jane, 85
Corss, Mary H. *See* Booth, Mary
Cowley, Charles, 155
Craddock, Ida, 169, 203n26
Cragin, George and Mary, 11, 23–25, 29–34,
     136, 178n1; charged with adultery, 34; com-
     plex marriage and, 38, 58; conversion to
     perfectionism, 29–30; death of Mary,
     44–46; Noyes and, 25, 29–34, 44, 47; at
     Oneida Community, 35; Smith adultery
     affair and, 30–32, 45
Crosby, James L., 112
Cunningham, Jane, 94
Cupid's Yokes (Heywood, 1878), 169

Davis, Andrew Jackson, 11, 60, 63, 161–162;
     annulment of marriage, 160–162; Bennett
     trial and, 169; Booths and, 81, 91; criticism
     of, 136, 139; marriage to Mary Davis, 64–
     68, 161; Philanthropic Convention (Utica)
     and, 108–109; race and, 164; Randolph on,
     75, 110–111, 164; on sexual expectations in
     marriage, 71; spiritualism of, 65–66; views
     on marriage, 63, 66–68, 75–76, 105, 108–
     109, 161
Davis, Mary Fenn Robinson (formerly Love),
     11, 60–62, 104, 139; annulment of marriage,
     160–162; Booths and, 81; divorce of, 63–64,
     161; free love philosophy and, 7–8; mar-
     riage to Andrew Davis, 64–68, 161; mar-
     riage to Samuel Love, 62–63;
     Philanthropic Convention (Utica) and,

108–109; on sexual expectations in marriage, 71; spiritualism of, 62; views on marriage, 105–109, 112
Davis, Paulina Wright, 144
divorce, 3, 5; adultery as reason for, 5, 23, 66–67, 99, 125, 135, 159–160; for "false" marriages, 108–109; increased rates of following Civil War, 134–135; of Marie and Lyman Case, 99–100; marriage following, 125; McFarland-Richardson case and, 124–125, 156–157; New York law and, 3, 6, 40, 63–64, 66, 71, 117, 125, 135, 139, 159–161; *New York Tribune* debate over, 49; Stanton on, 112, 126; women's rights movement and, 53, 63, 104, 112; Woolsey on, 135
Dixon, William Hepworth, 136, 140, 178n1
Dodge, Catherine DeWolf, 64
Dwight, Timothy, 13, 17

Ellis, John B., 136–140
Esoteric Anthropology (Nichols), 76
Essay on Divorce and Divorce Legislation (Woolsey, 1869), 136
Eulis! The History of Love (Randolph, 1874), 162–163
Evarts, William, 152–153

false marriage. *See* "true" versus "false" marriage
Familistere, 117–119; in *Papa's Own Girl*, 119–121
Farnham, Eliza, 107, 114–115
Finney, Charles Grandison, 15, 24–25, 27
Foster, Lawrence, 38–39
Foster, Stephen S., 106, 110
Fourier, Charles, 7, 49–50
Fourierism, 8, 49–50, 53; Modern Times community and, 54; women's autonomy and, 121–122
Fowler, Orson and Lorenzo, 70–72, 75, 81
Fox, Kate and Margaret, 62
"free" conventions: Buffalo convention, 111; Rutland convention, 105–108; Utica Philanthropic Convention, 108–111
Free Love and Its Votaries (Ellis, 1870), 136–140
Free Love Club, 93–95, 111, 118
free-love philosophy, 2, 9, 12–13, 57, 59, 75–76, 111–112, 169, 173n4; adultery and, 62, 75–76, 120, 146, 158–159; Andrews and, 10, 57–58,

67, 77, 101, 127, 152, 154; anti-obscenity laws and, 145, 169–170; attacks against, 136–139, 141–142, 145, 152, 156–157, 163–165; Beecher accused of, 152, 155; Beecher-Tilton affair and, 116, 152–153, 155–156; Booths and, 80, 92; Branch and, 7, 9, 94, 101, 105–109; Case family and, 98–99; Chase and, 113; criticisms of marriage and, 109, 111–113, 120, 142, 145, 158; Davises and, 7, 68, 107–109, 164; "free" conventions and, 105–111; Free Love Club, 93–95, 118; Howlands and, 117, 122; Hull family and, 146–147, 149; marriage and, 7–9, 58, 63, 68, 75–76, 103–109, 111, 151, 156, 175n25, 182n2, 182n11; Modern Times community and, 54, 57, 59; Nicholses and, 63, 75–77, 101; Owen and, 70; phonography and, 203n26; prostitution and, 109, 194n26; race and, 110; Randolph on, 75, 110, 163–164; Sawyer and, 149–151; sexual frequency and, 76; as social freedom, 116; spiritualism and, 62, 110, 148; spiritual love, 80; Stanton accused of, 125–126; Tilton accused of, 152–156; Underhill and, 95, 167; Unitary Home and, 9, 95, 97–101, 112; women's rights and, 9, 102, 127; women's rights movement and, 9, 102, 103–109, 111–113, 133; women's suffrage and, 129, 170; Woodhull and, 10, 132, 154; "Wood-Hull" vanguard of, 142, 148, 151
Fugitive Slave Act, 46, 81, 113
The Fugitive Wife (Chase, 1861), 113, 126

Gage, Matilda Joslyn, 170
Gay, Elizabeth Neall, 104, 108
Ginzberg, Lori, 104
Glover, Joshua, 81, 86
Godin, Jean-Baptiste André, 117–119, 121–122
Goodell, William, 108
Gordon, Mary Ann, 52, 54
Gottschalk, Louis M., 90, 100
Gove, Hiram, 1
Gove, Mary. *See* Nichols, Mary Gove
The Great Harmonia (Davis, 1855), 66–67
Greeley, Horace, 49, 55
Green, Harriet Cornelia, 27–28, 35, 65
Green, William, Jr., 27–28, 35–36, 65, 67
Greenback Party, 164
Greene, Beriah, 17
Griffing, Charles S. S., 78
Grimké, Sarah, 104

harmonialism, 65–66, 70, 110
Hathaway, Samuel G., Jr., 21
Hawthorne, Nathaniel, 5
Hendricks, Leonard, 98
Heywood, Ezra H., 169
Hills, Alfred C., 95
History of American Socialisms (Noyes, 1870), 49
Hoffman, Christian, 122
Holton, Harriet, 28–29
Hooker, Isabella Beecher, 128, 134, 171
Horowitz, Helen Lefkowitz, 2
Howland, Edward, 99–100, 117–119, 121–123
Howland, Marie Stevens (formerly Case), 11, 53, 94, 98–101, 117–124, 160
Hubbard family, 37, 40–42, 44
Hubbard Seymour, Tryphena, 37–44, 47, 58, 180n3
Hull, Elvira, 11, 143, 147–149
Hull, Mary Florence, 164–165
Hull, Mattie (formerly Sawyer), 11, 149–151, 164–165
Hull, Moses, 10, 11, 142–143, 146–151, 164–166; Beecher-Tilton affair and, 146; on marriage, 143, 146–147, 165; Randolph and, 163; Sawyer and, 149–151
Human Love (Randolph and Randolph, 1860), 73–74
Hunt, Richard P., 53
Hunter, Tera, 160
Hussey, Esther B., 57

individual sovereignty, 7, 53–55, 58, 105, 112, 130; Beecher-Tilton affair and, 155; women's rights movement and, 63, 103, 105

Jackson, Sarah, 69
Jackson Female Seminary, 51
Jacobs, Harriet, 4
James, Henry, Sr., 49, 55, 169
Jewett, Helen, 17
Johnson, Horace, 164–165
Johnson, Mary. *See* Cragin, Mary
Journal of Public Morals, 17
June, Jennie, 94

Kapp, Caecilie, 168
Kelley, Abby, 106

Laight Street church, 16
Lathrop, Wealthy Ann, 50

Latourette, James, 25
Latter-day Saints, 9–10, 175n25
Lazarus, Marx Edgeworth, 50, 54, 96–97
"legalized adultery," 1–2, 4, 7, 17, 57, 78, 101, 105, 132
Leland, Theron C., 53–54, 169
The Life-line of the Lone One (Chase, 1857), 114
The Lily, 56
Love, Mary. *See* Davis, Mary Fenn Robinson
Love, Samuel Gurley, 62–63, 66, 125, 161
Love and Parentage (Fowler, 1844), 72
Love vs. Marriage (Lazarus, 1852), 54, 96

Magdalen Society, 14
The Magic Staff (Davis, 1857), 68, 161
male continence, 37, 43, 72
marriage, 2–3, 5, 157; adultery as metaphor for loveless marriage, 1–2, 7–10, 13, 49–50, 55–56, 58, 62, 67, 70, 73–74, 77, 92, 101–102, 107, 112–113, 116, 120, 147, 156–159, 171, 173n2, 183n25, 203n11; among former slaves, 134, 160; among marriage reformers, 84, 91–92, 98–99, 118, 121, 167–168; Andrews on, 50–51, 54–58, 127; Beecher-Tilton affair and, 156; Chase's views of, 113–114; as civil right, 160; companionate marriage, 3; compared to prison, 43, 113, 143; complex marriage (*See* complex marriage); contrasted with free love, 58; Davises' views on, 61–63, 66–68, 75–76, 105–109, 161; debated in *New York Tribune*, 54–55; effect of marriage reformers on, 158–159; egalitarianism in, 60; during Enlightenment era, 3; false (*See* "true" *vs* "false" marriage); following adultery, 135–136; Fowlers' views on, 70–72, 75; free love philosophy and, 7–9, 58, 63, 68, 75–76, 103–109, 111, 151, 156, 175n25, 182n2, 182n11; homogeneity of marriage reformers, 11–12; Howlands on, 120–122; Hull on, 143, 146–147, 165; Latter-day Saints and, 9–10, 175n25; Lazarus on, 54–55; love and, 2–3, 8, 58, 67, 70, 84, 107, 112, 126, 159; marriage treatises, 68–76; McFarland-Richardson case and, 124, 132; Modern Times community and, 54; monogamy and, 5, 23, 27–28, 62, 68, 107–108, 132, 160; moral reform view of, 69, 76–77; motherhood and, 109; mutual desire in, 61–62, 68, 157, 160;

Nicholses' views on, 75–76; Owen on, 69; phrenology and, 69–70; prostitution as metaphor for, 1, 8–9, 67, 102, 104, 107–109, 112–113, 126, 132, 142, 193n4; race and, 75, 110, 160; Randolph's views on, 72–75, 162–164; religion and, 69; remarriage following divorce, 125; same-sex relationships and, 88, 91, 168–169; sex within, 12, 61, 71–73, 80, 84, 92, 101, 103–104, 108–109, 146; slavery and, 4; slavery as metaphor for, 1, 9, 12, 47, 51–52, 56–57, 104–107, 109, 113, 124; spiritualism and, 62, 68, 75; Stanton on, 126; Stowe on, 140–141; Tilton on, 126; true (*see* "true" versus "false" marriage); Unitary Home and, 8–9, 98, 100–101; women's rights movement and, 2, 53, 62–63, 103–109, 141–142; women's rights within, 2, 60–62, 69, 77, 101, 103–109, 158–159; women's suffrage organizations and, 124–125; Woodhull on, 129–130; Woolsey on, 135–136. *See also* adultery; divorce
Marriage (Nichols and Nichols, 1854), 76
Marriage and Parentage (Wright, 1854), 71, 103
marriage treatises, 68–76; race and, 72–73
Mary Lyndon (Nichols, 1855), 1, 101–102
McDowall, John R., 14–18
McDowall's Journal, 14
McFarland, Daniel, 124–127, 132, 156
McFarland-Richardson case, 124–127, 132, 139, 156–157
McKim, James Miller, 108
Men's Moral Reform Society, 17
middle-class women: campaigns against immorality and, 16–17
Miller, Charlotte, 34–35
Miller, Elizabeth Smith, 170
Miller, John, 34–35
Modern Times community, 36, 53–54, 57, 159; criticism of, 139; free love at, 57, 59, 75; Free Love Club and, 93; marriage at, 54
Moore, Hannah Augusta, 152–153
Moral Physiology (Owen, 1830), 69
moral reform, 16–17, 23; antislavery and, 17–19, 23; criminalization of adultery, 14, 19–23; marriage and, 6–7, 69; perfectionism and, 23; prostitution and, 6, 17; racial prejudice and, 18–19; Second Great Awakening and, 15; seduction and, 20–21; sexual double standard, 22–23. *See also* New York Female Moral Reform Society

Morris Pratt School, 165
Mott, Lucretia, 108
Moulton, Emma, 152
Muller, Antoinette, 99
mutual criticism, 32, 56, 136
My Wife and I (Stowe, 1871), 140–142

National Liberal League, 169
National Woman Suffrage Association, 124–126, 134, 168; Woodhull and, 128, 132
New England Female Reform Society, 20
New Harmony, 69
Newman, John Henry, 97
New York Female Moral Reform Society (NYFMRS), 16–17; criminalization of adultery and, 20–21; Mary Cragin and, 25; perfectionism and, 27–29
New York State, 15; attempted criminalization of adultery in, 19–23, 71, 135; ban on remarriage in, 5, 125; divorce laws of, 3, 6, 40, 63–64, 66, 71, 117, 125, 135, 139, 159–161; prostitution in, 15–16
New York State Lunatic Asylum, 40
New York Tribune, 49–50, 53; debate over marriage in, 54–56
New York Vigilance Committee, 17
Nichols, Mary Gove, 1, 49, 54, 56, 101, 115; free love philosophy and, 63, 75–77, 101; views on marriage, 1, 75–76
Nichols, Thomas L., 1, 54, 101, 115; free love philosophy and, 63, 75–77, 101; views on marriage, 75–76
Noyes, George, 35
Noyes, Harriet, 23, 31
Noyes, John Humphrey, 6–7, 11, 23, 25–50, 135, 165–166; on adultery, 32, 41; Andrews and, 56–57; beliefs on conventional marriage, 27–32, 34–35, 46–48, 58; comparison of slavery and marriage, 46–47; complex marriage and, 7, 35–37, 39, 41, 47, 165; Cragins and, 25, 30–32, 44–45; criticism of, 136; criticism of utopian movements by, 49; establishment of Oneida Community, 35; Putney Community and, 32–34; religious experiences of, 25–27; spiritualism and, 45; as teacher of perfectionism, 25, 27, 29; Unitary Home and, 96

obscenity laws. *See* anti-obscenity laws
Oneida Community, 7, 35–48, 75, 159, 165; abandonment of complex marriage,

Oneida Community (*continued*)
40–41; Achilli and, 97; adultery and, 40; birth control at, 37, 43; charged with 'seduction,' 41–42; child rearing at, 43; complex marriage practiced at, 35–39, 42–44, 58, 165; contrasted with Latter-day Saints, 10; criticism of, 136–138; domestic violence at, 39–40; Mary Cragin's influence in, 45–46; mutual criticism at, 32, 56, 136; phonography and, 52; spiritualism and, 62; Tryphena Hubbard Seymour at, 37–40, 42–44; women's power in, 44, 47–48, 56. *See also* Noyes, John Humphrey
Owen, Albert K., 118, 122
Owen, Robert Dale, 69–70, 72

Pantarchy, 170
Papa's Own Girl (Howland, 1874), 119–122, 140
Parkhurst, Henry M., 53
People v. Faber, 161
perfectionism, 23, 27; marriage and, 27–28, 30, 32–34; Noyes as teacher of, 25, 27; "Oberlin perfectionism," 25; viewed as dangerous, 28. *See also* Noyes, John Humphrey; Oneida Community
Pfaff's Cellar, 93, 100, 117
Phalanx movement, 36, 50, 113
phonography, 2, 52–53, 93, 167–168
phrenology, 69–70
Pillsbury, Parker, 78, 110
Pitman, Isaac, 2, 52
Plumb, Charles M., 64, 90
Post, Amy, 170
Progressive Union Club, 93–95
prostitution, 15, 17, 177n13; attempts to criminalize, 22; free love and, 109; marriage as prostitution metaphor, 1, 8–9, 67, 102, 104, 107–109, 113, 126, 132, 142, 193n4; seduction and, 20–21
Putney Community, 32–34

Randolph, Mary Jane, 73–74
Randolph, Paschal Beverly, 11, 72–75, 109–110, 162–164; Civil War and, 114; on Davis, 75, 110–111, 164; race and, 12, 164; "Wood-Hullites" and, 163
Rebecca Ford (ship), 44–45
Reconstruction, 118

Richardson, Abby Sage (formerly McFarland), 124–126, 132, 139, 156–157
Richardson, Albert, 124, 139
Rose, Ernestine, 106, 108
Ruggles, David, 17–18, 23
Rutland "free" convention, 105–108
Ryan, E. G., 86

Sage, Abby. *See* Richardson, Abby
same-sex relationships, 88, 91, 168–169, 189n27
Sawyer, Mattie. *See* Hull, Mattie
The Scarlet Letter (Hawthorne, 1850), 5
Second Great Awakening, 15, 23
seduction, 20–23; Booth/Cook seduction case, 82–86; criminalization of, 22–23, 82, 177n22; Oneida Community charged with, 41–42
Seneca Falls women's rights convention, 53, 57, 62–63; Declaration of Sentiments of, 53, 62–63
Seventh Commandment, 5, 14–15, 17–18, 41
Seventh Commandment Society, 17
sexual double standard, 21–23, 84, 128–129, 130; Hull family and, 147; slavery and, 18
Seymour, Henry J., 37–44, 180n3
Skaneateles colony, 37
Skinner, Harriet, 165
slavery, 4, 46, 51, 174n11; Fugitive Slave act, 46, 113; marriage among former slaves, 134; marriage and, 4, 12, 46–47; marriage as slavery metaphor, 1, 9, 12, 47, 51–52, 56–57, 104, 105–107, 109, 113, 124; moral reform and, 17–18, 46, 106; sexual double standard and, 18; sexual morality and, 17–18, 46–47. *see also* antislavery movement
Slavery and Marriage: A Dialogue (Noyes, 1850), 46–47, 49
Smith, Abram C., 30–31, 34, 44–45
Smith, Augusta Ann, 168
Smith, Gerrit, 90
Smith, Joseph, 10
social freedom, 116, 147–151; Beecher-Tilton affair and, 156; Randolph on, 75, 163–164
Social Palace, 117–119; in *Papa's Own Girl,* 119–121
Social Solutions (Godin, 1886), 117, 121–122
Spencer, Theodora Freeman, 170
spiritualism, 45, 62; criticism of, 110–111; of Davis, 65–66; free love and, 62, 110, 148; of

Hull, 143, 165; Hull's marriage and, 148–149; marriage and, 62, 68, 75; of Randolph, 72; Woodhull and, 129, 145–146; "Wood-Hullite" branch of, 142–143, 148, 151, 159, 166

Spiritual Wives (Dixon, 1868), 136

Spring Street church, 16

Stanton, Elizabeth Cady, 63, 112–113; anti-Comstock activities of, 169–170; Beecher and, 125; Beecher-Tilton affair and, 144, 154; on divorce, 112, 134; McFarland-Richardson case and, 124–126; sexual double standard and, 129; Woodhull and, 128

Stedman, Edmund Clarence, 98, 100

Stedman, Laura, 98

Stevens, Marie, 53, 94. *See also* Howland, Marie

Stoddard, Evelyn T., 167–168

Stone, Lucy, 63, 103–104, 124–125

Stowe, Harriet Beecher, 140–142, 159

subordination, 32

Swedenborg, Emanuel, 65–66, 136

Tappan, Lewis, 15, 27, 69

Tiffany, Joel, 106

Tilton, Elizabeth: Beecher-Tilton affair and, 116, 144–145, 152, 155

Tilton, Theodore, 90, 116, 126–127; Beecher-Tilton affair and, 144–145, 151–156; Woodhull and, 128–130, 153–155

Topolobampo colony, 118, 122, 123

Tremont Temple, 155

"true" versus "false" marriage, 8, 62, 67–68, 77, 104–109, 159; Davises and, 60, 63–64, 66, 68, 105–106, 108, 161–162; divorce and, 108–109; false marriage as adultery, 62, 68, 120, 147, 158; Randolph and, 73, 75; same-sex relationships and, 91; spiritualism and, 143

Truth, Sojourner, 18, 23

Tyson, Louisa, 51

Underhill, Edward Fitch, 11, 53, 93, 95, 111, 114, 167–168; Unitary Home and, 95–97, 112

Underhill, Evelyn, 167–168

Underhill, Martha Maria, 53

Underhill, Mary Post, 98

Unitary Home, 8, 95–102, 111–112, 159; Howlands and, 117

Utica Philanthropic Convention, 108–111

Vanderbilt, Cornelius, 127

Waisbrooker, Lois, 169

Wakeman, T. B., 169

Warren, Josiah, 128

Wayside Blossoms (Booth, 1865), 87–90

Weld, Charles, 25

White, Ellen Harmon, 142–143

Whiting, Leon, 99

Women's National Loyal League, 114

women's rights movement, 9, 53, 103–109; Andrews and, 57–58, 63, 127; Anneke and, 81, 168; anti-obscenity laws and, 145; Civil War and, 114–115; divorce and, 63, 104, 112; free love philosophy and, 9, 102–109, 111–113, 127, 133, 139; individual sovereignty and, 103; marriage and, 57, 62–63, 112; spiritualism and, 62; Stowe on, 141–142; suffrage and, 124–125; Unitary Home and, 97–98; women's moral authority and, 107; women's rights within marriage, 60–62; Woodhull and, 132–133

women's suffrage movement, 124–125; free love and, 129, 170; Woodhull and, 127–128, 132–133

Woodhull, Canning, 128–129

Woodhull, Victoria, 11, 127–133; arrested for obscenity, 145; Beecher family and, 142, 144–145; Beecher-Tilton affair and, 10–11, 116, 143–145, 152–153, 156; Cowley and, 155; as "free lover," 132; Latter-day Saints and, 10; on marriage, 129–130, 132, 143; McFarland-Richardson case and, 132; Randolph and, 163; spiritualism and, 145–146; Tilton's biography of, 128–129, 153; women's suffrage and, 127–128

Woodhull and Claflin's Weekly, 10, 127, 142–143, 146–147

"Wood-Hullites," 142–143, 148, 151, 159, 166; Randolph and, 163

Woolsey, Theodore Dwight, 135

Worden, Marcus LaFayette, 42–43

Wright, Henry Clarke, 71, 103, 107–108

Wright, Martha Coffin, 105

Wunderlich, Roger, 54

Wust, Louis, 90–91

ACKNOWLEDGMENTS

I am grateful to many individuals and institutions for supporting this project. It was partially inspired by Lucretia Mott, about whom I have written, and who had a very long and happy marriage. It was also inspired by the Oneida Community Mansion House, a short drive from my home in central New York State. Spencer Klaw's *Without Sin* hinted at the challenges of complex marriage for couples who joined the community, and piqued my interest in competing notions of adultery as sin and love.

This project would never have been completed without financial and moral support from the Dean's Office of the Maxwell School of Citizenship and Public Affairs at Syracuse University. Former Senior Associate Dean Michael Wasylenko has always been a strong advocate for my career. The Appleby-Mosher Fund enabled a research trip to Wisconsin. Dean David Van Slyke gave me the time to finish the book. Andrew London and Mary Pat Cornish smoothed the way in the final stages. I am grateful to work with such a great group in the dean's office, who all care deeply about research and teaching. This project also received financial support from the History Department, and I benefited from early feedback from my colleagues in a lively departmental workshop.

I received research assistance from Molly Jessup (who also helped me in her role as the Oneida Community Mansion House's museum educator), Davor Mondom, and Claudia Smith. Marjorie Galelli translated Mathilde Anneke's letters, written in nineteenth-century German, so that I could read Anneke's real-time perspective on the decline of the Booth marriage.

Many friends and colleagues offered feedback and suggestions. Thanks to Bonnie Anderson, Kathleen Brown, Kristin Celello, Kate Culkin, Lori Ginzberg, Matthew Grow, Nancy Hewitt, Kathi Kern, Michelle Kuhl, Bonnie Laughlin-Schultz, Charles LeWarne, Janet Lindman, Alison Parker and Rochester-area U.S. Historians (RUSH), Hélène Quanquin, John Reidl, Kimberley A. Reilly, Marcia Robinson, Erik Seeman, the late Giles

Wayland-Smith, and Victoria Wolcott. The bloggers at Religion in American History (http://usreligion.blogspot.com/) created a welcoming intellectual community. John L. Crow pointed me toward Paschal Beverly Randolph, and Emily Suzanne Clark offered book recommendations. Thanks to Leigh Fought and Doug Egerton for brainstorming the title.

Penn Press sent the manuscript to outstanding readers, including Patricia Cline Cohen, Pamela Haag, and an anonymous reviewer. They have made the book better in every way. Peter Agree gave me great advice and encouragement, and I appreciate his dedication to the project. I am delighted to be working with him and all the wonderful people at Penn Press.

I enjoyed searching for examples of adultery in archives across the United States, and staying with friends and relatives along the way. I spent a wonderful month in the collections of the American Antiquarian Society, and I am grateful to the staff and to a Kate B. and Hall J. Peterson fellowship for the opportunity. I appreciated the help of Joshua Ranger, University Archivist, Polk Library, at the University of Wisconsin, Oshkosh, and to the amazing Wisconsin system, which sends archival materials around the state. I also gave an initial talk about my research to an audience of students and faculty at UW-Oshkosh. Thanks to Michelle Kuhl, Jeff Pickron, Clio, and Eliza for making it happen! I also overstayed my welcome with Jill Faulkner, Clara McNeal, and Colin McNeal when I traveled from Los Angeles to the Special Collections Research Center, Henry Madden Library, at California State University, Fresno, which has a lovely reading room. My parents, David and Joanne Faulkner, provided housing, food, and childcare during a trip to Manuscripts and Archives, Sterling Memorial Library, Yale University. Bob Cohen is a great host for visits to Philadelphia. I appreciated Kate Culkin's hospitality on a snowy trip to the Rare Book and Manuscript Library at Columbia University. I always rely on the fantastic Special Collections Research Center at Bird Library, Syracuse University. We are lucky to have such a great resource on campus.

I also want to thank the people and institutions who granted permission to publish the images included in this volume, especially Julie Herrada, Kate Hutchens, and the University of Michigan Library; Marie Lamoreaux and the American Antiquarian Society; Abigail Lawton and the Oneida Community Mansion House; Lisa Marine and the Wisconsin Historical Society; David Rosado and the New York Public Library; Adam Wallace and the Special Collections Research Center, California State University,

Fresno; and Grace Wagner, Nicole Westerdahl, and Special Collections Research Center, Syracuse University.

I dedicate this book to my wonderful, amazing daughter Mae, who loves history and did not care that the book's topic made this dedication an odd one. I cherish the love and support of Andrew Wender Cohen, and his commitment to the past, present, and future of marriage.